SOUTHEAST ASIAN SECURITY IN THE NEW MILLENNIUM

THE NATIONAL BUREAU OF ASIAN RESEARCH

NBR is a nonprofit, nonpartisan organization devoted to bridging the policy, academic, and business communities with advanced, policy-relevant research on issues confronting the Asia-Pacific region. Through publications, conferences, television programs, and other projects, NBR serves as an international clearinghouse on a wide range of issues, from trade and investment to national security. NBR does not take policy positions, but rather sponsors studies that promote the development of effective and farsighted policy. Recent projects have focused, for example, on the Asia-Pacific Economic Cooperation (APEC) forum, Russia's changing role in Asia, China's most-favored-nation status, and the evolving security environment in Southeast Asia.

NBR's research agenda is developed and guided by a bipartisan Board of Advisors composed of individuals drawn from academia, business, and government including thirty-four U.S. senators and representatives. NBR was established in 1989 with a major grant from the Henry M. Jackson Foundation.

SOUTHEAST ASIAN SECURITY IN THE NEW MILLENNIUM

Richard J. Ellings and
Sheldon W. Simon, Editors

M.E. Sharpe
Armonk, New York
London, England

An East Gate Book

Copyright © 1996 by The National Bureau of Asian Research

Library of Congress Cataloging-in-Publication Data

Southeast Asian Security in the New Millennium : a study of The National Bureau
of Asian Research / Richard J. Ellings and Sheldon W. Simon, editors.
p.   cm.
"An East Gate Book."
Includes bibliographical references and index.
ISBN 1-56324-658-9 (hardcover : alk. paper).—ISBN 1-56324-659-7 (pbk. : alk. paper)
1. National security—Asia, Southeastern.
2. Asia, Southeastern—Politics and government—1945–   .
I. Ellings, Richard J.
II. Simon, Sheldon W., 1937–   .
III. The National Bureau of Asian Research (U.S.).
UA830.S34   1996
355'.033059—dc20
96-12786
CIP

Printed in the United States of America

The paper used in this publication meets the minimum requirements of the
American National Standard for Information Sciences—
Permanence of Paper for Printed Library Materials,
ANSI Z 39.48-1984.

∞

BM (c)   10   9   8   7   6   5   4   3   2   1
BM (p)   10   9   8   7   6   5   4   3   2   1

Contents

Acknowledgments

This book found inspiration in a National Bureau of Asian Research (NBR) study many of our authors undertook for the office of International Security Affairs of the U.S. Department of Defense in 1991–92. That study was conducted as part óf the East Asia Strategic Initiative, America's strategy for the region developed as the post–Cold War era began to unfold. The members of this team, which was organized by Richard Ellings and directed by Sheldon Simon, included Kenneth Pyle, Donald Emmerson, Clark Neher, William Turley, Harlan Jencks, and Peter Soverel.

The articles for this present volume are new and original, with one (partial) exception. An earlier and shorter version of Karl Eikenberry's piece was published in the spring 1995 issue of *Parameters*.

The editors owe a tremendous debt of gratitude to all of our distinguished authors for their patience and willingness to revisit their work. We owe an equal debt to the NBR staff, in particular Jen Linder, who is NBR's latest star manager, editor, and juggler of innumerable projects; Sara Robertson, NBR's managing editor; and Helen Schneider, Henry M. Jackson Foundation intern and graduate student in China studies at the University of Washington. They assisted in every responsible way to transform a stack of raw essays into a volume. Without their persistence, considerable and capable editing, research, administrative finesse, and sense of humor the essays would still be heaped on a shelf. At various stages other NBR staff, including Bruce Acker, Marie Pielage, Gavin Williams, and Tom Wilson, lent valuable assistance.

With this book Sara Robertson adds another publication to her impressive editing record. She has edited the work of most of America's finest specialists on contemporary Asia to the terrific benefit of all of us who care about the region and care that policymakers and others may understand more clearly and with greater felicity the research and views of these specialists.

We are also deeply appreciative of Douglas Merwin and his colleagues at M.E. Sharpe, particularly Dorothy Lin and Angela Piliouras, for their patience while we went through drafts and solved the typical problems associated with putting together a collection of new essays, and for their wonderful support of the M.E. Sharpe/NBR series on Asian topics.

Richard Ellings, Seattle
Sheldon Simon, Tempe

Commonly Used Abbreviations

ADB	Asian Development Bank
APEC	Asia-Pacific Economic Cooperation
AFTA	ASEAN Free Trade Area
ARF	ASEAN Regional Forum
ASEAN	Association of Southeast Asian Nations
AWACS	Airborne warning and control system
BITAC	U.S.-Malaysian Bilateral Training and Consultative Group
C3I	Command, control, communications, and intelligence
CBM	Confidence-building measure
CCP	Chinese Communist Party
CGDK	Coalition Government of Democratic Kampuchea
CIS	Commonwealth of Independent States
CMC	Central Military Commission (China)
CSCAP	Council for Security Cooperation in the Asia Pacific
CSCE	Conference on Security and Cooperation in Europe
CTBT	Comprehensive Test Ban Treaty
EAEC	East Asian Economic Caucus
EAGA	East ASEAN Growth Area
EEZ	Exclusive economic zone
EPA	Economic Planning Agency (Japan)
EPG	Eminent Persons Group
EU	European Union
FDI	Foreign direct investment
FPDA	Five-Power Defence Arrangements
GATT	General Agreement on Tariffs and Trade
IADS	Integrated Air Defense Systems
ICBM	Intercontinental ballistic missile

IISS	International Institute for Strategic Studies (London)
IM&S	Indonesia, Malaysia, and Singapore
IMT	Indonesia, Malaysia, Thailand
IRBM	Intermediate–range ballistic missile
ISIS	Institutes of Security and International Studies
LDP	Liberal Democratic Party (Japan)
MFN	Most-favored nation
MIRV	Multiple independently targetable reentry vehicle
MITI	Ministry of International Trade and Industry (Japan)
MoF	Ministry of Finance (Japan)
MTCR	Missile Technology Control Regime
NAFTA	North American Free Trade Agreement
NATO	North Atlantic Treaty Organization
NEACD	Northeast Asia Cooperative Dialogue
NGO	Nongovernmental organization
NIE	Newly industrializing economy
NPA	New People's Army (Philippines)
ODA	Official development assistance
PAVN	People's Army of Vietnam
PBEC	Pacific Basin Economic Council
PECC	Pacific Economic Cooperation Council
PKO	Peacekeeping operations
PLA	People's Liberation Army (China)
PLAAF	People's Liberation Army Air Force (China)
PLAN	People's Liberation Army Navy (China)
PMC	(ASEAN) Post-Ministerial Conference
RIC	Regionally industrializing core
RIMPAC	Rim of the Pacific
SEANWFZ	Southeast Asian Nuclear Weapons–Free Zone
SDF	Self-Defense Forces (Japan)
SOM	(ASEAN) Senior Officials Meeting
TPDA	Three-Power Defense Arrangement
UNCLOS	United Nations Convention on Law of the Sea
UNTAC	United Nations Transitional Authority in Cambodia
VCP	Vietnam Communist Party
WTO	World Trade Organization
ZOPFAN	Zone of Peace, Freedom, and Neutrality

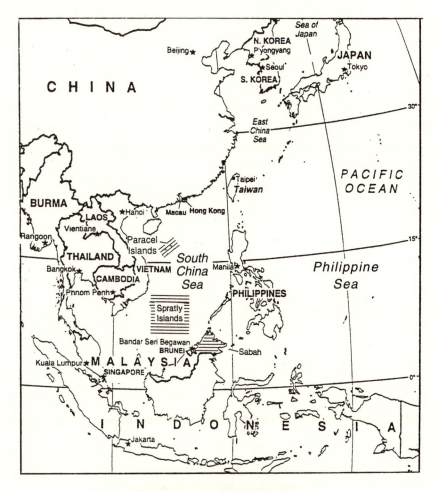

**Boundaries and Major Territorial
Disputes in Southeast Asia**

SOUTHEAST ASIAN SECURITY IN THE NEW MILLENNIUM

1

Introduction

Richard J. Ellings and Sheldon W. Simon

A vibrant Southeast Asia straddles the twentieth and twenty-first centuries with great reasons for optimism. There are no major military conflicts or immediate, ominous threats in the region. This generally peaceful environment is enabling many of the region's economies to be world leaders in economic growth. Most Southeast Asian nations are taking the opportunity to integrate themselves more fully into the world economy and to liberalize their investment and trade regimes. At the same time, however, they are modernizing their armed services and forging alignments with neighbors and selected regional powers to respond to trends they perceive as potentially destabilizing.

Following the dramatic geopolitical changes wrought by the end of the Cold War, Southeast Asian nations have pursued successful strategies for growth. Middle classes are expanding at prodigious rates, and intra- and interregional trade is proliferating as well. As a consequence, Southeast Asians' standards of living are reaching heights that seemed unimaginable just a couple of decades ago. Even in Indochina reforms are under way and economies are on the move.

While Indonesia, Singapore, Malaysia, and Thailand have received proper attention for leading this growth, they have not received the consideration they probably deserve for the broad distribution of this new income among their populations. These economies, along with several in Northeast Asia, are the only ones in the world with both high growth *and* declining income inequality.[1]

Political change is under way as well in Southeast Asia, although that change is perhaps not as dramatic as in nations to the north such as the Republic of Korea and Taiwan. For the most part, Southeast Asian nations have progressed toward democratic rule. The most remarkable political change has occurred in the Philippines, beginning with the "people's power" revolution of 1986 in which Ferdinand Marcos was replaced by civilian leaders in national elections. Modest signs of pluralism have appeared in Vietnam; there are now competitive local elections and real debate takes place between factions within the Vietnam Communist Party. Thailand has also committed to democracy, although tense civil-military relations and money politics cloud the political horizon. Malaysia continues to have a mix of competitive elections and curtailed civil liberties; the result has been a comparatively accountable Malaysian government faced with the difficult task of moderating relations among contentious ethnic groups. Even considering the ever-mercurial situation in Cambodia, the relative political stability and direction of domestic politics bodes well for Southeast Asians as they look to the new millennium.

Improved relations among nations in the region also give reason for optimism. The Cold War is over in Southeast Asia, unlike in Northeast Asia, and there is no immediate internal or external threat in the region similar to the kind that attracted intense attention and involvement of the United States and other powers from the 1950s to the 1980s. The Association of Southeast Asian Nations (ASEAN) is incorporating the Indochina states and is likely to include Myanmar (Burma) soon. Military cooperation is expanding as well.

Moreover, there is evidence of enhanced cooperation between Southeast Asian nations and other Pacific Rim players. The region is experimenting with a variety of joint initiatives, including bilateral and multilateral arrangements to discuss a wide variety of issues and to conduct military exchanges and exercises. Southeast Asians initiated the Asia-Pacific Economic Cooperation (APEC) process, which is now seeking to liberalize trade in the region, and the ASEAN Regional Forum (ARF), which is a venue founded in 1994 for discussing security issues. These are the two salient, multilateral experiments in East Asia since the establishment of ASEAN in 1967.

Therefore, both on the surface and in many deeply rooted ways, the turn of the twenty-first century seems a time for bright hopes for the region. Yet paradoxically, rapid change within and outside Southeast Asia has recently increased the level of insecurity in the region. Three developments—the end of the Cold War, which reduced markedly America's justification for a strong military presence in the region; the rise of China (particularly) and Japan; and high but differential rates of growth among Southeast Asian nations themselves—have raised numerous concerns and spawned military modernization and a moderate arms competition.

Economic growth and the development of trade are increasingly important factors for evaluating Southeast Asia's regional security. Connections between nations are based as much on economic concerns as they are on security issues, since economic development is of primary concern to Southeast Asian leaders. Rates of growth reflect the success of these efforts. Southeast Asian trade is growing prodigiously. Estimates by the Pacific Economic Cooperation Council (PECC) of average annual growth of exports (1995–96) for key Southeast Asian nations are as follows: Vietnam, 22.9 percent; Malaysia, 21 percent; the Philippines, 18.3 percent; Thailand, 16.6 percent; Singapore, 13.3 percent; Indonesia, 10.3 percent. PECC's estimates for real economic growth (GDP) for these countries in the 1995–96 period are likewise impressive. Their composite annual growth rate for the period is forecast to be 7.7 percent.[2]

The Chinese and U.S. economies are the two major "engines" driving this growth. Chinese imports grew by more than 25 percent per year in 1992 and 1993 and continue to grow fast, albeit at a somewhat reduced pace.[3] The United States is also intimately connected to Southeast Asian growth. In a mutually beneficial relationship, trade with Southeast Asia is an important aspect of the U.S. economy. American firms have invested more than $108 billion in East Asia, and two-way trade between the United States and the Asia-Pacific region was $425 billion in 1994.[4] This amount was 36 percent of total U.S. trade and was over 40 percent greater than U.S. trade with Europe.

The role of outside powers such as the United States is critical in assuring peace and prosperity in Southeast Asia. On the other hand, outside powers pose challenges as well. Will the region be an arena of increasing but healthy economic engagement by Chinese, Japanese, American, and European firms, or will the region be coveted by governments, especially China, and thus become an arena for dangerous contention? If stripped of an overarching clash among outside great powers, will disputes among Southeast Asian states themselves destabilize the region?

Particularly problematic for policymakers responsible for security in the region is the interplay of traditional state-to-state relations and various forms of transnational and multilateral linkages. To what extent do the new multilateral arrangements, together with trade and investment flows and the explosion in communication and information links, alter the geostrategic landscape or even the manner in which states conduct defense policies?

And what should America's role be in the region? Although reconfigured by the end of the Cold War and important recent developments in the region, American interests remain considerable. Southeast Asia is *strategically* important to the United States for three reasons: it is an increasingly significant market and supplier for the U.S. economy; it will likely be an area of intense competition, both economic and political, between great powers such as China and Japan, and therefore a potential arena for global instability; and it is a strategic transit area for supplies of Middle Eastern oil and the nexus of other U.S. interests in the Indian Ocean and its littoral states. The United States has myriad political interests in Southeast Asia as well, stemming, for example, from millions of American citizens with family ties to the region and from the production in the region of vast quantities of illicit narcotics that tear at American society.

This volume analyzes Southeast Asian security from several levels of analysis: domestic politics and economics; traditional state-to-state relations and balance-of-power considerations; the new multilateralism; and transnational forces. In so doing, this volume also seeks to refine our understanding of security in Southeast Asia for the post–Cold War period, building in part on the work in *East Asian Security in the Post–Cold War Era*, edited by Sheldon Simon and published in 1993.

In his chapter in this volume Professor Simon analyzes the development of regional cooperation. In the post–Cold War era, international relations among Asian states are moving from a bilateral framework toward a multilateral one. He shows that economic and political–security components of international relations in Asia are not yet deeply integrated, but instead operate on different, yet parallel, tracks.

On the economic track, Southeast Asian countries have responded to market forces and to fears that other trading regions will be increasingly closed to them by forming the Asia-Pacific Economic Cooperation (APEC) forum. Simon argues that as regional multilateralism matures and the nations in Asia become increasingly reliant on each other as sources of trade and investment, the United States will find itself marginalized and unable to use trade as leverage to pursue its interests.

U.S. influence in the political-security arena is also declining, as relations among nations in Southeast Asia are no longer exclusively brokered through unilateral ties with the United States. Instead, groupings such as the ARF are becoming important venues for security discussions. The goals of these regional groupings are to foster transparency on strategic issues in order to build trust, to distance members from U.S. strategies that are not compatible with Asian political developments, and to serve as a regional bloc to counter China. Simon recommends that U.S. policymakers encourage these regional groups, with U.S. participation in them, to deal with security concerns. He believes that the United States, the sole remaining superpower, will continue to be an important and welcome participant in Asia's political, economic, and security future and should continue to be involved as a trade and investment partner and security guarantor in the region.

Professor Donald Emmerson also examines the issues surrounding the development of multilateral links with an innovative, stimulating examination of ASEAN and three states which he argues form ASEAN's security core. He defines ASEAN as a regional security regime. The maintenance of such a regime, he believes, depends on the presence of threats to stability, the resilience of the regime to challenges posed, and the ways that the states within the regime are ordered. The existence of an active regional security core is another way in which a security regime can be maintained. Emmerson avers that Indonesia, Malaysia, and Singapore make up such a regional security core within ASEAN. This core is not institutionalized, but has proven central, stable, and active enough in regional security issues to be considered primary in keeping the region secure from external and internal hegemony. Looking at the interplay of these three states, Emmerson shows how strategic balance among various levels of contending interests has been maintained in Southeast Asia, and offers insights into the future of cooperation in the region.

The perpetuation of the regional security regime relies on the presence of challenges, both internal and external. In his chapter, Emmerson outlines the history of challenges to ASEAN and the role played by the "core" states. He argues that ASEAN will continue to face internal challenges, such as the instability of Indochinese states and Myanmar, and external challenges, particularly the rise of China, in the context of a relative superpower vacuum in the region. Emmerson concludes that the "core" states of Indonesia, Malaysia, and Singapore show promise in handling the delicate job of leading ASEAN without monopolizing it or otherwise undercutting its effectiveness.

Colonel Karl Eikenberry objectively explores the question of the Chinese "threat." China's increasing role as a regional arms supplier, as well as its own military buildup, are sources of some concern among its Southeast Asian neighbors. The area of contention generally perceived to be the most threatening involves the Spratly Islands in the potentially oil-rich South China Sea. China's tenuous internal stability is also a cause for some concern among neighboring Southeast Asian nations, as it holds the potential for inconsistencies and unpredictability in China's foreign policy.

Eikenberry believes that the trepidation engendered by China's rapid economic growth, military modernization program, and the uncertainty of the political situation following Deng Xiaoping's death has been overstated. In arguing that China's power and motivations for using force have been exaggerated, he examines such indicators as China's defense expenditures, force structure, and national wealth. Although there are countries in Southeast Asia that are vulnerable to the Chinese military threat, his conclusion is that limits to Chinese military power, at least in the short term, will mitigate against Beijing's inclination to use force. In the face of continuing destabilizing economic reforms, China's internal situation is likely to absorb the central leadership's attention. In addition, Eikenberry argues that the Chinese are not as dissatisfied with the international, particularly regional, status quo, as is often alleged. They have more to gain by continuing to be active participants in normal international economic and political affairs than is worth risking in military adventures.

Eikenberry further suggests ways in which the United States can bolster stability in the region. The United States should make every effort to facilitate increased Chinese involvement within the international economy as well as to encourage the continued development of subregional, issue-specific forums that will strengthen the ties between China and its Southeast Asian neighbors. Maintaining that China has a strong stake in peace in the region and that there are numerous shared concerns between the United States and China, Eikenberry holds that security ties between the two countries should be increased and regularized. Finally, Eikenberry, like other contributors to this volume, recommends a continuation of the U.S. presence in the region for stability and sustained economic growth.

Central to the issue of stability and America's presence in Asia is the U.S.–Japan alliance, which is the focus of Professor Kenneth Pyle's insightful and timely contribution to this volume. His chapter outlines the relationship between the United States and Japan and assesses developments in Japanese foreign policy, particularly Japanese efforts to redirect its course in Southeast Asia. Pyle reviews the roots of Japan's dependence on U.S. security guarantees in the "Yoshida Doctrine," which enabled the Japanese to direct their efforts to developing their economy. Because of Japan's stunning economic successes, combined with the end of the Cold War and the shifting balance of power in Southeast Asia, Japanese leaders are necessarily reassessing their role in regional affairs.

Since the Plaza Accord of 1985, Japan has dramatically increased its economic role in Asia. A series of economic policies, including careful deployment of foreign direct investment and official development assistance, has given shape to a strategy that seeks to "lay the basis for a soft regionwide integration of economies under Japanese leadership." Already Japanese firms have been successful at creating production and distribution networks linking Asian economies. Although this engagement has led to increasing contact between Japanese nationals and the rest of the world, Japan continues to face obstacles to regional political leadership due to the legacy of its aggressive actions during World War II and the resistance among many Japanese to accept international responsibilities.

Pyle believes that Japanese participation in multilateral military efforts, such as the Persian Gulf War and the United Nations peacekeeping mission in Cambodia, has begun to erode Japan's isolationism. Japan is already centrally connected to Southeast Asian regional economic development, and Pyle argues that Japan will inevitably become involved in multilateral security policymaking as well. As Japan becomes an active participant in regional security structures, the nature of U.S.–Japan relations will undoubtedly change. The United States should encourage an expanded Japanese role in regional cooperation, while still maintaining the U.S.–Japanese alliance as a stabilizing force in the region.

In his study of the security issues in Thailand and the Philippines, Professor Clark Neher notes that with the end of the Cold War the twin threats of superpower involvement and communist-led insurgencies in the region no longer dominate. Instead, "economics is in command and ideology is in decline"; there has been a shift in security concerns from direct military confrontation to securing access to resources and emerging markets. Moreover, as other contributors have noted, the fluidity and uncertainties of the new international system have encouraged Thailand and the Philippines to engage in regional multilateral discussions that are adding rapidly to the changing dynamism of Asian security.

Thailand and the Philippines face the same security issues as many of the other states in the region, such as rapid rearmament, ocean disputes (for example, Thai fishing disputes with Malaysia and the Philippine claim on the Spratly Islands), and possible instability caused by the reduced security role of the United States in the region. However, there are sharp differences between these two countries' internal development. Thailand's economy is flourishing, which has in turn provided a solid basis of support for the growth of democratic institutions. In the Philippines the unstable, oligarchic political structure has done less to encourage economic growth and foreign investment. In an environment where economics has a central role in international relations, the Philippines has far to go before it can become a major player in regional decision making. By contrast, Thailand has been active in regional economic and security discussions and has been involved in Indochina's development and the Cambodian peace process.

Vietnam has also made an effort to enter multilateral discussions with its Asian neighbors. Essentially "friendless" after the collapse of the Soviet Union, Vietnam scrambled to find its place in the new world order. In his chapter in this volume Professor William Turley outlines Vietnam's two major efforts in the post–Cold War period. First, the Vietnamese have tried to shift from a strict defense posture and concern with military development to efforts in diplomacy and reconciliation. Second, they have increased their economic cooperation with other ASEAN countries, Japan, and the West in an attempt to "extract maximum benefit from merger with the world market economy." Similarly, changes in the international environment have forced Vietnam to be more accommodating toward China, Vietnam's traditional security concern.

Vietnam views its Southeast Asian neighbors as more than important economic allies for trade and regional development. The Vietnamese hope that regional cooperation in ASEAN and other fora will serve as a counterbalance especially to Chinese but also to Japanese and U.S. power. Such cooperation is important because the Vietnamese military is at present simply not equipped to handle a major, or long-term, conflict. The potential for armed hostility still exists, however. Turley identifies the disputes along the Cambodian border and with China in the South China Sea as two important regional hot spots. Although the Vietnamese are trying to improve their relations with other states in the region and are committed to security and peace in the region, they do not trust all of their neighbors equally.

On the domestic front, Vietnam is working to liberalize its economy without turning to pure capitalism. Turley dispels the popular belief that Vietnam's economic reforms have not been accompanied by political reforms. On the contrary, he believes that although Vietnam is not likely to be governed by a multiparty system soon, it has ceased to be a revolutionary state and its leaders have begun to reform the political system. Turley asserts that having normalized relations with Vietnam, the United States should continue to work closely with Vietnam in this period of dramatic change and promise.

The countries of Southeast Asia are responding quickly to immediate challenges as well as the longer-term potential threats to the region. Spurred by reduced U.S. credibility in the region, continued and relative Japanese timidity, and increasing Chinese assertiveness, these countries have once again shown a remarkable capacity for successful experimentation in diplomacy and international organization. The establishment in 1994 of the ASEAN Regional Forum (ARF), designed as a venue for discussing security issues and strengthening trust through work on confidence-building measures, is the salient example. By including the Asia-Pacific's great powers, the ARF is an ambitious effort to regularize consultations among ASEAN members and the players that both pose the greatest potential threats to the region and offer the greatest potential source of countervailing power to those threats.

In other words, Southeast Asians appreciate—in spite of their best efforts to organize themselves—their vulnerability to outside states. They have not given up completely on the United States as the ultimate balancer and guarantor, but have soberly faced the question of U.S. reliability. With able leadership from within their ranks, Southeast Asians have sought flexibly to enhance their long-term chances for peace. The studies in this volume suggest that as helpful as Southeast Asian initiatives are, peace will also depend upon the independent decisions of the Asia-Pacific's great powers.

Notes

1. *The East Asian Miracle*, World Bank Policy Research Report, Oxford: Oxford University Press, 1993, pp. 3–4.

2. *Pacific Economic Outlook, 1995–1996*, U.S. National Committee for Pacific Economic Cooperation, 1995. Export figure for Thailand is for 1995; 1996 estimate was not provided.

3. Ibid., p. 9.

4. *U.S. and Asia Statistical Handbook 1995*, Washington, DC: The Heritage Foundation, 1995.

2

The Parallel Tracks of Asian Multilateralism

Sheldon W. Simon

As the Asia-Pacific region approaches a new millennium, regional international relations are moving away from Washington-centered bilateralism to a more diffuse multilateral structure. This new structure consists of both economic and political-security components, which currently run along separate tracks. The structure is quite comprehensive in that almost all Asia-Pacific states are involved, although it is not completely inclusive. For example, Russia, North Korea, the Indochinese states, and Burma (Myanmar) in early 1996 are not yet members of economic regional groups. Nor are North Korea, Burma, and Taiwan members of the new regional security gathering. (In all probability, however, Burma, Vietnam, Laos, and Cambodia will join both types of Asia-Pacific organizations by the turn of the century.)

Economic regionalism in the Asia-Pacific region, in contrast to Europe, has been driven by market forces rather than politics. The European Union (EU) evolved over a thirty-five-year period through top-down political decisions. Economies were linked through negotiations among West European governments. In Asia, economic regionalism has been a product of market forces through which capital from Japan, the United States, and Europe has created linkages among Asian economies via transnational corporations and technology transfer. Again, unlike Europe, this market-led regionalism is open to interaction with states outside the Asia-Pacific region on the basis of reciprocity. The European model is rejected in Asia as too rigid, institutionalist, and discriminatory.[1]

Open economic regionalism in East Asia is partially driven by fears that other regionalisms will be closed. Asian states fear being shut out of the North American Free Trade Agreement (NAFTA) as well as the European Union. They are attracted, rather, to the concept of global free trade embodied in the General Agreement on Tariffs and Trade (GATT) and its successor, the World Trade Organization (WTO). Asian states have initiated policy consultations among themselves as well as some coordination to establish such common goals as the gradual elimination of trade barriers. They hope to accomplish these tasks through ASEAN (Association of Southeast Asian Nations) Free Trade Area negotiations and Asia-Pacific Economic Cooperation (APEC) forum plans. At this stage, however, no member-state is willing to consider sharing authority with a supranational mechanism that could make binding decisions, as in the EU.

One of the most striking features of Asian economic growth has been mutual economic penetration. In the aggregate this has led to remarkable rates of economic growth in the region over the past fifteen years. But it has also led to friction with respect to the distribution of trade benefits, particularly between the United States and Japan and the United States and the newly industrializing economies (NIEs). America has been running large annual deficits with the Asia-Pacific region—currently around $80–$90 billion—since the early 1980s. To ameliorate this financial drain, Washington has pressed its Asian trading partners to open their markets further to U.S. products, in the case of Japan (until autumn 1994) even insisting that some U.S. exports be guaranteed shares of Japan's market (e.g., government procurement, automobile parts, computer chips). U.S. bilateral negotiations with Japan, China, South Korea, and Thailand in particular have created political tensions that threaten to undermine the generally favorable U.S. relationship with Asia in the post–Cold War period.

Despite these frictions, Asia-Pacific economies are of vital importance to the United States. American trade across the Pacific is one-and-a-half times as large its counterpart with Europe. Exports to APEC countries account for 2.6 million jobs in the U.S. economy. Approximately half of all U.S. exports go to Asia, and about 60 percent of U.S. imports come from that region. Thirty percent of U.S. overseas investment goes to APEC countries.[2]

The other parallel track of Asian multilateralism lies in the political-security realm. Although America's Cold War–originated bilateral security arrangements remain in place, their relevance for such new security concerns as the South China Sea islands disputes, overlapping maritime exclusive economic zones (EEZs), and regional burgeoning arms buildups is now problematic. These issues must be confronted multilaterally. The Clinton administration, unlike its Republican predecessor, has accepted this new reality and is encouraging regional security discussions both as an active participant through membership in the new ASEAN Regional Forum and as a benevolent onlooker in the case of the several Indonesian-sponsored workshops convened to help resolve the Spratly Islands conflict. The important point to emphasize here is that U.S. bilateral security commitments to Japan, South Korea, Thailand, the Philippines, and Australia ensure a sustained U.S. military presence in the western Pacific; however, the uncertainty about conditions that could lead to the use of these forces in a post–Cold War setting has motivated the creation of new multilateral fora to deal with new security concerns.

The Declining U.S. Position in the Asia-Pacific Region

The United States plans to sustain important political-security and economic positions in the western Pacific. However, as a declining hegemon, it can no longer do so either unilaterally or bilaterally. Its allies now share the costs of maintaining forward-deployed U.S. forces on their soil, with Japan paying virtually all local costs after 1995 and the Republic of Korea (ROK) paying approximately 35 percent of these costs.[3]

Since trade drives American foreign policy toward the Pacific Rim in the post–Cold War era, the U.S. Department of Commerce and the Office of the U.S. Trade Representative seem to take precedence over the departments of both State and Defense. And U.S. economic pressure on Japan to open its markets has been exerted even at the potential cost of weakening the bilateral security relationship. Thus the Clinton administration places the need to protect foreign patents, copyrights, and intellectual property at the top of its foreign policy agenda in dealing with Thailand, Indonesia, China, and South Korea. It also presses for more open markets throughout the region. The United States believes that the Pacific's economic dynamism is at least partly based on the export emphasis of virtually all its economies. Unlike Europe, so far Asia does not appear to be sliding toward protectionism or inward-looking regionalism. Washington hopes to ensure that this economic openness continues. President Clinton has consciously used the American military presence as a lever to open regional markets further for U.S. products. At the November 1993 APEC meeting in Seattle, he stated: "We do not intend to bear the cost of our military presence in Asia and the burdens of regional leadership only to be shut out of the benefits of growth that stability brings."[4] Thus, under Clinton, the United States has brandished its security role as a good for which improved trade and investment access should be exchanged.

Another point of contention between the United States and several of its Asian partners is Washington's emphasis on human rights as a condition for economic assistance and favorable political relations. Increasingly, U.S. aid is allocated to nongovernmental organizations (NGOs) in recipient countries. Many of these NGOs are in conflict with their governments. In Indonesia, for example, $320,000 was recently given to the Indonesian Legal Aid Institute, one of the country's leading NGOs in the promotion of democratic reform. Such actions, though small in scale and impact, are seen by some as interference in Jakarta's internal affairs.[5]

Further complicating this issue is the fact that the U.S. vision of human rights is derived from North American and European histories, which emphasize the rights of the individual vis-à-vis governments. Asian experiences reverse these priorities, insisting that benefits for the collective (society) must come ahead of the individual; and government's primary responsibility and a basic "human right" must be economic development. Additionally, U.S. efforts to link workers' rights and environmental issues to trade are challenged in Asia as a form of American protectionism. Better wages and working conditions are seen as a way of raising costs and lowering the competitiveness of Asian products.[6]

Finally, it should be noted that the ability to use access to the American market as leverage is declining. By the early 1990s, 43 percent of Asia's exports were sent to other Asian states. Relative dependence on the U.S. market declined from 30 percent in 1986 to only 21 percent in 1991.[7] All the more reason for the United States to remember that "get tough" unilateralism will not fit in an era of economic globalization and regional multilateralism.

ASEAN: Early Links across the Tracks

Formed in 1967, the Association of Southeast Asian Nations was ostensibly created to promote economic and social ties among five anticommunist Southeast Asian states (Indonesia, Malaysia, Singapore, Thailand, and the Philippines—Brunei joined in 1984 and Vietnam in 1995). The more important, though unstated, purpose for ASEAN's creation was, however, political security. That is, each member, fearful of internal communist subversion possibly backed by Vietnam, China, and the USSR, and concerned that the United States would withdraw from Southeast Asia after the Vietnam War, concluded that their common domestic security could best be obtained through a united front.

Over the next several years, that front developed a regional security policy which declared Southeast Asia's long-term interest in Cold War nonalignment—the Zone of Peace, Freedom, and Neutrality (ZOPFAN)—and insisted that foreign bases (in particular the U.S. bases in the Philippines) were ultimately to be removed. This apparently anti-Western posture was not, in fact, what it appeared to be at first glance. Its primary goal was to preclude either the Soviet Union or China from establishing new bases in Indochina by insisting on ASEAN's neutrality. Gestures, such as ZOPFAN in the 1970s, were meant to reassure Beijing, Moscow, and Hanoi that the ASEAN states would not serve as a counterrevolutionary base against them. Therefore, there would be no need for these communist victors to subvert ASEAN regimes.

By the end of the 1970s ASEAN seemed almost moribund. Although the economies of the Association's members grew in that decade, the proportion of intra-ASEAN trade to its members' total trade actually declined. Once again, security concerns revived ASEAN's fortunes in the 1980s as the group coordinated diplomatic efforts against the Soviet-backed Vietnamese invasion of Cambodia. Leading annual UN condemnations of Vietnam's actions, ASEAN had achieved a major regional security victory by the end of the decade: (a) Vietnam had withdrawn its forces back to its own territory, abandoning designs for a Hanoi-controlled Indochina; (b) the Soviets were retreating from their forward politico-military position in Southeast Asia; and (c) both China and the United States had followed ASEAN's diplomatic lead toward the restoration of an independent Cambodia. By the early 1990s, ASEAN had become Asia's most successful example of regional cooperation. The path had been prepared for new regional endeavors.

APEC and Open Regionalism

APEC represents the culmination of a process of market-oriented, outward-looking policy reforms that began in the ASEAN economies in the 1980s. These reforms ultimately convinced ASEAN's most skeptical member—Indonesia—that an Asia-wide economic consultative body had become a necessity. Because the market economies of East Asia are trade-dependent, APEC was launched in 1989 in support of the GATT process of open regionalism—a commitment to nondiscrimination or the offer of most-favored-nation (MFN) treatment to all trade partners either inside or outside APEC who are willing to reciprocate. Thus APEC has been more concerned with the health of global trade than the creation of an East Asian trade bloc.[8]

Indeed most APEC members, with the exception of the United States, Australia, Singapore, and possibly Indonesia, prefer that the organization confine its activities to discussions of trade and investment liberalization and related topics. There is little sentiment to institutionalize this forum by creating a permanent bureaucracy or allocating decisions on these matters to the membership as a group. Thus APEC has no decision-making capability. Nevertheless it has established ten working groups capped by a distinguished array of well-known economists and other intellectuals drawn from its members. This Eminent Persons Group (EPG) has taken two years to devise a free trade blueprint for the region, a recommendation guaranteed to generate controversy. The ten working groups are less controversial. They have already produced useful reports on APEC investment patterns and a tariff data base for all members.[9]

The United States may have a different agenda for APEC, however. The Clinton administration sees APEC as a vehicle for opening Asian markets. It is thought that if there is a regional commitment to trade liberalization through APEC, then U.S. efforts to deal with bilateral trade imbalances with Japan, China, and Thailand should be eased. However, any special U.S. bilateral trade arrangements may be at the expense of other APEC partners. This occurred in Japan's negotiations with the United States on both beef, at the expense of Australia, and plywood, at the expense of Indonesia and Malaysia.[10] U.S. behavior reinforces the apprehensions of the ASEAN countries that Washington is out to "hijack" APEC and turn it into a free trade area dominated by the large economies.

Certainly the results of the November 1994 APEC meeting in Jakarta could be read in this light. The meeting ended with a call for regionwide trade and investment liberalization in two phases, with industrial countries eliminating all barriers by 2010, and less-developed states doing so by 2020. The August 1994 EPG Report also took note of potential conflicts between APEC and such subregional arrangements as the ASEAN Free Trade Area (AFTA) and the North American Free Trade Agreement (NAFTA), urging that these latter bodies equalize the preference arrangements they offer members with the larger APEC.[11] This is in keeping with APEC's commitment to open regionalism: equal benefits to outsiders providing they reciprocate. Parallel recommendations have been made for investment policy through a separate APEC committee report, which requested that members provide nondiscriminatory treatment to foreign investments, that is, that they treat foreign investors the same as domestic investors. This recommendation is also consonant with GATT principles.[12]

The free trade proposals forwarded by the Eminent Persons Group are interpreted as particularly advantageous to the United States because they call for reciprocity, a procedure the United States has advocated in bilateral negotiations with its Asian trade partners. Reciprocity would require trade partners to open their markets to each other on an equal basis. As U.S. negotiators insist, this would level the playing field. Thai officials, reflecting the concerns of other ASEAN states, have reacted cautiously, however, fearful that equal treatment for foreigners would drive some local industries out of business. Malaysia and the Philippines have openly criticized the EPG proposals, claiming that, if implemented, they would move APEC toward a trade bloc, diminishing ASEAN's importance within the larger Pacific group.[13] Nevertheless, with Indonesian president Soeharto's support, the free trade timetable could well prevail—even though it may be inconsistent with GATT principles against discrimination and despite Malaysian prime minister Mahathir Mohamed's objection to APEC's becoming a trade bloc instead of a "loose forum."[14]

Subregionalism: AFTA and the EAEC

A major reason for ASEAN reticence over Pacific-wide free trade is the belief that it would supersede ASEAN's own plans for a free trade area. Similarly, Malaysia's East Asian Economic Caucus (EAEC) initiative has been stalled by Washington's objection that it would split APEC into Asian and non-Asian camps. The communiqué that came out of the July 1994 ASEAN Foreign Ministers Meeting virtually ignored the EAEC. This stalemate appears unresolvable since Japan has stated it cannot support the Caucus unless the United States removes its objection.[15]

The successful conclusion of the Uruguay Round of GATT negotiations has accelerated the AFTA timetable of tariff reductions in order to keep ASEAN consistent with the new World Trade Organization. AFTA negotiators have shortened the time from fifteen to ten years so that intra-ASEAN tariffs on industrial and agricultural goods will be reduced to a maximum of 5 percent by 2003. These reductions, combined with new subregional economic cooperation among Indonesia, Malaysia, and Singapore; the Philippines, Indonesia, and Malaysia; and Thailand and Indochina, should help to keep Southeast Asia an attractive investment region. Moreover, the ASEAN economic ministers have also agreed to expand AFTA's coverage to include raw agricultural products and the services sector. This expanded AFTA should cover virtually all intra-ASEAN trade, which currently accounts for 20 percent of the total trade of ASEAN members.[16]

The primary obstacle to harmonious American participation in Pacific economic regionalism remains the EAEC. Prime Minister Mahathir has downgraded his original 1990 proposal, which would have created a separate ASEAN-led bargaining group for Asia-Pacific economic diplomacy, to a more modest consultative group within APEC. EAEC proponents have also sought to reassure North America and Australia that the Caucus would remain committed to an open, multilateral trading system. Other potential EAEC members such as South Korea, Singapore, and, of course, Japan, would also ensure that the group did not create a protectionist bloc within APEC. Washington's continued objection, therefore, may be overdrawn. The United States could earn considerable good will within the region by endorsing the EAEC. Such an endorsement would be an effective follow-up to America's renewal of China's MFN status. Moreover, the real target for EAEC proponents may be less the United States than Japan. That is, the EAEC may well be a device to open Tokyo's market to Asian exporters rather than a way of diminishing the importance of the non-Asian members of APEC.

Regionalism and Asian Security

The second track of Asian-Pacific regionalism in the post–Cold War period lies in the political-security realm. Pacific-wide security discussions are a new phenomenon. They evolved in the aftermath of the Cold War and emerged from the U.S. military drawdown in the Pacific. While American forces remain in fixed bases in both Japan and South Korea, they have left the Philippines even though the ASEAN states did not desire a complete U.S. departure from Southeast Asia. In fact, all six ASEAN states in varying degrees have helped the United States maintain a low-profile air and naval presence in their vicinity through a relationship known as "places not bases."[17] Memoranda of understanding have been signed bilaterally with all ASEAN members—except the Philippines—through which U.S. ships and planes in small numbers have rights of access to specific ports and airfields for repair, provisioning, and joint exercises. Through these arrangements the United States remains the dominant sea and air power throughout the western Pacific, not just in Northeast Asia where its only bases are located. The low-key U.S. presence in Southeast Asia is designed to alleviate local anxieties about putative regional threats without compromising sovereignty or offending nationalist sentiments. Nevertheless, U.S. efforts in late 1994 to discuss with the Philippines and Thailand the prospect of permanent offshore prepositioned military supplies in their vicinity were rejected as a vestige of the old Cold War dependence on outsiders for regional security. That era has ended.

Although a U.S. military presence remains, it is no longer a sufficient guarantee of security nor is it appropriate for such concerns as territorial disputes, local arms buildups, and ethnic tensions. Only discussions among the region's members can address these effectively. These discussions help to create a habit of dialogue and transparency among regional actors, thus providing reassurance about intentions even as military capabilities increase.[18] South Korea's establishment of diplomatic relations with three of its former adversaries (China, Russia, and Vietnam), even as it gradually builds a military capacity for regional—not just peninsular—action, is an example of efforts to establish this new dialogue of reassurance.

ASEAN's decision to become the core of an Asia-Pacific security discussion forum emerged from two realizations. The first was that the region's economic linkages to Northeast Asia meant that developments in the North Pacific directly affected Southeast Asia. The second was a desire to preempt the creation of a Pacific-wide security group in order to have some control over its agenda. ASEAN feared the prospect of being subordinated to the United States, Japan, Korea, and China if any combination of the latter initiated regional dialogue before ASEAN could.

Initially through post-ministerial conferences and then through the ASEAN Regional Forum (discussed below), ASEAN and its dialogue partners have developed an Asia-wide discussion agenda for the 1990s whose primary aim seems to be transparency. Information on arms transfers, acquisitions, and indigenous arms production; military deployments and exercises; and defense doctrines are all fair game for a cooperative security dialogue. This agenda was originally developed by government-funded think tanks in the ASEAN states, consisting primarily of academic researchers whose recommendations were then transferred for action to the official level.[19] The ultimate purpose of transparency is, of course, reassurance. Accumulated mutual confidence is a prerequisite to resolving difficult issues such as territorial and resource disputes. That ASEAN—an organization that has assiduously avoided any semblance of security responsibilities since its inception—should emerge as the primary institution for wide-ranging Pacific security discussion is a real measure of how much change the post–Cold War world has induced in Asia. ASEAN is founding a new regional security order centered on itself to replace (some would say supplement), at least partially, the old system based on bilateral security ties with the United States.[20] Emblematic of this new arrangement is the fact that the 1976 ASEAN Treaty of Amity and Cooperation has become the basis of security ties among neighbors. The Indochina states are adhering to it as a first step toward joining ASEAN itself.

An additional explanation for Asian decisions to create their own security mechanisms is a growing realization that America's post–Cold War foreign policy goals may not be entirely compatible with Asian political developments. The Clinton administration has placed democracy and human rights near the top of its global agenda. This means that Washington has become increasingly concerned with how Asian states are governed. From the target government's viewpoint, this comes perilously close to direct interference in its internal politics and a challenge to governing elites. Insofar as American human rights concern focuses on labor conditions, it is also seen as an effort to raise business costs in the region and/or justify U.S. protectionism against Asian products. Either way, Washington's human rights agenda is one more indication that the purely military security concerns of the Cold War have ended, and a much more complex U.S. relationship with the Asia-Pacific region has begun.[21]

The country in Asia whose security intentions seem the most imponderable is China. On the one hand, even traditional adversaries such as Malaysia, Indonesia, and South Korea see the PRC as a newly awakened capitalist giant with which trade and investment provide mutual profitability. On the other, China is perceived to be a regional great power inexorably developing economic and military capabilities that will permit it to restore its traditional influence over the region. In general, Asian states have responded by trying to encourage China's outward-looking commercial policies in hopes of nurturing a political-business elite with a strong stake in maintaining regional stability.

A litmus test for Beijing's intentions is its policy toward the future of the potentially oil-rich Spratly archipelago in the South China Sea. China remains the only one among six claimants (the others are Vietnam, Malaysia, Taiwan, Brunei, and the Philippines) that has refused to endorse a pledge to refrain from using force to settle incompatible claims. Moreover, it has also refused to engage in multilateral discussions about creating a development regime for the Spratlys, although it appears to have endorsed the idea in principle.

China has focused its Spratly confrontation on Vietnam, thereby hoping not to antagonize the ASEAN states. However, in July 1995 Vietnam joined ASEAN. Hanoi has already agreed to the 1992 ASEAN declaration on the South China Sea asking all parties to the dispute to exercise restraint and settle their differences peacefully. Thus China appears on the diplomatic defensive with ASEAN, which sees Beijing and not Hanoi as a threat to the region. This alignment vis-à-vis the South China Sea reverses the situation of the 1980s, when Vietnam was regarded as the predator and China as one of the region's protectors against a Moscow–Hanoi alliance.

Nevertheless, China insists that Vietnam is at fault, having sunk eighty to one hundred oil wells in the South China Sea area claimed by Beijing. China alleges that most of Vietnam's annual 35 million barrels of offshore crude production comes from disputed areas. To prevent further Vietnamese drilling in a block given by China to the U.S.-based

Crestone Corporation, the Chinese navy has deployed warships that interdicted the resupply of Vietnam's rig.[22] Competitive exploration and drilling in overlapping blocks is one of the most dangerous features of the Spratly conflict. Military confrontation in the South China Sea between Hanoi and Beijing occurred in 1988. It could occur again.

Moreover, in February 1995, the Philippines discovered Chinese installations in the eastern extremities of the Spratlys only 100 miles from the Philippines' Palawan Island. This is the first indication that the PRC has extended it physical presence in the island chain beyond the islands Beijing disputes with Vietnam. Additionally, Chinese warships in the vicinity appear to be protecting the islands from any Philippine efforts to remove the Chinese structures.

Bilateral discussions between Manila and Beijing and a strong ASEAN declaration of support for the Philippines' appeal to prohibit the occupation of additional islands have led to a more conciliatory Chinese stance. At the July 1995 ASEAN Post-Ministerial Conference (PMC) in Brunei, Foreign Minister Qian Qichen of China appeared to make a significant concession. For the first time China agreed to *multilateral* discussions on the South China Sea islands. This was followed by a second agreement to discuss the disputes on the basis of recognized principles of international law, including the 1982 Law of the Sea.[23] This second concession could open a diplomatic Pandora's box, for under the latest Law of the Sea, the Philippines could claim that Mischief Reef—on which Beijing has built a communications station—is, in fact, within the Philippines' 200–mile exclusive economic zone.

China also appears to have conceded on another dimension of the South China Sea dispute. On July 24, 1995, the U.S. State Department issued a statement emphasizing "an important national interest" in ensuring "the freedom of navigation in the South China Sea . . . and in the principle that international disputes be resolved by peaceful diplomatic means." While this position has always been implicit in U.S. policy, the statement's timing—which coincided with the ASEAN PMC—was clearly designed to support the Association's stance on the Spratly Islands. The American statement was followed by a Chinese demurral that "China attaches great importance to safe and free passage in the international sea lanes there, therefore . . . there will be no problem. . . ."[24]

Trends in Defense Cooperation

China, Vietnam, and the Philippines are not the only states along the Pacific Rim that suspect each other's intentions. Indeed, the single most important obstacle to the creation of a genuine Asia-Pacific security concert is a persistent absence of trust among neighbors. Illustrative of this anxiety was a recent complaint by an Indonesian parliamentary official that Malaysia's military exercises featuring the capture of an island by that country's new rapid-deployment force could be interpreted as an indirect threat to Indonesia because of island disputes between the two countries. Singapore and Thailand were also reported to express concern, for they too have unresolved territorial claims against Malaysia.[25] All this despite the fact that these states are close collaborators within ASEAN on security issues.

Malaysian defense acquisitions are fairly typical of arms buildups throughout the Pacific over the past decade as economic prosperity has permitted the region's militaries to acquire modern air and naval components. Unlike the period through the early 1980s, East Asian armed forces are expanding their tasks beyond counterinsurgency and border protection to control of air and sea spaces in their vicinities. These new capabilities have become particularly important since the 1982 Law of the Sea Treaty was activated in November 1994. Under this new maritime regime, littoral states acquire a 200–mile exclusive economic zone whose protection depends on an oceangoing navy and long-range air force.

In this context, Malaysia has taken delivery of Russian MiG-29s and American FA-18D fighters as well as two new British frigates. In the pipeline are submarines, three dimensional defense radars, and a new fleet of fast patrol boats. All are justified in terms of developing an EEZ defense capability. Malaysian officials do not stop there, however. Former defense minister Datuk Sri Najib Tun Razak noted that "our added capability means we are contributing to regional security. A stronger Malaysia in military terms means a stronger ASEAN." Moreover, similar upgrades by Singapore, Indonesia, Thailand, Australia, or further away, South Korea, are all acceptable to their neighbors so long as they exclude weapons of mass destruction. Minister Najib also reiterated the importance of a continued American military presence and regular joint exercises with regional forces so that they can work together on a bilateral basis.[26]

Other forms of defense cooperation are emerging, too. A major breakthrough in Philippine-Malaysian relations has occurred, considerably easing the long-term enmity that had prevailed between the two countries over an unresolved Philippine claim to the Malaysian province of Sabah. Indicative of Malaysia's willingness to see the claim essentially as an issue in domestic Philippine politics rather than as a problem between the two states, Minister Najib and Philippine defense secretary Renato de Villa concluded a bilateral defense cooperation pact in September 1994. The agreement provides for regular joint military exercises, an exchange of military information to encourage transparency, and the possible joint use of each other's defense locations. The latter would include repair and service, thus providing for the repair of Philippine C-130 transport aircraft at Malaysian facilities.[27]

Japan, too, may be moving gradually toward a regional defense capability. A high-level advisory committee report to the Japanese government in the summer of 1994 recommended not only a greater commitment to UN peacekeeping operations but also improved surface warfare, sealift, and air defense capabilities through the acquisition of air refueling tankers. These capabilities would provide Japan with longer-range deployment opportunities.[28] As if to underline these new considerations, for the first time Japan and South Korea began to plan for training exchanges. And the two countries' navies exercised jointly for the first time in June 1994 during the six-nation Rim of the Pacific (RIMPAC) exercises near Hawaii.[29]

The ASEAN Regional Forum (ARF)

As the Cold War wound down in the 1980s, international relations theorists began to explore alternative security approaches. The old idea of a concert of countries was resurrected, although on a regional rather than global basis. The Conference on Security and Cooperation in Europe (CSCE) was revitalized as a device to bridge the North Atlantic Treaty Organization (NATO) and the now-defunct Warsaw Pact. In Asia, discussions were initiated in nonofficial think tanks to explore security arrangements *with* rather than against states.[30] These new dialogues, many of which included government participants in their private capacity, emulated such economic communities as the Pacific Economic Cooperation Council (PECC) and the Pacific Basin Economic Council (PBEC). That is, they conceptualized security in a broad manner, going beyond narrow military considerations to economic development and commercial linkages—all the while emphasizing cooperative approaches.

During the 1980s, as noted above, East Asian states also experienced sustained economic growth. Resources became available to expand defense establishments beyond counterinsurgency and close-in territorial defense to the protection of adjacent sea and air space out to the 200–mile EEZ enunciated in the 1982 Law of the Sea Treaty. Overlapping maritime jurisdictions and the need to collaborate on fishery poaching and antipiracy led to intense discussions in such regional groups as the ASEAN Institutes of Security and International Studies (ISIS).[31] These discussions included academic policy specialists from throughout the region addressing issues that were considered too sensitive for official meetings. The ASEAN-based fora laid the groundwork for subsequent governmental negotiations on such issues as collaboration in the exploitation of South China Sea resources and peaceful settlement of the Spratly Islands claims.

The ASEAN Regional Forum evolved gradually from ASEAN ISIS meetings to the ASEAN Post-Ministerial Conferences, which inaugurated security discussions in 1992, to a Senior Officials Meeting (SOM) in July 1993, which, in turn, announced the creation of an annual Regional Forum to begin the following year. Virtually every state along the Pacific Rim is now included except North Korea and Burma. Particularly noteworthy has been Japan's enthusiastic participation, marking the first time Tokyo has engaged in multilateral security discussions. This new policy may symbolize a break from Japan's traditional exclusive reliance on the United States in all security matters. It may constitute the beginning of an independent Japanese voice in Asian security matters. Japanese security analysts have recently written of cooperative security arrangements that will supplement the Japan–U.S. Security Treaty: "Japan may need, for example, to provide such cooperation as transportation and rear support for the United States guarding the major shipping lanes."[32] Thus the presence of U.S. bases in Japan will be seen more directly as a Japanese contribution to regional stability.

In its early stages, the ASEAN Regional Forum will probably not go much beyond a venue for the discussion of security transparency and confidence-building measures (CBMs). Regional problems that were addressed by the ASEAN Senior Officials Meeting in March 1994 prior to the July ARF included Cambodia, South China Sea issues, relations with Burma, and nuclear issues on the Korean peninsula. The SOM's recommendation to the ARF was to be as inclusive as possible, that is, to engage disputants in proactive negotiations when feasible to resolve international disputes. Singapore's *Straits Times* perhaps best articulated the Asia-Pacific's hope for the new forum on March 2, 1994:

> What the region needs is a permanent forum to facilitate consultative processes, promote confidence-building measures, and whenever necessary, set up the machinery to investigate disputes. This implies, of course, constant dialogue and interaction so that members acquire a better appreciation of each other's security concerns.

The 1994 Bangkok ARF took several important steps: (1) it established the forum as an annual event; (2) it endorsed ASEAN's Treaty of Amity and Cooperation as a code of conduct among ARF members, thus formalizing a kind of nonaggression undertaking among them (this was understood to be a CBM and a basis for political cooperation); and (3) studies were commissioned for the July 1995 ARF in Brunei on such issues as nuclear nonproliferation, further CBM prospects, the creation of a regional peacekeeping training center, exchanges of nonclassified military information, antipiracy issues, and preventive diplomacy.[33] These topics are so broadly gauged that they could cover virtually all possible security issues along the Pacific Rim.

Some countries proffered specific security issues, reflecting their own priorities. South Korea proposed consideration of a Northeast Asia Security Cooperation forum that would parallel Southeast Asian security discussions. Australia presented a paper on defense cooperation among the region's militaries, which could induce "habits of cooperation" and lead to a "framework for regional security." An ASEAN report called for the exchange of defense white papers as a transparency measure. Japan and the Philippines proposed a regional arms register. And, while Vietnam requested multilateral negotiations on the South China Sea, the Chinese contribution was limited to an expression of interest in scientific cooperation around the Spratly Islands.[34]

Among the most important of these suggestions was the South Korean plan for a ministerial-level security forum for Northeast Asia, which would include the two Koreas, Japan, China, Russia, and the United States. Like the ASEAN Regional Forum, its Northeast Asia subgroup would first focus on CBMs and preventive diplomacy based on nonaggression and nonintervention agreements. With progress toward the settlement of the Korean nuclear standoff achieved in October 1994, prospects for a Northeast Asian security dialogue may be improving. It would provide a mechanism for bringing Russia back into regional security discussions as well as a way of linking Japan and both Koreas in political discourse for the first time. China may be the least interested in such an arrangement, however. In general, Beijing has preferred to deal with security matters on a bilateral basis and has not responded positively to transparency proposals such as foreign observers at its military maneuvers or joint exercises.[35]

Indicative of security problems facing the Asia-Pacific region are those that were dropped from the Bangkok ARF statement because they were considered too controversial or premature. These included the creation of a regional security studies center, the exchange of military observers among neighbors, the sharing of defense white papers, and the establishment of a maritime data base that would facilitate the protection of sea lanes. Nor were the futures of Cambodia or Burma mentioned in the final statement, although the situations in both countries were discussed in the ARF meeting. Dissension prevailed, with Thailand opposing any effort to assist in the development of a more professional Cambodian army, while the United States and Australia argued that assistance to that army may be necessary if the Khmer Rouge is to be defeated and internal security restored.[36] For Thailand, a more stable Cambodia could mean a neighbor less susceptible to Thai economic interests and political pressure.

In July 1995 the second ARF was convened. The momentum set by the 1994 meeting continued. An ASEAN proposal to exchange annual statements on defense policy was adopted by the larger body, a step toward transparency. Track Two studies of sensitive issues such as arms control were delegated to nongovernmental and strategic studies institutes which would present their findings and recommendations to future annual ARF meetings. ARF decisions will be made through consensus. Based on ASEAN leadership, the ARF is to evolve gradually through three broad stages:

> namely the promotion of confidence building, developing of preventive diplomacy, and elaboration of approaches to conflicts. The ARF pro-

cess is now at Stage I. . . . Stage II, particularly when the subject matters overlap, can proceed in tandem with Stage I.[37]

Three intersessional Working Groups have been established and
will report to the July 1996 ARF meeting in Indonesia. Each consists
of an ASEAN state and a non-ASEAN member. Malaysia and Canada
will investigate peacekeeping operations; Indonesia and Japan will
work on CBMs; and Singapore and the United States will cover search
and rescue operations.[38] ARF participants were also encouraged to
declare support for the 1976 Treaty of Amity and Cooperation in
Southeast Asia. The participants further understood that ASEAN will
remain the core group for the ARF, all other members affiliating only
as individual countries. This understanding is designed to address
Malaysia's concern that the ARF not be deflected from a focus on
ASEAN security interests by larger powers.

Concluding Observations

The United States will remain an important player in Asia's political
economy and security future. However, it will be seen increasingly to
be an outsider as the nations of the Asia-Pacific region turn more and
more to each other for trade and investment. The U.S. market can no
longer be the primary engine of growth for Asia-Pacific development.
As a heavily indebted mature economy, it cannot absorb the export
surpluses that characterized Asian development in the Cold War era.
Thus Asian states increasingly turn to one another as both suppliers
and markets. Japan's trade surplus with the rest of Asia exceeded its
surplus with the United States for the first time in 1993. Taiwan,
South Korea, Singapore, and even Malaysia are becoming major investors in their neighbors' development. Japan's direct investment in
Southeast Asia has soared in the 1990s as the strong yen has led a
number of manufacturers to locate in other parts of the region. These
economic dynamics are occurring outside the U.S. relationship with
the Asia-Pacific region.

Along the security dimension, while a U.S. naval and air presence in
the Pacific remains welcome for its calming and deterrent effects, its
importance for the settlement of local conflicts over South China Sea
jurisdictional claims, Cambodia's future, Burma's fate, illegal migration among neighbors, and a host of other political tensions is mar-

ginal. Regional political-security disputes will be negotiated in regional fora such as ASEAN, or handled exclusively among the disputants. Any American role in dispute settlement will be marginal.

Because multilateral approaches to Asia-Pacific economic and security issues are still in their infancy and, therefore, weakly institutionalized, U.S. involvement as a trade and investment partner as well as a security backer continues to be essential. Where the stakes are particularly high in Northeast Asia (e.g., the Korean Peninsula), there will be no substitute for an American presence. Similarly, to reassure the region that Japan need not become an independent military player, all Asian states prefer that the Japan–U.S. Security Treaty remain in force. On the other hand, in Southeast Asia, where the stakes for military confrontation are lower, mulitilateral discussions and approaches may bear fruit over time. While the United States certainly remains first among equals along both economic and security dimensions in the Asia-Pacific, the region's future will be increasingly dominated by the preferences of its Asian members.

Notes

1. For recent discussions of these distinctions, see Tsuneo Akaha, "Asia-Pacific Regionalism: The Economic Dimension," a paper prepared for the International Studies Association—West meeting, The University of Washington, Seattle, October 15, 1994; and Richard Higgott, "Introduction: Ideas, Identity and Policy Coordination in the Asia-Pacific," *The Pacific Review,* vol. 7, no. 4, 1994, pp. 367–379.

2. *Asahi shimbun* (Tokyo), July 8 and November 6, 1993.

3. For an extended assessment of the U.S. position in the Pacific, see Sheldon W. Simon, "U.S. Policy and the Future of Asian-Pacific Security," *The Australian Journal of International Affairs,* vol. 47, no. 2, October 1993, pp. 250–262.

4. Quoted by Kyodo News Service (Tokyo), November 19, 1993, in Foreign Broadcast Information Service (hereafter referred to as FBIS), *Daily Report: East Asia,* November 23, 1993, p. 4.

5. Nigel Holloway, "Seed Money," *Far Eastern Economic Review,* August 18, 1994, p. 18.

6. Statement by Foreign Minister S. Jayakumar of Singapore as carried by *The Straits Times,* July 28, 1994.

7. Sean Randolph's presentation to The Heritage Foundation's Asian Studies Center Symposium: *The New "Malaise": Clinton Adrift in Asia,* Washington, D.C.: The Heritage Lectures, June 21, 1994, p. 15.

8. Richard A. Wilson, "APEC: The Next Step Toward a New Pacific Community," *CAPA Report No. 12,* San Francisco: The Asia Foundation, November 1993.

9. Mohammed Ariff, "The Multilateralization of Pacific-Asia," a paper prepared for the Fourth Defence Services Asia Conference, Kuala Lumpur, April 21–22, 1994, p. 3.

10. Ibid., p. 11.

11. "APEC Set to Consider Ambitious Plan to Create World's Most Open Trade Area," *The Asian Wall Street Journal Weekly,* August 8, 1994, p. 4.

12. Kyodo News Service, September 10, 1994, in FBIS, *Daily Report: East Asia,* September 12, 1994, p. 2.

13. *The Nation* (Bangkok), September 7, 1994, in FBIS, *Daily Report: East Asia,* September 7, 1994, p. 80; Kyodo News Service, September 21, 1994, in ibid., September 21, 1994, pp. 2–3; and *The Bangkok Post,* September 24, 1994, in ibid., September 26, 1994, p. 2.

14. *The Asian Wall Street Journal Weekly,* September 26, 1994, p. 2.

15. Kyodo News Service, July 23, 1994, in FBIS, *Daily Report: East Asia,* July 25, 1994, pp. 8–9.

16. Adam Schwarz, "Local Heroes," *Far Eastern Economic Review,* October 6, 1994, pp. 14–15.

17. The evolution of this new U.S. security relationship with Southeast Asia is discussed by Donald K. Emmerson, "U.S. Policy Themes in Southeast Asia in the 1990s," in David Wurfel and Bruce Burton, eds., *Southeast Asia in the "New World Order": Rethinking the Political Economy of a Dynamic Region,* Basingstoke, England: Macmillan Press, 1995.

18. Hee Kwan Park, "Multilateral Security Cooperation," *The Pacific Review,* vol. 6, no. 3, 1993, p. 253.

19. David Dewitt, "Common, Comprehensive, and Cooperative Security," *The Pacific Review,* vol. 7, no. 1, 1994, especially pp. 9–11.

20. Donald Crone, "New Bilateral Roles for ASEAN," in Wurfel and Burton, eds., *"Southeast Asia in the New World Order": Rethinking the Political Economy of a Dynamic Region.* Also see Sheldon W. Simon, "Realism and Neoliberalism: International Relations Theory and Southeast Asian Security," *The Pacific Review,* vol. 8, no. 1, 1995.

21. See Sheldon W. Simon, "East Asian Security: The Playing Field Has Changed," *Asian Survey,* vol. 34, no. 12, December 1994; and Charles McGregor, "Southeast Asia's New Security Challenges," *The Pacific Review,* vol. 6, no. 3, 1993, p. 269.

22. "Dispute over South China Sea Provides a Test for China's Regional Intentions," *The Asian Wall Street Journal Weekly,* July 25, 1994, p. 12.

23. Agence France-Presse (Hong Kong), August 14, 1995.

24. *The South China Morning Post,* July 25, 1995; and Xinhua, July 30, 1995, in FBIS, *Daily Report: East Asia,* July 31, 1995, p. 7.

25. Antara News Agency (Jakarta), October 10, 1994, in FBIS, *Daily Report: East Asia,* October 11, 1994, p. 84.

26. Interview with Defense Minister Najib in *The Sunday Times* (Singapore), July 24, 1994.

27. *The Sunday Chronicle* (Manila), September 25, 1994.

28. Kensuke Ebata, "More Active Security Role Urged for Japan," *Jane's Defence Weekly,* August 27, 1994, p. 4.

29. Kyodo News Service, June 14, 1994, in FBIS, *Daily Report: East Asia,* June 14, 1994, pp. 8–9.

30. For a review of these security studies, see Paul Evans, ed., *Studying Asia Pacific Security,* Toronto: University of Toronto, York University Joint Centre of Asia Pacific Studies, and Jakarta: The Centre for Strategic and International Studies, 1994.

31. The most recent review of ASEAN ISIS activities may be found in Pauline Kerr, "The Security Dialogue in the Asia Pacific," *The Pacific Review,* vol. 7, no. 4, 1994, pp. 397–409. This consortium of private, though often government-sponsored, think tanks was formed in 1988, and includes all ASEAN states except Brunei.

32. Satoshi Morimoto, "The Future of Japan-U.S. Security," *Secutarian* (Tokyo), July 1, 1994, in FBIS, *Daily Report: East Asia,* October 20, 1994, pp. 15–16.

33. Kyodo News Service, July 25, 1994, in FBIS, *Daily Report: East Asia,* July 26, 1994, p. 9.

34. These proposals are summarized in *The Bangkok Post,* July 25, 1994, in FBIS, *Daily Report: East Asia,* July 25, 1994, pp. 17–18.

35. Nayan Chanda, "ASEAN: Gentle Giant," *Far Eastern Economic Review,* August 4, 1994, p. 16.

36. A review of the ARF Cambodia debate was carried by Kyodo News Service, July 26, 1994, in FBIS, *Daily Report: East Asia,* July 26, 1994, p. 13.

37. This description of the July 1995 ARF meeting is drawn from the August 1 Chairman's statement as carried by Pacific Forum's *Pac Net,* no. 29, August 18, 1995.

38. Bandar Seri Begawan RTB Sukmainder Television in English, August 1, 1995; and the *Bangkok Post,* August 2, 1995, pp. 1–2.

3

Indonesia, Malaysia, Singapore:
A Regional Security Core?

Donald K. Emmerson

The Association of Southeast Asian Nations (ASEAN) is a regional security regime. A *regional security regime* may be defined as a formal or informal arrangement for cooperation among adjacent or mainly adjacent states to maintain their sovereignty in conditions of peace among themselves and with outsider states.[1]

I include sovereignty in this definition to make clear that regional security regimes are not solely interested in peace. Peace without sovereignty (capitulation) and sovereignty without peace (war) are suboptimal outcomes for a security regime. I realize that in the implied formula "security = peace + sovereignty," realpolitik supersedes *moralpolitik.* An idealist might prefer to define security as "peace + democracy" or "peace + justice." But a definition should summarize the way things are, not how they ought to be.

For nearly three decades since the birth of ASEAN in 1967, being a member has meant being at peace with fellow members and with outsiders. Co-occurrence is not cause, and many conditions facilitated this happy outcome. Yet by no means least among these are the range of interactions and the habit of consultation that the Association has fostered among its members. By the mid-1990s well over 200 ASEAN meetings were being convened annually on all manner of social, economic, and political topics, while private firms and nongovernmental organizations extended and tended their own networks of contacts and activities across an expanding "ASEAN region"—the space on maps filled by the

Association's five, then six, and eventually seven member states. (Indonesia, Malaysia, the Philippines, Singapore, and Thailand founded ASEAN, adding Brunei upon its independence in 1984 and Vietnam in 1995.)

Even before the advent of European colonial rule, the languages, religions, and institutions of the societies that ASEAN would come to encompass differed greatly. Britain, France, Holland, and the United States divided and appropriated Southeast Asia—all of it save Thailand—and turned its societies and their elites away from each other and toward distant metropoles. After these dependencies gained independence, some of their leaders tried to cooperate. But their efforts foundered. In the early-through-mid-1960s, while Malaysia and the Philippines bickered over who owned northeastern Borneo (Sabah), Brunei's, Malaysia's, and Singapore's relations with the largest Southeast Asian country, Indonesia, ranged from tense to violent.

The creation of ASEAN did not preclude discord among its members: Singapore triggered public outcries in Jakarta in 1969 and Manila in 1995 by executing, respectively, two Indonesian marines for sabotage and a Filipina maid for murder. What made such flare-ups noteworthy, however, was not their severity but their rarity—blips on a baseline of almost routine intramural amity, at least on the surface.

The existence of ASEAN was not enough to keep its territory safe from threats by outsiders: had Maoism not failed, had Mao's successors not focused on their lagging economy, had they not opened it to foreign trade and investment, the history of ASEAN's relations with China could have been less peaceful. Yet the Association's members played an important diplomatic role in countering the one external threat they did appear to face: the chance that Vietnam, having occupied Cambodia in 1978, might lean on an ASEAN member, Thailand, as the next "domino" in line. The Association has been, and remains, a successful instance of what, ironically, its leaders have never acknowledged it to be—a regional security regime.[2]

This chapter consists of a series of linked conceptual arguments, along with evidence on their behalf: first, that notions of challenge and resilience can help explain the success of ASEAN as a security regime; second, that one aspect of resilience is the extent to which regime members are ordered in a way that helps sustain the regime; third, that one such pattern entails the idea of a security core made up of some but not all members; fourth, that whether such a core can be said to exist will depend on the centrality, stability, and activity of its putative constituents compared with other members of the same regime; and fifth, that inside ASEAN, along these three dimensions, Indonesia, Malaysia, and Singapore have begun to resemble, although they do not solidly constitute, a regional security core.

Explaining Success: Challenge and Resilience

As aids to explaining the success of a regional security regime, a pair of broad propositions comes to mind: the achievement of peace among its members, or between them and outsiders, should be *challenged* enough to warrant the regime, but not so much as to demoralize it; and the regime should be *resilient* enough to withstand such challenges. From the birth of ASEAN in 1967 until Vietnam became its seventh member in mid-1995, the Association succeeded as a security arrangement largely because these conditions were met.

Will ASEAN continue to succeed by these criteria? The answer will depend in part on the implications of two developments: China's rise to prominence in East Asia; and ASEAN's expansion to encompass Vietnam and, prospectively, Cambodia, Laos, and Myanmar (Burma) as well.

Challenge

Will ASEAN close ranks to counter the threat that Chinese power may entail? Will China's rise thus raise the ASEAN states' ability to maintain the security of Southeast Asia against northern encroachment, much as Vietnam's invasion of Cambodia in 1978 animated and unified them successfully against it? Or will the Chinese challenge exceed the Association's ability to respond, inducing its members to acquiesce, one by one, to northern hegemony? Will enlarging ASEAN to encompass more countries increase its ability to speak clearly for and mobilize, if necessary, all of Southeast Asia, and thus more effectively counter Chinese designs? Or will its enlargement undermine the coherence of the grouping, and hence its ability to speak at all?

China's economic transition from socialism, beginning in the late 1970s, turned the world's largest country into a juggernaut. In subsequent years no documented East Asian economy grew faster, even in per capita terms.[3] If the data on gross domestic product (GDP) that underlie this conclusion about the recent past are recalculated at purchasing power parity and projected into the future at a 4.9 percent average annual rate of growth for 1994–2015, China emerges with the world's largest economy by 2007. And if this happens, the same methodology and assumptions yield this prediction: by 2003, China's military outlays will have surpassed American military expenditures for the first time and more than doubled those of Japan.[4]

Long-run statistical omens of hegemony should not be taken too seriously; too many unforeseen things can happen in the meantime. Controlling for purchasing power in this instance is especially problematic.[5] Yet no sensible observer would deny the possibility that a belligerent and powerful China could someday challenge ASEAN beyond its capacity to respond, and in so doing deprive it of the optimal challenge it might need to continue succeeding as a regional security regime.

One may counter that real success implies not a manageable challenge but none at all, as potential enemies are prevented from threatening the regime by its military strength. The sheer firepower of its members might indeed deter all potential adversaries from challenging such a regime. But the longer it is not challenged at all, other things equal, the greater the chance that it could atrophy for lack of a raison d'être. An arrangement to maintain security presupposes a felt need to do so. The nature of the challenges causing such a need to be felt do not have be military; they could be economic, cultural, or even demographic, as in the challenge of illegal immigration.

Any projection of the future security of Southeast Asia should include an assessment of the chance, nature, and timing of a Chinese challenge to ASEAN. This chapter will cite evidence for China's rising maritime profile in Southeast Asia. But my focus here is on the second, or purely internal, aspect of ASEAN's success as a security regime: its *resilience,* especially in relation to Indonesia, Malaysia, and Singapore. I make this choice mainly because China has its own chapter in this volume, but also because so much more attention has been paid in Western media to China's prospects than to ASEAN's—notwithstanding the dynamism of most Southeast Asian economies.[6]

Resilience

A regional security regime is an arrangement to maintain the sovereignty of member states in conditions of peace. Such an arrangement can exist, as it does in ASEAN, in the absence of any deep consensus about exactly how this should be done. Yet there must be a minimum common understanding of regional security, if not the best way to approach it, to ensure that regime members are not always working at cross-purposes, which would undermine the regime. Over the life of ASEAN, if any concept has embodied that minimum shared outlook among members, it is resilience, which entered ASEAN's vocabulary as a translation of *ketahanan,* an Indonesian word.

A second term, neutrality, has proven much more controversial. But it has garnered enough support among ASEAN members to become, if not a part of their thinking on regional security, a concept they must deal with and cannot publicly repudiate, especially given its popularity in Malaysia, where it originated. Neutrality faces outward toward the external powers whose disagreements and rivalries make it possible, or, at any rate, attractive. Resilience, in contrast, looks inward at the capacity of a regional regime to maintain itself against external and internal pressures and conditions that could defeat or divide it.

The Indonesian concept of resilience entered the lexicon of ASEAN early in the life of the Association as a national, not a regional, approach to security. Resilience did not imply the presence within the resilient country of a force sufficiently large and well armed to deter invasion; *ketahanan* was to be distinguished from *pertahanan,* or defense. *Ketahanan* was above all a socioeconomic prescription for internal security through development. By fostering economic growth, a state could improve public welfare—income, health, education—and a more prosperous society would be less vulnerable to internal subversion by communists on the left or Islamists on the right. Thus did Indonesia link *pembangunan* through *ketahanan* to *keamanan,* that is, development through resilience to security.[7]

The men who installed the "New Order" regime in Indonesia in the mid-to-late 1960s did not want ASEAN to maintain regional security proactively through multilateral diplomacy, let alone by means of collective defense. Soeharto and his colleagues saw ASEAN as a passive insurance policy against interstate disorder that would enable them to spend less, not more, time and energy on regional affairs. And that would let them focus on what was important: rescuing Indonesia's badly debilitated domestic economy and getting it to grow again. This Indonesian formula for national resilience—development over diplomacy—was then generalized into a more or less ASEAN-wide priority.

The stronger all member economies became, the more secure the region would be.

Proponents of *ketahanan* assumed that the prime threats to national security were internal. But the success of the strategy undermined this assumption. As ASEAN's economies grew (the Philippines partly excepted) internal threats waned, as actually or allegedly insurgent Communists were destroyed, split up, or lost support and were co-opted. In the outlying provinces of particular states, local resistance persisted under other banners: ethnicity, religion, a way of life endangered from the center. In Indonesia in the 1990s, for instance, Jakarta's authority remained under pressure in East Timor, Irian Jaya, and Aceh, listed in decreasing order of magnitude. But by and large across the ASEAN region internal security had been achieved.

Meanwhile economic growth had enabled ASEAN's members (the Philippines again partly excepted) to buy more expensive and deadlier air and naval weapons systems designed for use not on insurgents but against another state. Over the life of ASEAN, as internal threats subsided, members became more inclined to rethink resilience in interstate terms. By seeming to create a "power vacuum" in Southeast Asia, the local ebbing of British, then American, and then Soviet/Russian military power sped this process of reframing resilience. Internal security and economic development were in no sense displaced as policy priorities; they continued to occupy the tops of member states' agendas. But rising up alongside these imperatives were new views of resilience as a regional goal requiring proactive interstate diplomacy as well.

Defining a Core: Centrality, Stability, Activity

The resilience of a regional security regime can mean different things to different observers. One subset of such meanings concerns the distribution of power and influence inside the regime. These values may be concentrated in one or two member states, for example, or dispersed across several or more. In a regime with many members, power and influence may be so dispersed as to render the regime incapable of concerted action. Yet the more members a regime has, the more representative it is. This is the dilemma posed by the incorporation of Vietnam into ASEAN in 1995 and the prospect of further expansion to include Cambodia, Laos, and Myanmar. The Marxist-Leninist experiences of the Indochinese states and the long "Burmese road to socialism" have no counterparts among the basically capitalist founders of ASEAN and Brunei. When they join, these newcomers will also bring with them long histories and memories of conflict. Even without the addition of Cambodia, Laos, and Myanmar, one may imagine ASEAN being enervated, for example, by rivalry between Bangkok and Hanoi, or between Hanoi and Jakarta, or among all three.

Definition

Resilience, in short, implies coherence. Power should be distributed among member states centripetally enough to ensure the regime's integrity and its ability to respond to security challenges without falling apart. This chapter takes up one of these possible patterns: the existence within a regime of a *regional security core* made up of *one or more adjacent states that display centrality, stability, and activity on security matters relative to other states belonging to the same regime.*

When the core of a regime consists of a single state, that state need not surpass all other regime members on each dimension—centrality, stability, and activity. But its overall strength on these counts should give such a core state more influence over regional security than any other member of the regime. If a core comprises two or more contiguous members, they too need not outrank or outperform all other members on each variable. But, taken as a group, such core states should be more influential on security issues than any other state or grouping of adjacent states in the regime.

The member or members of a regional security core should, first, be more *central* than other regime members to the discussion and handling of regional security issues. Second, the core member or members should be reasonably *stable*. Stability in the case of a single-state core refers to the political stability of that state. A state that is politically unstable is likely to be so engrossed in its internal problems and appear so volatile to other regime members as to render its role on regional security ineffectual, divisive, or both. A case in point is Indonesia from its civil war in the mid-to-late 1950s to the dismemberment of its "Guided Democracy" in the mid-to-late 1960s.

Stability in a core made up of two or more states refers not only to these states' domestic politics but also to their relations with each other. They need not be bosom allies united by a single vision for the region. To the extent that core-member views on regional security are diverse and reflect the variety of outlooks in the larger regime, a core whose states' outlooks vary may actually enjoy greater legitimacy in the eyes of extra-core members. But intra-core relations cannot be so unstable as to preoccupy core members to the detriment of their ability to contribute energy and resources to the security of the regime. Beyond some threshold, unstable relations among adjacent states make them part of the problem of regional insecurity, not its solution, as exemplified by Indonesia's confrontation with Malaysia in the early-to-mid 1960s.

Third, compared with other states in the regime, the member or members of a regional security core should be distinctively *active* in trying to shape and maintain regional security. Such activity could include propounding approaches to regional security, convening forums to discuss it, and taking steps to resolve disputes, shows of force, and other conditions that may endanger it. Examples of such initiatives drawn from ASEAN's history include the Kuala Lumpur Declaration of 1971; the Indo-Malaysian "Kuantan principle" announced in 1980; the "Jakarta Informal Meetings" hosted by Indonesia in the 1980s to resolve the Cambodian war; the Sino-Indonesian and Sino-Taiwanese meetings hosted by Singapore in 1985 and 1993, respectively, to help reconcile these pairs of states; and the series of workshops that Indonesia has convened since 1989 to reduce tensions over the Spratly Islands.

Centrality has multiple meanings. Some are relatively structural in the sense of being hard to change. Others are relatively contingent in that policies can alter them. Three characteristics of centrality are particularly important: location, prominence, and longevity. Inside a regional regime, one or more countries may be central to the management of security by virtue of where they are, how big they are, or how long their top leaders have held office—or two or all three of these things.

Longitude and latitude—location—do not dictate destiny. But where a country physically happens to be is a constant, not a variable. What can change is what that location signifies. Depending partly on events and trends, a country may be seen to be advantaged, disadvantaged, or still otherwise affected by where it is. Normally the address of a house does not vary. But the dwelling's condition, occupants, and neighbors can and do change, and depending on these contingencies, the value of the property may rise or fall.

Still partly structural but more contingent than location is a country's prominence—the size of its territory, population, and economy relative to the size of other regime members on these dimensions. A country's borders are more changeable than its location, and so therefore is the extent of its territory. The disintegration of Pakistan in 1971 and of the Soviet Union in 1991 created smaller sovereign states but did not move them to new addresses. Countries, in any case, rarely break up. In contrast, the sizes of their populations change from day to day, depending partly on policies regarding migration and reproduction, and indirectly on policies that by speeding or slowing economic growth alter incentives to migrate or reproduce. Changes in population size, on the other hand, typically vary less from year to year than changes in GDP.[8]

Third and more contingent still is the longevity of political leadership in a country—how long a leader has remained in office compared with that of other regime members. The influence of a long-incumbent head of government or foreign minister need not exceed that of a counterpart who has just come to power and expects to be replaced fairly soon. A president-for-life may behave in ways that alarm the neighbors and reduce their willingness to cooperate, thus undercutting his influence. Sukarno's appetite for confrontation with Malaysia in the 1960s illustrates the point. But longevity in principle enables a leader to accumulate resources that can translate into influence: experience, contacts, and a consistency of outlook and policy that can make his state more influential by virtue of its being more reliable.

Dynamics

While structural and contingent centrality are analytically distinct, they are empirically related. During the Vietnamese occupation of Cambodia in 1979–89 Thailand was a "front-line state," in the sense that its physical position adjacent to Cambodia made it possible to imagine Vietnam using Cambodia as a staging area to launch cross-border raids intended to deny Thai sanctuary to the Khmer Rouge rebels, or, less plausibly, to march on Bangkok. Contingent Vietnamese action thus revalorized Thailand's structural location in a way that made the kingdom more obviously central to a settlement of the Cambodian imbroglio. Similarly contingent ASEAN responses—diplomatically isolating the Vietnamese and fostering Khmer opposition to their occupation of Cambodia—reinforced the perception of Thailand's more or less fixed border with Cambodia as a front line.

Feedback effects between structural and contingent centrality can also be discerned in the evolving security role of Indonesia. Structurally, Indonesia is the most prominent ASEAN country by virtue of its objective size. Yet Jakarta is not a party to the dispute over the Spratly Islands that dot the South China Sea. That controversy involves China, Taiwan, and four ASEAN states—Brunei, Malaysia, the Philippines, and Vietnam. Jakarta's structurally based sense of general entitlement, together with its contingent neutrality on this issue, encouraged Jakarta to invite all six Spratly disputants to a series of workshops to discuss and resolve their conflicting claims. By acting on their country's structural importance, Indonesian leaders in turn underscored it.

Feedback need not be positive. Should other ASEAN members view Jakarta's move to manage the Spratly issue as a failure, they may become less amenable to Indonesian intervention to resolve some future dispute to which they are parties. The fate of an initiative may make it riskier for the initiating government to assume that its country's prominence structurally entitles it to lead the region in diplomacy.

My purpose here is to discourage a static understanding of regional security cores. Because of the importance of contingent activity in augmenting or undermining structural centrality and stability, cores can shrink, expand, break up, or strengthen, among other scenarios. The same regime could have more than one core, so long as multipolarity does not sap the regime's ability to maintain regional peace. Peering into ASEAN's future, for example, one could picture an expanded bipolar security regime with Indonesia and Vietnam as southern and northern *primus inter pares,* respectively. One could even imagine a tripolar arrangement incorporating Thailand, although that pattern could prove too shaky to last.

Note, however, that even these speculations rest in part on a recognition of relatively structural power: Vietnam's large population, for example, or Thailand's economic size and central location in mainland Southeast Asia. The differing endowments of states give them unequal chances to become and remain core members.

"Front-line state," in contrast, is a removable label. By definition such a state is located near some epicenter of actual or threatened violence. When violence wanes, the site becomes less dangerous, and the state's claims based on its front line proximity to conflict lose persuasiveness. What insecurity creates, security can take away.

In this sense, the repatriation of Vietnamese troops from Cambodia in 1989 and the negotiation of a settlement in 1991 weakened the centrality of Thailand to ASEAN as a security regime. The winding down of the Cambodian war and the retreat of Vietnam as a danger to ASEAN, in effect, relocated Thailand on policy maps—away from the fulcrum of policy and back toward the geographic periphery of Southeast Asia as a security field. The subsequent shift in policy attention from war-torn Cambodia to the Spratlys, and the visibility of Indonesia in efforts to resolve the latter issue, raised the possibility that a recentering of ASEAN as a security regime might be under way.

I do not mean to slight Jakarta's earlier peacemaking role. Having been designated by ASEAN as its interlocutor with Vietnam, Indonesia was hardly absent from diplomacy to end the Cambodian war. One need only recall the series of informal meetings convened by Jakarta to discuss that conflict, or the Franco-Indonesian origins of the 1991 Paris peace conference that laid the basis for damping it down. Yet Indonesia's undoubted contribution to that outcome ought not to obscure the crucial importance of Thailand in rallying ASEAN to "contain" Vietnam.

Vietnam is now inside ASEAN. If Cambodia, Laos, and Myanmar are also allowed to join, the case for identifying Thailand as central to Southeast Asian security could improve. Accepting these new entrants—all on the mainland and all contiguous to Thailand—will extend the Association's land border with China westward to Bangladesh. The need to manage the risks created by ASEAN's enhanced proximity to China could raise the security importance of Thailand as the premier economy wholly on the Southeast Asian mainland and thus, structurally, a natural leader there, pending the rise of Vietnam. Bangkok's historical experience in dealing with China may further encourage Thai leaders to aspire to play the go-between role with regard to Beijing that Indonesia played in representing ASEAN to Hanoi. The mainland location of the most likely future members of ASEAN could also, while benefiting Bangkok as a would-be regional security core, disadvantage Jakarta as a candidate to play the same role.

But, as I have noted, ASEAN could evolve into a security regime with more than one core. And who is to say that Myanmar, Cambodia, Laos, and Vietnam will accept Thai leadership? One ought not underestimate the difficulty of weighing structure against contingency in anticipating the dissolution, shifting, and reconfiguration of regional security cores. Their metaphorical and many-dimensional character, simultaneously structural and contingent, makes them easier to suppose in theory than to discover in practice, let alone to predict inside future regimes.

In the light of the above definitions, illustrations, and caveats, I may now state my conclusion: *In the 1990s Indonesia, Malaysia, and Singapore emerged to form a new though provisional and fragile core inside ASEAN's regional security regime.* (Henceforth, to save space, "Indonesia, Malaysia, and Singapore" will be abbreviated "IM&S.")

Three Dimensions of Centrality: Location, Prominence, Longevity

Location

The geometric center of Southeast Asia lies in the southern South China Sea north of Brunei. That is where a line drawn diagonally from the northwesternmost edge of Myanmar to the southeasternmost tip of Indonesia intersects a second diagonal running from the northeasternmost tip of the Philippines to the southwesternmost edge of Indonesia. This maritime center of Southeast Asia is also the midpoint of ASEAN, since the northwest-to-southeast axis is the same whether it is drawn from Myanmar, which does not (yet) belong to ASEAN, or from Thailand, which does.

A ruler, a pencil, and a map pale as indicators of regional security cores compared with the mental maps used by political leaders in making regional policy. If physical centrality were all that mattered, regional security leadership would reside in Brunei. That enclave sultanate did chair ASEAN's Standing Committee and host its Ministers Meeting, Post-Ministerial Conference, and Regional Forum in 1995. But these roles fell to Brunei by virtue of the alphabet, not the map. (Thailand chaired the committee and hosted these meetings in 1994. By first-letter rotation, since Vietnam was not then an ASEAN member, Brunei was designated to do so in 1995, Indonesia in 1996, and so on.)

Nevertheless, the map does matter. The length of ASEAN's water-crossing borders greatly exceeds the length of those that lie on land. If the outermost limits of the ASEAN states are linked in straight lines to form one unbroken boundary, the sea predominates inside it. All of ASEAN's members have frontage on the South China Sea.[9]

Knowing that the heart of the ASEAN region is maritime still does not tell us which state in the region is geographically most central to it. To answer that question, one may rank the Association's members according to the number of other members they abut. Adjacency is obvious on land but not on water. Maritime borders are especially controversial in the South China Sea where so many of them are contested. Yet excluding water borders from adjacency makes no sense in an archipelagic space such as the one that ASEAN occupies. One need but stand on the soil of water-surrounded Singapore and look at Malaysian or Indonesian land to see the continental bias in the notion that only land makes neighbors. Arbitrarily, but I think reasonably, the status of neighbor may also be granted to countries whose coasts are within, say, fifty miles of one another.

By this definition, Malaysia is adjacent to five other ASEAN members, Indonesia to three, Singapore and the Philippines to two apiece, Brunei and Thailand to one, and Vietnam to none. One need not believe that location is destiny to argue that IM&S are geographically well suited to being seen as central to ASEAN.[10]

Prominence

IM&S are central not only because of their location but by how large their largest member looms in the ASEAN region. Indonesia has 56 percent of all the land inside the Association. Adding Malaysia and Singapore brings the proportion to two-thirds. Indeed, half of all the land in Southeast Asia lies in IM&S. Incorporating inter-island, continental-shelf, and extended-economic-zone waters into this comparison only augments the proportional dominance of Indonesia and IM&S. Indonesia towers over the region's demography too; of all the people inside ASEAN, nearly half live in Indonesia, and slightly more than half in IM&S.[11]

The disparity in size inside IM&S is extreme. With 187.2 million people on 1.9 million square kilometers of land, Indonesia makes Malaysia (19.0 million and 0.3 million, respectively) and Singapore (2.8 million and 0.001 million) appear small and microscopic. But all three countries have enjoyed similarly rapid economic growth. On an annual average in 1970–80 and again in 1980–93, Indonesia doubled the world average for gains in GDP. Malaysia did better, and Singapore better still, though even Singapore did not outpace Indonesia by more than 1.1 percent annually on average in either period. As a group from 1970 to 1993, IM&S outperformed the rest of ASEAN and the rest of Southeast Asia, notwithstanding Thailand's nonpareil record in 1980–93.[12]

Partly because of these consistently high rates of economic growth, IM&S in 1993 supplied nearly three-fifths of ASEAN's total GDP and more than half of Southeast Asia's.[13] Trade had buoyed this growth and been buoyed by it. IM&S accounted in that year for three-quarters of ASEAN's merchandise exports and over 70 percent of Southeast Asia's. Singapore and Malaysia were the first and second largest exporters in Southeast Asia, while Indonesia, in fourth place, lagged behind third-place Thailand only slightly.[14]

It is not coincidental that IM&S are the only economies that flank the Straits of Singapore and Malacca, the historic corridor linking the Pacific and Indian oceans and channeling commerce between Europe and the Middle East on the one hand and Northeast Asia on the other. Air traffic and deep-draught container ships have reduced the importance of this shallow and congested corridor for through-trade, but archipelagic Indonesia has benefited from the dispersion. The port of Bangkok is too far north and too congested to compete with Singapore as a center for transshipments. A canal across the Isthmus of Kra in southern Thailand has been proposed periodically, but so long as it remains unbuilt, the various channels through Indonesian waters will have no competing routes for ships unable or unwilling to ply the Malaccan route.

Mainstay cargoes in such ships include liquefied natural gas (LNG) and oil. From gas-processing complexes on Sumatra, east-coast Malaya, and north-coast Borneo (and in years to come from wells off the Natuna Islands in the South China Sea), Indonesia and Malaysia will continue to supply Northeast Asia with natural gas—arguably the key transitional fuel from (dirty) petroleum to (clean) hydrogen-based energy in the twenty-first century.

The Natuna field contains some two-fifths of all Indonesian gas reserves. Exploiting it should permit Indonesia to retain its position as the world's leading exporter of LNG. The size of the field, its proximity to shipping lanes and the contested Spratly Islands, and its importance in honoring Jakarta's long-term commitments to supplying energy-hungry Japan, South Korea, and Taiwan should make all the more compelling the interest of Indonesia in maintaining regional security. And that will in turn imply an active and ongoing Indonesian role in keeping the peace in and around the ASEAN region. From its base at Ranai on Greater Natuna the Indonesian air force already launches surveillance flights over the South China Sea.

The stake of Singaporeans in a peaceful neighborhood is not hard to understand, given their extreme vulnerability to any disruption in external trade. But Malaysians too live in a remarkably extroverted economy. In 1991 Malaysia was the third most foreign-trade-dependent state in the world after Singapore and Hong Kong. If this pattern persists, when China reabsorbs Hong Kong in 1997, Singapore and Malaysia will become the world's most and second most extroverted economies by this measure.[15]

Another trade-related condition that has helped the plausibility of IM&S as a regional security core in Southeast Asia is the unusually high proportion of intra-ASEAN trade for which Malaysia and Singapore are responsible. As a proportion of total ASEAN trade, trade among ASEAN states has not been impressive. A mere 18 percent of total ASEAN trade was conducted among the Association's six members in 1993. But Malaysia and Singapore together, in equal amounts, accounted for more than three-fourths of this intra-ASEAN trade. (Thailand and Indonesia contributed some 17 and 6 percent, respectively.)[16] And if the nexus of its members' economic intercourse is to be found in ASEAN's maritime south, it follows that their interest in the regional security needed to protect and expand that nexus should enlarge the roles of Malaysians and Singaporeans as keepers and planners of regional peace.

Preliminary evidence on investment in and trade with Vietnam, ASEAN's latest member, further highlights the roles of Singapore and Malaysia. Thailand, while very active in Laos and Cambodia, has lagged behind in the race among ASEAN members to supply Vietnam with goods and capital. And the greater Singapore's and Malaysia's stakes in ASEAN's new northern economic frontier become, the greater the interest in regional security these two maritime countries are likely to have.

Noteworthy too is the prominence of IM&S in three sub- and cross-national "growth zones," or regionally industrializing cores (RICs), inside ASEAN: Sijori, which connects Indonesian Riau and Malaysian Johor through Singapore; IMT, named after its participating countries' initials, which is meant to link Medan (Indonesia), Penang (Malaysia), and Phuket (Thailand); and the still mainly-on-paper East ASEAN Growth Area (EAGA) comprising Indonesian North Sulawesi, Malaysian Sabah, and Philippine Mindanao.

Thailand has expressed an interest in organizing a still protean RIC on the mainland, a "Golden Quadrangle/Pentagon/Hexagon" that would connect segments of Thailand with adjacent or nearby parts of three or more of its neighbors (Cambodia, China, Laos, Myanmar, and Vietnam). But the roughness of the terrain at one logical nexus of such a zone—where China, Laos, Myanmar, and Thailand come together—and the shallowness, narrowness, and difficulty of navigating the full length of the other—the Mekong River—compare poorly with the access the sea affords at the hearts of the southern RICs.

Piracy is a constraint in these maritime cases, notably in EAGA, the least developed of the sea-focused RICs. But that reinforces the regionalizing logic being argued here. The more they hope to develop maritime trading and investment zones among themselves and with their neighbors, the more IM&S are likely to address the regional insecurity that piracy illustrates.

Longevity

Augmenting the structural case for the centrality of IM&S is a highly contingent aspect of core status: how long a country has been led by the same leader. Table 3.1 compares the time spent in office by ASEAN's incumbent heads of government as of 1995 and by its foreign ministers since 1984. My previously noted supposition is that, other things equal, the influence a state can exert in foreign affairs will be greater the longer its leader retains power.

Longevity in office does not determine influence. For most of forty years—from 1948 when he became defense minister, through his presidency in 1974–81, to 1988 when he quit heading the state party— General Ne Win had the power to shape his country's regional security policy. Yet at no time during this long period was Burma (now Myanmar) a core state in this regard in Southeast Asia. A leader of long standing may be ignored by neighboring leaders, lack sufficient interest in regional security affairs to try to influence them, purposely shun external engagements including international regimes, or be too preoccupied with domestic challenges to have time for regional affairs.

Table 3.1

A Leader's Years—Time in Office, ASEAN Government Heads and Foreign Ministers

Part A: Summary
Tenure in Office

Country	Tenure of Head of Government as of Oct. 1995 Time (in years)	Median Tenure of Foreign Ministers Jan. 84–Oct. 95 Time (in months)	Number of Foreign Ministers Jan. 1984– Jan. 1995
Brunei	28	141	1
Indonesia	27	71	2
Malaysia	14	46	3
Singapore	5	56	3
Philippines	3	12	7
Thailand	0.25	14	6

Part B: Details
Tenure in Office

Office and Name of Office Holder	Head of Government (HG) as of Oct. 95 Time (in years)	Foreign Ministers (FMs) since Jan. 84 Time (in months)
Brunei		
HG Hassanal Bolkiah	28	
FM Mohamed Bolkiah		141
Indonesia		
HG Soeharto	27	
FMs Ali Alatas		79
Mochtar Kusumaatmadja		62
Malaysia		
HG Mahathir Mohamed	14	
FMs Abdullah Ahmad Badawi		56
Abu Hassan Omar		46
Ahmad Rithauddeen		39

(Table 3.1 continued)

Office and Name of Office Holder	Head of Government (HG) as of Oct. 95	Foreign Ministers (FMs) since Jan. 84
	Time (in years)	Time (in months)
Singapore		
HG Goh Chok Tong	5	
FMs S. Jayakumar		21
Wong Kan Sen 64		64
S. Dhanabalan		56
Philippines		
HG Fidel Ramos	3	
FMs Domingo Siazon		5
Roberto Romulo		35
Raul Manglapus		56
Salvador Laurel		19
Pacifico Castro		12
Arturo Tolentino		9
Carlos Romulo		5
Thailand		
HG Banharn Silpa-archa	0.25	
FMs Kasem Kasemsiri		3
Thaksin Shinawatra		9
Prasong Soonsiri		25
Arsa Sarasin		18
Subin Pinkayan		7
Siddhi Savetsila		79

Notes: Foreign ministers, including the one acting FM (Pacifico Castro), are listed in reverse chronological order. Vietnam is omitted because it joined ASEAN only in July 1995. Foreign ministers are listed from January 1984 because that is when Brunei joined ASEAN, because this chapter is focused on ASEAN's most recent decade, and for space reasons. For convenience in calculation it is assumed that foreign ministers always entered or left office in mid-month. Medians are used instead of means because of outlier values.

Sources: Asia 1984 Yearbook through *Asia 1995 Yearbook,* Hong Kong: Review Publishing [1988–95]; *Far Eastern Economic Review* [1984–87]; relevant embassies, Washington, DC.

But continuity at the top does allow for the accumulation of knowledge and experience, the maintenance of consistent policies, the projection of a regional vision, and—not least in an Asian context—the possession and use of seniority. And to the extent that the already proven ability of a leader to remain in office raises the probability that he or she will retain power in the future, neighboring leaders will be less inclined to dismiss his or her proposals.

Democracy implies turnover. In 1995, as Table 3.1 shows, the heads of the two most democratic governments in ASEAN[17]—Prime Minister Banharn Silpa-archa of Thailand and President Fidel Ramos of the Philippines—had the least time in office. Conversely, by far the most senior statesmen in the region were the rulers of authoritarian states: Brunei's Sultan Hassanal Bolkiah and Indonesia's President Soeharto. The relatively low figure of five years in office for Singapore's Prime Minister Goh Chok Tong is deceptive. Goh's predecessor, Lee Kuan Yew, had filled that office continuously for thirty-one years (1959–90)—a feat of durability unduplicated, to my knowledge, by any other prime minister before or since.[18] Nor did Lee's relinquishing the prime ministership mean leaving the government. Instead he became senior minister, a position created for him. He still held it in 1995. On major decisions, including matters of regional security, the senior minister's views remained extremely influential.

If years as formal head of government as a criterion of longevity are replaced with years of continuous influence on a member state's foreign policy over the twenty-eight-year life of ASEAN (to 1995), the Association's cofounders, Lee Kuan Yew and Soeharto, rank first in longevity at twenty-eight years apiece, which is twice the next longest span—fourteen years—achieved by Prime Minister Mahathir Mohamed of Malaysia. The sultan of Brunei ranks third at eleven years, with Philippine president Ramos and Thai prime minister Banharn lagging far behind. Ever since it was established in 1976, the ASEAN secretariat has been located in Jakarta. But the political stamina of Soeharto, Lee, and to a lesser extent Mahathir are additional reasons to locate the institutional memory of ASEAN in IM&S. The numbers and tenures of foreign ministers shown in Table 3.1 point to the same conclusion: continuity of leadership as a condition of influence is another reason to find plausible the evolution of these three states into a potentially resilient regional security core.

Stability: Disparity, Balance, Compensation

As a subset of ASEAN, IM&S are anything but homogeneous. Indonesia and Singapore are polar opposites by spatial size—a key dimension of structural centrality. And were it not for Brunei, whose population is even smaller than Singapore's, Indonesia and Singapore would also stand at opposite ends of a list of ASEAN members ranked by demographic size. As for Malaysia, while hardly a miniature state, it too is dwarfed by Indonesia on these dimensions.

Given Singapore's and Malaysia's proximity to Indonesia, and without knowing anything else about the two countries, one might think that because of its obvious superiority in land and population size, Indonesia must enjoy complete policy dominance over its two neighbors. From this, one might further infer that whatever stability IM&S display must be hegemonic, that the two smaller states are cabooses with no choice but to be pulled along by Indonesian locomotive power.

This is not so. Not the least of the reasons why is that Singapore's and Malaysia's wealth has offset somewhat their physical and demographic disadvantages alongside Indonesia. Conversely, Indonesia's strategic advantage in sheer numbers of people has been attenuated by their poverty compared to the relative wealth of Singaporeans and Malaysians.

Table 3.2 documents the point. In 1993 the ASEAN member with the least area and the smallest population—Singapore—had the most wealth. At the same time, the ASEAN state with by far the most area and population—Indonesia—had the least wealth. Malaysia fit the same pattern by combining, Singapore-style, relatively smaller size with greater wealth. This pattern may be called "balanced disparity," that is, the tendency among two or more interacting states for conditions that enhance and limit state power to be distributed in mutually offsetting ways. Indeed, as Table 3.2 shows, across ASEAN as a whole in 1993 disparities of size and wealth were almost exactly balanced. If the Philippines were larger in area than Thailand, and if Brunei were smaller in population than Singapore, the relative wealth of any ASEAN member in 1993 could have been inferred from its relative spatial or demographic size merely by turning either of the latter two rankings upside down.

Although wealth in the sense of per capita product is a more readily changeable dimension here than either of the size variables, the balanced disparity of ASEAN is not recent. It is a structural feature dating from the inception of the Association.[19] Balanced disparity is a matter of degree, however, and disparities within ASEAN have never been perfectly balanced across all relevant variables. One can at least imagine, for example, a security regime whose member economies' absolute (not per capita) size is perfectly inversely correlated with their size by area or population. But ASEAN fails this strict test. Unquestionably

Table 3.2

Balanced Disparity—Size and Wealth, ASEAN States and Most/Least Wealthy States in Northeast Asia

Country	Area (thousands of km^2)		Wealth (GNP/cap in U.S. $, 1993)		Population (millions of people, 1993)	
	Amount	Rank	Amount	Rank	Amount	Rank
			ASEAN States			
Singapore	1	6	19,850	1	2.8	5
Brunei	6	5	17,000	2	0.3	6
Malaysia	330	3	3,140	3	19.0	4
Thailand	513	2	2,110	4	58.1	3
Philippines	300	4	850	5	64.8	2
Indonesia	1,905	1	790	6	187.2	1
			Most and Least Wealthy States in Northeast Asia			
Japan	378	3	31,490	1	124.5	2
China	9,561	1	490	0	1,178.4	1

Notes: Not shown, but taken into account in the rankings for Northeast Asia, are Hong Kong, Taiwan, Macao, South Korea, North Korea, and Mongolia. Vietnam is excluded because it was not a member of ASEAN in 1993.

Sources: "World Development Indicators," *World Development Report 1995,* New York: Oxford University Press for the World Bank, 1995, pp. 162–163, 228; "Countries of the World," *1995 Information Please Almanac,* Boston, MA: Houghton Mifflin, 1994, pp. 157–158 (Brunei). Wealth figures for China and Brunei are, respectively, a preliminary estimate and an estimate of GDP per capita in 1992.

in 1993 Singapore was prosperous in per capita terms, but its economy barely surpassed in absolute size the historically laggard economy of the Philippines. Despite widespread poverty, the Indonesian economy was absolutely the largest in ASEAN.[20]

The conditions along which balanced disparity can be measured are not sealed off from one another. The size of a country's economy is positively influenced by the size of its population. What matters is what enhances and limits state power. Compared with the economic size of a country, its per capita product is a better indicator of the presence or absence of wealth that could be used, for example, to purchase weapons and hire and train military personnel—that is, to acquire the means to project state power and protect against its projection by other states. For the absolute size of a country's economy tells us nothing about the abundance or scarcity of material value, including the actual availability of resources for power projection and defense.

The governments of two countries with identical per capita products can, to be sure, spend very different sums on their militaries. Nevertheless, comparatively within ASEAN, having an unusually high per capita product implies a high priority on outlays for defense. In 1990–91, for example, defense spending in Singapore and Brunei, by far the wealthiest members of ASEAN in per capita terms, exceeded by 129 and 125 percent, respectively, their outlays on education and health combined. The priority on defense by this measure in ASEAN's next wealthiest and spatially next smallest member, Malaysia, was next highest at 71 percent. In contrast, the group's two poorest and most populous states at that time, Indonesia and the Philippines, spent on defense only 49 and 41 percent, respectively, of their education and health disbursements.[21]

One may explain this pattern as a product of availability and intent: the spendability of "surplus" resources in small, well-off societies already enjoying relatively good education and health, and a strategy to invest disproportionally in defense in order to compensate for the weakness that smallness implies. Conversely, other things (as always) being equal, the development-minded leaders of bigger and poorer societies who would like to enlarge their militaries may be doubly restrained. In such countries the urgency of antipoverty spending may have made resources for defense spending relatively unavailable. At the same time, knowing that their countries' larger size already makes them hard for a small neighbor to swallow may make such spending seem less urgent, especially if internal threats to national security are few and apparently manageable.

So long as these bigger, poorer states do not become so alarmed by the rapidly rising deadliness of their smaller, richer neighbors as to engage them in a destabilizing arms race, balanced disparity can improve regional security. Critical to such a benign outcome is the evolving mix of deterrence and reassurance within the regime, and within the core inside the regime.

Activity: Deterrence, Reassurance, Initiative

During the Cold War the literature on international security showcased the idea of deterrence. But even during that long pseudo-peace between military superpowers, deterrence alone could not explain the security behavior of states. Military security has two sides. Deterrence is one of them, but the other is reassurance, and they are intimately related. In a pattern of balanced disparity between two states, one may strive to reassure itself with moves to compensate for its unique weakness, as when Singapore's leaders through outlays on advanced weaponry, compulsory service, and combat-readiness invested in a "poisoned shrimp" strategy meant to make their city-state extremely painful for even a whale such as Indonesia to swallow. Viewed as a deterrent, that same strategy could cause the whale to think twice before opening its mouth.

Conversely, the poverty of Indonesia compared with Singapore may deter the former while reassuring the latter, if—and it is a big "if"—Indonesian leaders are so committed to developing their domestic economy and raising local welfare in concert with outsiders as to view Singapore as a partner for cooperation, not a shrimp for dinner. The uncertainty in this logic should not be minimized. Singaporean leaders remember that the extreme poverty of Indonesia under its first president, Sukarno, hardly prevented him from excoriating "neocolonial" Malaysia, which initially included Singapore, and smuggling saboteurs across its borders. Balanced disparity is merely structural, and structure without agency cannot make history.

Japan and China are listed in Table 3.2 to show how unbalanced is the disparity between them as potential members of a future Northeast Asian security regime. China is in the Northeast what Indonesia is in Southeast Asia—much larger spatially and demographically than it is in economic terms. But Japan's great wealth, and therefore its great capacity to arm itself, is not so well balanced by reassuring smallness of area or population, especially in view of rising pressures in and on Tokyo to revise or ignore its constitutional renunciation of the means of making war.

Unlike Singapore in ASEAN, Japan is far from being the smallest of the eight Northeast Asian states by area; it is the third largest. In the meantime, rapidly rising Chinese outlays on defense, notwithstanding the country's poverty, have hardly reassured Japan. Compared with Southeast Asia, Northeast Asia is grossly underorganized. A Northeast Asian security regime does not exist. The region has no "Association of Northeast Asian Nations," nor any equivalent security arrangement. Poorly balanced disparities between the wealthiest and largest countries in Northeast Asia are one reason why.

Spending and Procurement

I have noted that structure without agency cannot make history. We may ask then: Inside ASEAN as a maturing security regime, has the balancing of disparities of wealth and size been accompanied by cooperative behavior, or not? For example, has an arms race taken place?

The aggregate evidence on this score is encouraging. Admittedly, in 1985–92 real military spending increased in five out of six ASEAN countries. The exception was large and poor Indonesia, where the figure actually shrank by 14 percent. While the other five member states also registered increases in real defense spending on a per capita basis, the Indonesian figure in these terms declined 9 percent. Finally, expressed as a proportion of a country's economic product, defense outlays fell over the seven-year period in every ASEAN member except Brunei and the Philippines.[22]

Indonesian restraint in these circumstances is remarkable. President Sukarno was a civilian who spent heavily on the military. President Soeharto is a former army general who reoriented Sukarno's priorities away from defense toward development. In 1960, military expenditure as a proportion of spending on education and health combined was a mere 11 percent in Singapore and a whopping 207 percent in Indonesia. By 1990–91, Singapore's outlays for defense—making the shrimp deadlier—had risen to 129 percent of education and health spending, while the figure for Indonesia had plunged to 49 percent of spending to improve the education and health of Indonesians. In no other ASEAN country (Brunei excluded for lack of data) did these proportions change nearly so much.

Balanced disparity helps to explain Indonesia's apparent unwillingness to engage in an arms race with its fellow ASEAN members. However much the Singaporean shrimp makes itself poisonous to others, it will always be, geographically and demographically, a shrimp. A Singaporean conquest of, say, Sumatra is not a credible threat in Jakarta. Indonesians may be annoyed to think that when Singapore shops for arms it may be protecting itself from the possibility of an Indonesian attack, for that would indicate a lack of trust. But so long as the purchases themselves do not include blatantly offensive or massively destructive matériel—aircraft carriers, say, or nuclear missiles—they do not create in Jakarta a felt need to protect Indonesia from prospective Singaporean aggression. And this is despite Singapore's "forward defense" plans to carry any future war quickly and deeply into enemy territory.[23]

A skeptic could question the indicator: figures on defense spending are hard to compare across countries. What they do and do not cover may vary from state to state. Governments may have reason to understate true expenditures on defense. Military budgets are especially sensitive in Singapore, conscious as its leaders are of the need to reassure Jakarta and Kuala Lumpur.

Inventories of combat aircraft are harder to conceal and easier to compare than the dollar-equivalent costs of a category as broad as "defense." The ASEAN states' inability to make their own warplanes has necessitated purchasing these typically big-ticket items in more or less public transactions with foreign suppliers. Also, because Singapore has concentrated on enlarging its air force relative to its army or navy, if the city-state and Indonesia have been involved in an arms race, it should show up in Table 3.3a, which compares the two countries' stocks of combat planes in 1977, 1984, and 1994.[24]

Table 3.3a contains only modest evidence of an arms race in ASEAN. In four of the six member states the absolute number of combat planes actually declined in one of the two periods (Malaysia in 1977–84, Brunei and Singapore in 1984–94) or in both of them (the Philippines).

The stunningly high density of combat planes per unit of territory in Singapore in 1994 could appear provocative in the eyes of its Indonesian or Malaysian neighbors. The near doubling of Singapore's air force in 1977–84 may well have played a role in Malaysia's decision to expand rapidly its own inventory of planes in 1984–94. But Indonesia, if it responded at all to the earlier Singaporean expansion, did so only modestly in the later period. The extent to which Singapore's stock of planes remained constant in 1984–94 may also have encouraged Jakarta's relative restraint over that same decade. Third smallest in absolute numbers in ASEAN in 1977, the Indonesian combat air force was still third smallest in 1994.

Table 3.3

The Piranha's Teeth—Size and Outwardness of Air Force, ASEAN States

Part 3A: Size
Numbers of Combat Aircraft

Country	Per 1,000 km² 1994	Number of Planes 1994	Percentage Change 1984–94	Number of Planes 1984	Percentage Change 1977–84	Number of Planes 1977
Singapore	155.0	155	−0.6	156	92.6	81
Thailand	0.4	191	12.4	170	6.9	159
Brunei	0.33	2	−66.7	6	NA	0
Malaysia	0.28	92	170.6	31	−9.7	34
Philippines	0.1	43	−47.6	82	−21.2	104
Indonesia	0.04	79	23.4	64	64.1	39

Part B: Outwardness
Numbers of Conventional (Noncounterinsurgency) Planes
(as a % of all craft controlled by each set of three states)

Countries	1994	1984	1977
IM&S	92.0	64.9	63.6
BP&T	57.2	38.0	25.1

Notes: These figures cover combat airplanes under air force control, excluding reconnaissance craft and helicopters but including combat-capable trainers. No percentage change is given for Brunei in 1977–84 because the zero value of the initial observation makes the concept inapplicable (NA). Some of the thirty-nine planes listed for Indonesia in 1977—all bought from Western countries—were not operational for lack of spares. At that time Indonesia also owned ninety older-model Soviet MiGs; these were in storage and presumed not operational. Vietnam is excluded because it was not a member of ASEAN during the period covered. IM&S = Indonesia + Malaysia + Singapore; BP&T = Brunei + the Philippines + Thailand.

Sources: "East Asia and Australia," *The Military Balance 1994–1995,* London: Brassey's for the International Institute of Strategic Studies, 1994, pp. 164–193; "Asia and Australasia," *The Military Balance 1984–1985,* London: International Institute for Strategic Studies [IISS], 1984, pp. 90–112; "Asia and Australasia," *The Military Balance 1977–1978,* London: IISS, 1977, pp. 52–68. In the rare instance of a discrepancy between a summary figure and its enumeration by type of aircraft, the latter took precedence, along with figures in immediately prior and subsequent years.

Finally, the maintenance of generally good relations between Singapore and Malaysia in 1984–94 warrants skepticism as to the actually destabilizing effect of one of the most plausible signs of an intra-ASEAN arms race in Table 3.3a, namely, Singapore's increased spending in the first period as a possible spur to Malaysia's in the second. Also, Malaysia's "reply" does not appear to have been further "replied to" by Singapore during that second period. Instead Singapore seems to have allowed Malaysia to close somewhat the gap in inventory between them.

I say "seems to" because the true number of combat aircraft in Singapore's air force in 1994 could conceivably have exceeded the listed figure of 155 planes. There have been unconfirmed rumors that the city-state has stationed combat aircraft in Taiwan. Singaporean forces do train there, But even if Singapore's inventory in 1984–94 did not remain flat, that would not necessarily indicate an arms race with its fellow ASEAN members. If Singaporean planes are being kept on Taiwan, their potential to implicate the city-state in a war with China seems at least as clear as their prospective use against any ASEAN state.[25]

Meanwhile neither Singaporean nor Indonesian additions to their stocks of combat aircraft in 1977–84 provoked Brunei into like behavior in 1984–94. Because Table 3.3 focuses only on air forces, one should not conclude that Brunei did not enlarge or improve its armed forces over the decade. Sultan Hassanal Bolkiah has equipped his small navy, for example, with costly and deadly Exocet surface-to-surface missiles. But one may speculate that Singapore's steeply rising air combat capability, far from worrying the sultan, reassured him as a prospective deterrent to his immediate neighbors, Malaysia and Indonesia. Among all the ASEAN states, Singapore is the sultanate's least probable future adversary. From Brunei's standpoint as a small state located near two much larger ones, no ASEAN country is more similarly positioned or more like-minded on matters of defense than Singapore. For some years now the sultan has let Singapore station military personnel—some 500 in 1994—in Brunei for training purposes.

The comparative evidence by type of plane summarized in Table 3.3b further damages the case for an ASEAN-wide arms race. In preparing Table 3.3b I grouped the combat aircraft listed in 3.3a under two designations: craft such as strike planes and interceptors that are suited to external warfare against an enemy state; and typically smaller and cheaper craft appropriate for counterinsurgency operations against a domestic foe. I then aggregated these data into two groups of countries: IM&S as a hypothetically emerging ASEAN security core, and the other three ASEAN states as of 1994.

The result? Although Brunei, the Philippines, and Thailand (BP&T) had significantly reoriented their air forces "outward" toward interstate warfare since 1977, their air arms in 1994 remained substantially focused on the prospect of insurgency. In sharp contrast, IM&S, already in 1977 more "outward-facing" than BP&T, had become almost entirely so by 1994.

BP&T may have been too preoccupied internally to respond by acquiring more obviously external-use aircraft. Or they may not have been worried enough by IM&S' greater and increasing tilt toward external use to speed up their own shift in that direction. Or both. And both possibilities undermine the idea that an ASEAN-wide arms race has been under way. Relevant too is the fact that long-range bombers, a more obviously outward-offensive weapon than fighter aircraft, were not to be found in the air force of any ASEAN state at any time in 1977–94—or in 1995, for that matter. There seems to have been a tacit agreement simply not to purchase them.

Singaporean and Malaysian purchases possibly excepted, it is hard to see an arms race escalating along the sides of the IM&S triangle. The concentration in IM&S of ASEAN's total inventory of outward-oriented combat aircraft—61.5 percent of all 435 such planes were under these three states' control in 1994—does represent a potential for intramural violence. But those planes may also deter such conflicts while helping keep ASEAN safe from extramural threats. The arms that make IM&S part of the problem of regional security also help to give these governments roles in any solution, and that is another reason to entertain the idea that IM&S could be evolving into a security core. I do not mean to slight the arms-based influence of Thailand. But if counterinsurgency craft are subtracted from the figures for 1994 in Table 3.3a, Singapore's air force considerably exceeds Bangkok's in size—155 to 115.

Bolstering the argument in favor of IM&S as a security core is the likelihood that more than twenty-five years of cooperation inside ASEAN has allayed the suspicions in each of these states as to the probability that weapons purchased by one are intended for use against the other. Conditions would have to change greatly before war among

IM&S could become conceivable. At the same time, however, the increasing extent and deadliness of these states' arsenals will make all the more valuable the intramural reassurance to be gained by cooperative measures.

Would substituting ships for planes in this analysis lead to a different conclusion? A Malaysian analyst, J.N. Mak, has reviewed the evidence for and against a naval arms race inside ASEAN. He sees a "naval build-up" that "has not become an arms race." But he has voiced concern that one could be triggered, for example, by Thailand's expansive naval ambitions, which include plans to acquire the first aircraft carrier in ASEAN in 1997. (That would break a threshold comparable to the taboo against long-range bombers in ASEAN-state air forces.) Mak recommends that arms modernization be monitored and, if possible, moderated through confidence-building measures of various kinds, lest the buildup become destabilizing.[26]

Restraint and Cooperation

Balanced disparity has not predetermined the coherence of ASEAN as a regional security regime or, within that regime, the emergence of Indonesia, Malaysia, and Singapore as a reasonably stable if fragile security core. Without the forbearance and willingness of Indonesia to allow itself to lag in the standings behind many of its fellow members, ASEAN might have seen—and could have been destroyed by—a real arms race, as Singapore's effort to compensate for weakness might have triggered a tit-for-tat competition in arms between the two neighbors.

Singapore's financial power helped it to develop the most effective air force in Southeast Asia. Meanwhile the much lower ratio of funds to needs in Indonesia constrained Jakarta's ability to support an air force proportional to its huge size. Over ASEAN's first decade, 1967–76, Indonesia used the respite from conflict with neighbors that ASEAN cooperation provided to concentrate on its own economic development. The success of ASEAN in promoting trust among members also made the nearly two-thirds increase in Indonesia's combat air force in 1977–84 easier for the neighbors to understand not as a provocation, but as the natural consequence of the archipelago's rapid economic growth, which had made upgrading Jakarta's air force more affordable. The fact that Indonesia had only the fourth-largest number of such planes in ASEAN in 1984, a stock smaller than that of its much smaller neighbor, the Philippines, further reassured the rest of ASEAN. By the same token, over the ensuing decade, the success of ASEAN as a cooperative security regime helped to warrant Indonesian patience and restraint in the face of sharply rising Malaysian procurements.

Extreme differences of size can generate suspicion and facilitate intervention and conflict, as they have off and on, for example, between India and the rest of the South Asian Association for Regional Cooperation. Or they can help engender interdependence through acknowledged complementarity. And no ASEAN member is more obviously complementary with its neighbors than Singapore is with Malaysia and Indonesia. This meshing of comparative advantages is illustrated in the Sijori RIC (regionally industrializing core) already referred to, which links Singapore's strength (in capital) with the strengths of Indonesia (in labor, natural resources, and land) and Malaysia (in natural resources and land). Complementarity even marks Indonesia–Singapore military relations in that Jakarta allows Singapore—and no other foreign government—to use an air training space in Sumatra to keep up the skills of the city-state's pilots. Nor do Singapore and Indonesia have any boundary disputes to inhibit cooperation between them.

Sijori is not the sole RIC in ASEAN. But it is the oldest and the best developed. Compared with the relative strengths of Singapore, Johor, and Riau in Sijori, those that distinguish Medan, Pinang, Phuket, and their hinterlands in the planned Indonesia–Malaysia–Thailand triangle are less obviously complementary, and the economic logic of the latter RIC accordingly less compelling. The economic coherence of IM&S in this sense should facilitate their emergence as a regional security core, at least to the extent that the material interdependence of these states raises the cost to them of failing to cooperate on questions of security as well.

Personalities and Departures

The personalities of the leaders of IM&S have played key roles in shaping relations among the three states. Comparing the relative personal amity between heads of government on each side of the triangle, Soeharto–Lee contacts appear to have been the most amicable, Lee–Mahathir interactions somewhat less friendly, and Mahathir–Soeharto meetings probably the least cordial of the three. In view of their striking differences—Soeharto the reserved Javanese pragmatist, Lee the didactically neo-Confucian meritocrat, and Mahathir the outspokenly Asianist Malay—one may wonder that they were able to get along at all. Yet they managed to cooperate over a long period of time.

Tensions among IM&S have simmered on more than one occasion, though never to the boiling point. In 1968 Singapore convicted and hanged two Indonesian marines who had infiltrated the city-state as saboteurs under Sukarno's policy of "confronting" the "neocolonial" Federation of Malaysia, which had included the city-state from 1963 until its expulsion in 1965. In Jakarta, demonstrations against the executions triggered anti-Singapore riots. In 1969, rioting in Kuala Lumpur between Malays and ethnic Chinese threatened to rekindle the racial mistrust—between Malaysia's politically dominant Malay community and the Chinese majority in Singapore—that had sped the ejection of Singapore from Malaysia only four years before.

Occurring so early in the life of ASEAN, before habits of cooperation had had time to form, the riots in Jakarta and Kuala Lumpur could have spun out of control. Had they done so, they could have crippled the nascent association. It is not coincidental that ASEAN was founded in Bangkok. In 1967 memories of Lee's bitter exit from Malaysia and Sukarno's confrontation with both neighbors were still fresh in Singapore, Kuala Lumpur, and Jakarta. Nor had Manila given up its dispute with Malaysia over Sabah. In fact, in 1968 Manila revived its claim to Sabah and was reported to be training guerrillas to infiltrate the territory. Of the five states planning to create and join ASEAN, Thailand was least implicated in such current or recent altercations.

The five founding heads of state or government had not been willing to travel to Bangkok to launch the new grouping in person. In leaving this to their ministers, they had hedged their bets. Not having visibly and personally committed themselves to the new association made it easier to disavow and dismantle the experiment should that have become necessary. And if ASEAN were to unravel, the coming apart seemed most likely to start in renewed acrimony among IM&S, given the bad record of relations between them.

As matters turned out, the worry was unfounded. Soeharto and Lee made sure that the furor surrounding the executions did not get out of hand, while Lee and then–prime minister of Malaysia Tunku Abdul Rahman kept the riots in Kuala Lumpur from being internationalized. This record of at least tacit cooperation deepened in ensuing years, as

Indonesia placed a far higher priority on repairing and enlarging its domestic economy than on scoring points abroad. The commitment to economic development in all three capitals helped to keep the IM&S triangle stable. No member of the triad was willing to jeopardize local growth by endangering regional peace. And that, in turn, bought time in which to heal the wounds that had been inflicted on their relations in the 1960s by Indonesian vilification of Malaysia-cum-Singapore and the latter two states' estrangement.

External conditions facilitated rapprochement. The departure of most British forces from Malaysia and Singapore could have triggered an arms race between these neighbors. Instead, the prospect of a destabilizing "power vacuum" encouraged them to codify in 1971, jointly with the United Kingdom, Australia, and New Zealand, a set of Five-Power Defence Arrangements (FPDA) based on the idea that the security of Singapore and the security of Malaysia were indivisible. NATO-style collective security was not the point of the FPDA; the five signatories merely agreed to consult one another in the event of a threat to any one of them. But the FPDA did facilitate Singaporean-Malaysian defense cooperation. Nearly a quarter-century later, in the mid-1990s, the two states were still exercising together at sea and in the air under the auspices of the Arrangements, and still contributing to and benefiting from the Integrated Air Defense System (IADS) organized under the FPDA. (Off and on since 1989 Malaysian and Singaporean army units have also conducted joint exercises.)

In Indochina in 1969, hastened by events in 1968 such as the Tet offensive and the start of peace talks in Paris, the United States began drawing down its forces in Indochina. Although the process would not be completed until 1973, it was not hard for ASEAN to read the writing on the wall: Washington probably would not or could not stay the course in Vietnam. Already in 1969 President Richard Nixon had, in the Guam Doctrine, encouraged Asians seeking regional security to rely on their own resources.

Absence and Ambivalence

In this context—an impending "power vacuum" warranting self-reliance—Malaysia orchestrated the Kuala Lumpur Declaration in 1971. Not since their Bangkok Declaration four years earlier had all of the ASEAN governments gathered to articulate a vision of regional security. In Kuala Lumpur the five foreign ministers professed their respective states' determination to secure recognition of, and respect for, Southeast Asia as a Zone of Peace, Freedom, and Neutrality (ZOPFAN) free from external interference of any kind. Acknowledging a trend toward establishing regional "nuclear-free zones" (African and Latin American efforts to this effect were noted), the ministers in Kuala Lumpur also cautiously agreed that they "should explore" how to achieve the neutralization of Southeast Asia as "a desirable objective."[27]

Peace and freedom were not a new agenda for ASEAN. Four years earlier the Bangkok Declaration had dedicated the grouping to regional "peace, freedom and prosperity."[28] But "neutrality" was new. Also new in the Kuala Lumpur document was the seed of what would later become an official ASEAN hope—that Southeast Asia could become not just a ZOPFAN but a Nuclear Weapons–Free Zone (SEANWFZ) as well. Among the five members, Malaysia would remain the most vocal proponent of both ideas.

The communization of Indochina in 1975 further spurred intra-ASEAN cooperation. Worried by Hanoi's rising power and Washington's retreat, Bangkok quickly repaired its ties with Vietnam's chief local counterweight, China. In 1975 Bangkok established formal relations with Beijing and asked U.S. forces to leave Thai territory—a withdrawal completed in 1976. That ASEAN should have held its first summit in the latter year was no coincidence; there was a felt need to take stock of these new circumstances. Nor was it coincidental that the meeting should have been convened in ASEAN's most imposing Southeast Asian state, Indonesia, or that this first summit should have been followed merely eighteen months later (1977) with a second one in alphabetically next-in-line Malaysia.

The Vietnamese invasion of Cambodia in 1978 and the Chinese incursion into Vietnam in 1979 further galvanized ASEAN against a possible northern threat. But the question was, which threat? While Soviet-backed Vietnam caused particular anxiety among the Thais, located as they were on the new front line against Vietnamese troops in Cambodia, policy elites in Malaysia and Indonesia tended to see China as a greater or longer-term danger. In addition to China's far larger area and population compared with Vietnam's, there were no resident "overseas Vietnamese" communities in Malaysia or Indonesia for Hanoi to manipulate, in contrast to the conceivable chance that Beijing might try to recruit from among "its" ethnic Chinese Malaysians or Indonesians a locally destabilizing fifth column.[29]

Again, within ASEAN, Malaysia led the effort to adapt to new circumstances. No member state had identified itself earlier or more clearly with a foreign policy of keeping a substantial and equal distance from major outside powers. Bangkok and Manila had been too close to Washington. Thailand and the Philippines had not only hosted American troops and bases, they had fought alongside the Americans against North Vietnam and the Vietcong. By 1970, in contrast, the neutralization of Southeast Asia had become official Malaysian policy, including the view that American forces ought to leave Vietnam.

Singapore, by comparison, appeared incapable of giving more than lip service to neutralization if that meant spurning protection by an extra-regional power. Singapore's geophysical inferiority made it too vulnerable to its immediate neighbors, and hence too inclined to rely on outside powers staying around to check one another and make any local state think twice before trying to dominate the region.

In 1976 Singapore's foreign minister, Sinnathamby Rajaratnam, clearly but wishfully generalized his own country's calculus into a strategy for all of Southeast Asia. "The only rational course for Southeast Asian nations," he contended, "is not to work for the liquidation of [a] great power presence in the region but rather to ensure a multi-power presence as a more agreeable alternative to a single-power dominance."[30] The British departure from Malaysia and Singapore and America's defeat in Indochina in the 1970s, the Soviet disinvolvement that began in the late 1980s, and America's Philippine exit not long after Soviet disintegration in the early 1990s, accompanied by the extreme reluctance of Japan to play a security role in Southeast Asia, all combined to make Rajaratnam's admonition seem academic. To the extent that a check-and-balance pattern of great-power participation in regional security could not be assured, a Singapore-type strategy for ASEAN was unrealistic.

As for Indonesia, one might have picked it to become ASEAN's most ardent champion of ZOPFAN. If any Southeast Asian state could be expected to fill whatever local "power vacuum" departing outsiders might leave behind, it was Indonesia. As a Singapore-in-reverse, the one plausible would-be hegemon in Southeast Asia had the least to fear and the most to gain from neutralization. Certainly Indonesia supported ZOPFAN, but somewhat less consistently and enthusiastically than Malaysia did. Why?

First, domestic economic rehabilitation and growth far outranked neutralizing the region as a priority on Soeharto's agenda. This context made unappealing a high-profile campaign for regional neutralization that could scare the Western donors, lenders, and investors on whom his country's economic success had come substantially to depend. Second, the Malaysian origin of ZOPFAN and its zealous pursuit by Kuala Lumpur initially limited Indonesia's commitment to the idea. As Mahathir would discover in 1990 when he launched the notion of an East Asian Economic Grouping without first consulting Soeharto, Indonesia's sense of regional entitlement tended to make surprise moves by other ASEAN states unwelcome in Jakarta. ZOPFAN had not been sprung on Indonesia, and most Indonesian diplomats felt comfortable advocating it. But well into the 1970s, if not beyond, it retained a distinctly Malaysian flavor.

Third, Soeharto had no desire to stoke his neighbors' fears of Indonesian hegemony, least of all after 1975 when Indonesian troops were parachuted into the far smaller "power vacuum" created by Portugal's abandonment of East Timor. In deference to Indonesia, all of its ASEAN colleagues voted against the subsequent United Nations General Assembly resolution calling for Jakarta to withdraw its forces from East Timor—all, that is, save Singapore, which abstained. The abstention sent two signals to Jakarta: we are not just another enclave to be absorbed at will, but we will not oppose outright what you have done. And before long, Singapore too was voting the Indonesian way on East Timor in the UN.

Fourth and finally, the value of actually putting ZOPFAN into practice, as opposed to admiring it as an ideal, was undercut by the concept's failure to discriminate among outside powers, which were not all equally suspect in Indonesian eyes. In the 1970s and 1980s the presence of the U.S. Seventh Fleet just "over the horizon" could not be officially endorsed in Jakarta for fear of betraying Indonesia's credentials as a leader of the nonaligned world. However close his ties to the Americans might have become, Soeharto would not renounce that reputation, which dated from the 1955 Bandung Conference that had placed the archipelago within a "Third World" between American and Soviet spheres of influence. Privately, however, Indonesian officials in the 1970s and 1980s acknowledged the usefulness of an ongoing American military presence inside ASEAN as a check against the expansion of Soviet and especially Chinese power.

Tilt and Convergence?

Sino-Soviet rivalry in Southeast Asia in the late 1970s reinforced this unofficial "tilting" of ZOPFAN: as Beijing and Moscow became more obviously part of the problem of foreign interference in the region, it became harder to deny that Washington might be part of the solution. The invasion of Cambodia by Soviet-supported Vietnam in 1978 and the brief counterinvasion of Vietnam by China in 1979 brought President Soeharto in 1980 to the Malaysian town of Kuantan where he joined Prime Minister Hussein Onn of Malaysia in enunciating the "Kuantan principle": for the sake of peace in Southeast Asia, the USSR and China—pointedly cited by name in the communiqué—should stop intervening in Indochina.

Malaysian and Indonesian views of China were not identical. In 1974 Kuala Lumpur had moved out in front of its fellow ASEAN members by becoming the first to establish full relations with Beijing. Indonesia, in contrast, had suspended ties with the People's Republic in 1967 and would not resume them until 1990. It took that long for Indonesian mistrust of China to abate. The anticommunist generals who had fathered the "New Order" reckoned that China had covertly backed the leftist conspirators who had murdered seven of their fellow officers in Jakarta in 1965. Fears of the chance of future subversion by Beijing—that China could turn ethnic-Chinese Indonesians into a fifth column—kept Sino-Indonesian relations on hold even after Deng Xiaoping's economic reforms, begun in 1978, showed that in China too domestic economic growth had taken priority over foreign adventures.

Meanwhile Singapore, aware of Indonesian animosity toward China and anxious not to give Jakarta any reason to treat the Chinese-majority city-state as a proxy for Beijing, kept its public promise to wait for Indonesia to exchange ambassadors with China before doing so itself. In 1990, less than two months after Sino-Indonesian ties were unfrozen, Singapore turned its trade office in Beijing into an embassy. But de facto relations between Singapore and China had already warmed in the form of rising trade and investment.

Lee was a frequent visitor to China, advising Deng's government on economic growth and committing Singaporean management and resources to transform the city of Suzhou near Shanghai into an economic growth center based on Singapore's own experience in attracting foreign capital. Singapore even took the initiative to host a watershed meeting between delegations from China and Taiwan. If China's economic opening and disengagement from Indochina had made possible its rapprochement with Indonesia, those assuaging events had freed Lee Kuan Yew to behave less circumspectly toward the mainland, notwithstanding his country's ethnic makeup.

The end of the Cold War and associated trends in East Asia had by the 1990s given a dated quality to the conventional wisdom about ASEAN's centrifugal vision on security: that Singapore and Thailand wanted an externally guaranteed balance of power that would keep outsiders involved in Southeast Asia, while Indonesia and Malaysia preferred an internally balanced region rid of foreign interference. (The Philippines was too preocuppied with domestic traumas and its love-hate relationship with the United States to have a regional vision, while Brunei, after joining ASEAN in 1984, kept its profile too low to disseminate a vision if it had one.)

Singapore's and Thailand's desire for an external balance of power, as contrasted with Indonesia's and Malaysia's preference for an internal equilibrium, calls into question the resilience of IM&S as a putative regional security core. But even in the 1970s this polarity was overdrawn. Not all of the major outside powers were equally welcomed by Singapore and Thailand as external balancers. Nor were outsiders equally unwelcome in Indonesian or Malaysian eyes. All four ASEAN states, including even Malaysia, were basically well disposed toward an American security role; they differed mainly over how unobtrusive or "over the horizon" it should be. This shared attitude softened the contrast in strategic outlook between Singapore and its two Malay neighbors.

Also, compared with Thailand, Singapore was less willing to entertain a security role for China. In Bangkok, China's willingness to back the Khmer Rouge against Vietnam appeared to serve Thai interests, given the chance that the Vietnamese, having seized Cambodia, could threaten Thailand as the next domino in their way. The long history of rivalry between ethnically Thai and Viet power in mainland Southeast Asia further favored China as a balancer in Bangkok's eyes. Located farther down the domino chain, Singaporeans were less directly threatened by Vietnam and more concerned to reassure Indonesians and Malaysians that the city-state's racial composition did not imply pro-China policies, let alone a desire to become a Trojan horse for China inside ASEAN.

Nor had neutralization's pioneer, Malaysia, wanted simply to exclude the big powers from Southeast Asia. Initially Malaysia had hoped that outsiders could guarantee the "N" (neutrality) in ZOPFAN—hardly an invitation to them to ignore the region. And although Australia, New Zealand, and the United Kingdom were not exactly big powers, the willingness of Malaysia to join with Singapore in the FPDA showed that the latter two states' visions of regional security were not so radically opposed.

Implicit in the rationale for maintaining the Arrangements, after all, was the threat of Indonesian hegemony. Among ASEAN members from 1984 until Vietnam joined, Malaysia's population was only half as large as the median for the Association as a whole.[31] Demographically, the only smaller states were Singapore and Brunei. Malaysia, Singapore, and Brunei too had a structural interest in using outsiders as protection against domination by Southeast Asia's largest power. By reducing this asymmetry, these smaller states' economic growth had balanced ASEAN's disparity in the abstract. But that did not preclude their trying to restrain Indonesian power more concretely by involving prospective balancers from beyond the region. Compared with Malaysia and Singapore, however, Brunei kept a very low profile on regional security matters. When the tiny sultanate joined ASEAN in 1984 it barely had enough trained diplomatic staff to establish relations with other countries, let alone shape regional affairs. This deficiency could have been remedied had the sultan wanted to exert regional influence, but he did not.

As for Indonesia, the one ASEAN country without formal defense ties to any outside state, its leaders understood full well what former foreign minister Mochtar Kusumaatmadja acknowledged in 1990: that the FPDA amounted to "insurance" against a "reversion" of Indonesia "to its old ways"—that is, to a neo-Sukarnoist policy of hostility toward Malaysia and Singapore. But that rationale, far from motivating the ex-minister to chastise his immediate neighbors, led him to criticize Thailand instead. He saw in Thai prime minister Chatichai Choonhavan's shift toward rapprochement with Indochina a desire to create a "Thai sphere of influence" in mainland Southeast Asia.[32]

Kusumaatmadja proposed a Three-Power Defense Arrangement among IM&S that could be phased in over a five-year period, as the FPDA was phased out. Under this TPDA, the minister said, IM&S could conduct joint exercises with Australia as "a friendly neighboring power." The three states on the Malacca Straits, he argued, already enjoyed "the closest kind of military co-operation in ASEAN." A TPDA would merely institutionalize the defense collaboration that IM&S had forged de facto over the preceding "five to ten years."[33]

IM&S did not pursue this idea. To have done so would have disturbed other ASEAN members, especially Thailand, by appearing to create an exclusive subregime inside the Association. It is noteworthy nonetheless that IM&S had sufficiently convergent interests and a strong enough record of prior cooperation in Kusumaatmadja's eyes to make a TPDA seem realistic, at least to him.

From Cambodia to the Spratlys

This was not the first time that an Indonesian had intimated dissatisfaction with Thailand over Cambodia. In March 1980 Jakarta and Kuala Lumpur had articulated the Indo-Malaysian Kuantan principle—that China and the USSR ought not interfere in Indochina—partly to warn the Thais not to cooperate so closely with the Chinese and their Khmer Rouge allies as to bring the latter back to power in Phnom Penh, for that could have threatened ASEAN by expanding Chinese power on the mainland.

A scant two months after the Kuantan meeting, however, a Vietnamese battalion crossed the Thai-Cambodian border in search of Khmer Rouge. Only after two days of fighting were Thai soldiers able to push the Vietnamese back. Hanoi's timing was poor: by crossing the Thai border just when the Vietnamese foreign minister was being hosted by his Indonesian counterpart in Jakarta, the Vietnamese embarrassed Indonesia. By doing so not long after pleasing Kuala Lumpur by announcing its acceptance of ZOPFAN and promising not to violate Thai sovereignty, Vietnam angered Malaysia. The upshot was to reunify ASEAN behind Thailand as the "front-line state."

Indonesia and Malaysia continued to support ASEAN's policy of isolating Vietnam, if less outspokenly than Singapore. With IM&S approval, ASEAN helped to make the Cambodian resistance more palatable to world opinion by sponsoring a Coalition Government of Democratic Kampuchea (CGDK) that incorporated two noncommunist Khmer factions to balance the Khmer Rouge, whose rule in Cambodia in 1975–78 had taken perhaps a million lives. Lee Kuan Yew spearheaded this anti-Vietnamese move by persuading the three groups to meet in Singapore in 1981, while Malaysia helped complete it by hosting the inauguration of the CGDK the following year.

For most of the rest of the 1980s Thailand's vulnerability to Vietnam-in-Cambodia continued to give Thai views special weight in the making of ASEAN policy toward Indochina. But behind this more or less Bangkok-led common front, the three Malacca Straits states were growing closer. In 1981 Malaysia's newly installed Prime Minister Mahathir Mohamed began his long tenure—longer than any other Malaysian premier—by distancing his Cambodian policy from Thailand's. Along their common land border, Thailand's pursuit of Muslim separatists southward and Malay pressure northward against the remnants of the Communist Party of Malaya had already abraded relations between the two ASEAN states. Mahathir announced that Vietnam was not a major threat to ASEAN, and that henceforth Malaysia would regard Indonesia as a much closer ally than Thailand, let alone the Philippines, which had still not formally withdrawn its claim to Sabah. As if to underscore this shift, Mahathir chose Jakarta as the first ASEAN capital he would visit and made clear that he had no plans to travel to Manila.[34]

Meanwhile, in the early 1980s, slumping global demand for Malaysian and Indonesian primary exports raised the value to Kuala Lumpur and Jakarta of Singaporean capital and access to the global economy, and the value to Singapore of Malaysian and Indonesian markets, labor, land, and natural resources. In 1982 Lee Kuan Yew took his top cabinet ministers to both neighboring capitals to negotiate a range of bilateral economic agreements. By the end of the year, for example, Singapore's and Malaysia's airlines were running hourly shuttles between the two cities. But Lee also stimulated security cooperation, for example, by extending Malaysian use of the Woodlands naval base in Singapore.

Lee also proposed that bilateral military exercises with Indonesia be made multilateral with other ASEAN members. Soeharto was cool to this idea, which would have risked making ASEAN seem like a military pact. But the proposal showed that Singapore's vision of an externally supported balance of power in the region did not preclude intraregional cooperation of the sort one might have associated more with ZOPFAN than with the FPDA: multilateral regional resilience to be built up among the ASEAN states themselves.

Over the course of the 1980s Indonesian attitudes toward such cooperation with Singapore and Malaysia warmed. By 1990, as quoted above, Jakarta's former foreign minister Kusumaatmadja could in effect agree with the proposal Lee had made eight years before, provided that gradually, as trilateral security ties among IM&S were deepened, the FPDA would be dismantled.

In the 1990s Malaysia and Singapore still could not accept this condition. The risks of giving up the Arrangements as a hedge against Indonesian good will seemed too great. Who knew what would happen to Indonesian foreign policy after Soeharto? Had not Kusumaatmadja himself acknowledged the possibility of "reversion" to the "old ways" of confrontation with neighbors? Nevertheless, over the 1980s and into the 1990s, the respective regional security visions of IM&S did tend to converge. ZOPFAN was, in effect, externalized.

Trends in the late 1980s and early 1990s had seemed, on the contrary, to open a ZOPFAN-facilitating "power vacuum" in Southeast Asia: the shriveling of Moscow's ability to keep subsidizing Hanoi followed by the unraveling of the Soviet Union itself; the disengaging of Vietnam and China from Cambodia; and the exit of American forces, which had earlier quit Indochina and Thailand, from the Philippines.

By the early-to-mid-1990s, however, one outsider had emerged as the prime candidate to fill whatever "empty" space the disinvolvement of outsiders had created in Southeast Asia: China. The ASEAN states generally, and IM&S in particular, regarded with anxiety the increasing ability and willingness of Beijing to project military power across maritime Southeast Asia on behalf of its claim to sovereignty over the entire South China Sea. In 1992, for example, China boosted military spending 12 percent, took delivery of two dozen long-range fighters from Moscow, built a runway on the Paracel Islands, upgraded its garrisons in the Spratlys, and authorized in a national law the use of "necessary force" to protect nearly 800,000 square kilometers of its "territorial waters" in the South China Sea—a zone that one internal Chinese document called "survival space," which sounds like lebensraum.[35]

In 1991 an Australian observer, Tim Huxley, doubted the prospects for security cooperation among the ASEAN states. The waning of Indochina as an external security issue would, he argued, "throw into sharper relief long-standing contentious relationships *within* ASEAN," notably between Singapore and Malaysia. Their already prickly relations, he feared, would get worse. The two neighbors were already involved, he believed, in an intra-ASEAN arms race that was gaining speed. Seen with the hindsight of 1995, Huxley's warnings appear somewhat overdrawn. One reason could be the absence in his account of China and the possibly solidifying effect of a felt threat from that direction.[36]

Candor and Action

From its inception in 1967, ASEAN had kept regional security off its formal agenda—for fear of resembling a military alliance, which might have provoked outsiders, and because its members' divergent views made discord on the subject too likely. It was an ad hoc meeting of member states that had issued the Kuala Lumpur Declaration proposing ZOPFAN in 1971, and they had been careful not to speak in ASEAN's name. Nor was the Indo-Malaysian Kuantan principle of 1980 an ASEAN idea.

By the early 1990s the taboo against taking public stands of security had been weakened in several ways. A quarter-century of intramural diplomacy and economic growth since ASEAN's birth had accustomed its members to cooperating as a group and lowered the risk of broaching the topic of security. Meanwhile the subject had become less sensitive externally as well. One of the three outsiders whom ASEAN might have disturbed by seeming to augur a military bloc—the USSR—had disappeared, and its Russian successor state was not a major player. The others had disengaged from the region—China and the United States from Indochina, the United States from Thailand and the Philippines.

These changes made ZOPFAN propitious by, in effect, inviting ASEAN to seize the day and fill the resulting "vacuum" from within, preempting outsiders. Meanwhile, however, the rise of China as the sole plausible external hegemon in Southeast Asia posed a choice for ASEAN's members: to join the Chinese bandwagon, siding with China in hopes of moderating its influence; or to balance the Chinese, forming a counterweight in hopes of checking that influence. Both options pointed away from an exclusively indigenous security arrangement as implied by the "N" in ZOPFAN and toward the reinvolvement of outside powers. If China were propitiated, its right to a say in Southeast Asian affairs would have to be acknowledged. If China were counterbalanced, the United States would have to be granted a greater role in the region. ASEAN's own military power alone could not, at least not yet, credibly deter Beijing. As for Russia and Japan, the first was too weak, the second was too inhibited, and both were historically too suspect to be cast in that supporting role.

Had the externalist or anti-ZOPFAN priorities of Thailand and Singapore diverged as much from Malaysia's and Indonesia's internalist or pro-ZOPFAN views as the conventional case for their polarity indicated, this dilemma over how to handle China should have been resolved by silence, as ASEAN's members continued to agree to disagree. Instead, ZOPFAN was externalized by, in effect, redefining it to incorporate external participation in Southeast Asian security. In 1990 Singapore signed an agreement with the United States to invite American forces back into the region. Singapore would host a small but ongoing contingent of American naval and air force personnel, mainly for logistical purposes but with a provision for the "rolling deployment" of U.S. combat planes. Singapore's move proved much less controversial in Indonesia and Malaysia in 1990 than it would have been earlier in ASEAN's history.[37]

Gathered in Singapore for their fourth summit in January 1992, ASEAN's leaders could have defended an exclusionary understanding of ZOPFAN against this invitation to welcome the U.S. military again. Instead, Indonesia and Malaysia joined the consensus in Singapore that the time had come to make security an explicit part of ASEAN's agenda, and not just for discussion among the five members but for consultation with their "dialogue partners" as well. These partners included the United States (and Japan) but not China (or Russia). Later that year, the ASEAN Ministers' Meeting and Post-Ministerial Conference with these and other such partners discussed security matters for the first time.

Initially Singapore's overture to the Americans did appear to ruffle Indonesian and Malaysian feathers. But before long both of the latter states had closed their own deals with the Americans—the Malaysians to repair U.S. warships and warplanes at Lumut and outside Kuala Lumpur, respectively, and the Indonesians to repair U.S. warships in Surabaya. Such low-key arrangements soon spread to all of the ASEAN states, excepting of course Vietnam, even after it joined the Association in 1995. And a few months after that accession, one knowledgeable American source was willing to predict that within a year a U.S. navy vessel would make a port visit to Vietnam.[38]

The case of Malaysia is particularly striking. No ASEAN state has spent more diplomatic energy promoting ZOPFAN, itself a Malaysian invention. Yet in September 1991, just five days before the Philippine Senate voted to terminate America's leases on Clark Field and Subic Bay within a year, Defense Minister Mohamed Najib bin Abdul Razak of Malaysia announced that his country was ready to expand the range and frequency of joint exercises, visits, and repairs already being implemented by a U.S.-Malaysian Bilateral Training and Consultative Group (BITAC). BITAC had been established in 1984, but its existence had not previously been revealed.[39]

For nine years BITAC had been kept secret at Malaysia's request. That Najib was willing in 1991 not only to acknowledge BITAC's existence publicly but to offer to enlarge it showed that Kuala Lumpur did not intend to use the Cold War's end as a chance to establish ZOPFAN by disinviting the United States from Southeast Asia. "We [Malaysians]," said Najib in 1991, "would like to see a fair degree of American military presence in the region." In Najib's estimation, this presence would have a "salutary countervailing effect" on regional security.[40]

This evolution in the Malaysian position should not be misunderstood. First, Malaysian military officers were considerably more willing to argue for an American regional security presence than was their volatile prime minister. It was Mahathir who would later in an off-the-cuff remark dismiss even the existing modest U.S. military profile in Southeast Asia as a waste of American money. Second, while Najib's judgment that American forces operating in Southeast Asia would have a "salutary countervailing effect" seemed to suggest that they could help check Chinese hegemony and thus were in Malaysia's national interest, he gave no indication that this interest was great enough to warrant Malaysia's making any concessions to the Americans in order to help them retain a local presence. Third, Najib's willingness to entertain an American security role did not prevent him from criticizing the United States for what he called its "big stick approach" to Southeast Asia, presumably a reference to American objections to the human rights records of Malaysia and other ASEAN states.[41] Nevertheless, ZOPFAN had been externalized. China's muscle-flexing in the South China Sea, as if to fill the "vacuum" left behind by the American exit from the Philippines, had made sensible a Malaysian tilt toward Singapore's views.

This is not to say that in the 1990s ASEAN chose to rely on American power to counterbalance a rising China. From the viewpoint of many in ASEAN the administration of President Bill Clinton seemed too preachy, prickly, and domestically preoccupied to be reliable. Nor were the ASEAN states passive. In 1989 Indonesia began to organize and host what would become an ongoing series of unofficial workshops to discuss the South China Sea disputes. These events brought together all six claimants to the Spratly Islands—Brunei, China, Malaysia, the Philippines, Taiwan, and Vietnam.

Jakarta saw no need to involve the United States in this initiative. Doing so would have made it harder for China to take part, and the Indonesians very much wanted the Chinese there. Internationalizing ZOPFAN did not presuppose cooperation with only one external partner. Nor did the ASEAN states see a reason to invite the Americans or any other third party to the meeting they held in 1995 in Hangzhou, China. There the Southeast Asians felt bold and unified enough to express directly as a group their concern over Chinese maritime ambitions.

The forging of large multilateral frameworks for Asian-Pacific security cooperation in the 1990s further illustrates the willingness of IM&S to act on the idea that regional security requires cooperation with outsiders. The Council for Security Cooperation in the Asia Pacific (CSCAP) was constituted in Kuala Lumpur in mid-1993. The ASEAN Regional Forum (ARF) held its first meeting in Bangkok a year later. Think tanks in IM&S had played key roles in the planning for CSCAP, whose organization had been stimulated by the Roundtable on Asia Pacific Security held annually in Kuala Lumpur. The Roundtable had been organized by Malaysia's Institute of Strategic and International Studies since 1987, first singly, later jointly with strategic studies centers elsewhere in ASEAN. CSCAP in turn encouraged ARF, which built upon the ASEAN Post-Ministerial Conferences that annually had brought the five Southeast Asian states together with their "dialogue partners," and had, as noted, been discussing security matters since 1992.

A Regional Security Core?

A fuller exposition of the relative contribution of IM&S to regional security diplomacy compared with other ASEAN member states would require me to violate the bounds of this already long chapter by also reviewing Thai, Filipino, and Bruneian security policies in some detail.

Certainly such a review would yield instances of initiatives taken by these states, especially Thailand. But it would not, in my judgment, dislodge my conclusion, which is based in any case not just on levels of activity but on centrality and stability too: by the 1990s Indonesia, Malaysia, and Singapore had begun to resemble a regional security core—embryonic, fragile, perhaps destined to be superseded by some other pattern, but a core nonetheless.

Even in 1995 IM&S were not a solidly harmonic triangle. Disagreements over territory, for example, still complicated two of the three bilateral sides. Malaysia claimed an uninhabited rock with a lighthouse on it controlled by Singapore. The periodic flaring of this controversy irritated the two claimants, but it was hard to imagine them coming to blows over it. Nor did Indonesia appear prepared to implement by force its claim to a pair of islands off the northeast coast of Borneo controlled by Malaysia. The third side of the triad was in this respect trouble-free, Singapore and Indonesia having long since agreed to their common border.

Future relations among IM&S will not be trouble-free. Underneath the surface of their cooperation, it is not hard to notice biases, sensitivities, and disagreements. Commenting on instances of intra-ASEAN squabbling, a Malaysian observer mused ruefully that "perhaps" his country had earned the "dubious distinction of having been involved in such situations more often than any other"—and with every other— member state.[42] On the other hand, for all Prime Minister Mahathir's or, for that matter, Senior Minister Lee's ability to ruffle the neighbors' feathers, one ought not discount the centripetal benefits of nearly thirty years of steady if fluctuating bilateral Indonesian-Malaysian, Malaysian-Singaporean, and especially Singaporean-Indonesian cooperation.

Illustrating the dynamics and evolution of the sensitivities among IM&S to each other's behavior are the differences between successive trips to Singapore by two Israeli leaders: President Chaim Herzog in 1986 and Prime Minister Yitzhak Rabin in 1993. The first visit triggered anti-Singapore demonstrations in Indonesia, Malaysia, and Brunei. These states' diplomatic heads of mission in Singapore were called home, but only for the duration of the visit. President Soeharto felt no qualms about visiting Singapore himself a few months later, albeit on his way back from Malaysia. Singapore's semiofficial *Straits Times* objected to Malaysia's objection and reasserted the city-state's right to its own foreign policy, but the controversy quickly died down.

In 1993 Singapore received Rabin after he had met with Soeharto in Jakarta. The Israeli premier's brief visit to Jakarta was downplayed in Indonesia, which like Malaysia and Brunei did not recognize Israel. Indonesian authorities did not announce the visit until some four hours after Rabin's departure. They termed it a "courtesy call" on Soeharto in his capacity not as Indonesian president but as head of the country then leading the Non-Aligned Movement. Soeharto's foreign minister quickly squelched rumors that diplomatic relations with Israel were under consideration. Inside IM&S, nevertheless, Jakarta's invitation legitimated Singapore's. Malaysia could not castigate the city-state's effrontery without criticizing a far larger and overwhelmingly Muslim neighbor, Indonesia.

But even if Rabin had not stopped first in Jakarta, Mahathir would not have broken off relations with Singapore, partly because of the desire he shares with Soeharto to co-opt, but not be co-opted by, potentially disruptive anti-Chinese Islamists at home.[43] Two years later, in 1995, Lee led a Singaporean trade mission to Israel and, at the United Nations in New York, Soeharto met again with Prime Minister Rabin, this time officially as the president of Indonesia, all without visible damage to inter-IM&S relations. Indonesia and Malaysia still recognized the Palestine Liberation Organization; Singapore still recognized Israel. About some things the three countries have agreed to disagree.

Overall in the 1990s, the Singapore–Jakarta connection worked remarkably well, considering how different the two countries were spatially, racially, and economically. Balanced disparity in this instance, and the complementarity it implied, facilitated cooperation. More important in policy terms were the good working relations that Lee Kuan Yew and Goh Chok Tong maintained with Soeharto. Singapore and Malaysia, on the other hand, were more like formerly estranged siblings—quick to bicker but slow to fight. Of the three personal dyads, probably the least warm was Soeharto's with Mahathir, whose behavior reportedly seemed too strutting and abrasive for the older man's Javanese taste.

After more than twenty-five years of getting along inside ASEAN, IM&S had not evolved into a trilateral entente and showed no signs of doing so. Even Sijori was less a triangle than a straight line linking Singapore north to Malaysia and south to Indonesia. But these limitations were not ruinous to IM&S as an emerging regional security core. If their activities were not always congruent, IM&S were not at such loggerheads as to countermand each other's influence within ASEAN as a security regime.

Looking back over ASEAN's history, had the balance of initiative on regional security shifted from Thailand, poised on the front line against Vietnam in the continental northern portion of Southeast Asia, to IM&S on a new front line against China in the maritime south? Not exactly. IM&S had already been influential within ASEAN, so when the shift came it was not sudden but incremental. Unlike the Cambodian war, the Spratlys pitted several ASEAN states against each other, blurring the clarity of a front line against China. China's "threat" to ASEAN could not be identified as solely maritime. Just as Jakarta had been named ASEAN's go-between with Hanoi when Vietnam appeared to threaten regional security, so could a show of Chinese power on the mainland someday bring Bangkok back into the diplomatic spotlight as an interlocutor with Beijing.

In the long run the ASEAN states were more likely to propitiate China than they had been willing to appease Vietnam, and that further qualified the sense in which a new front line had been drawn in the South China Sea. Also, despite ZOPFAN's externalization, IM&S did not all see China the same way, even by the mid-1990s. Nor was it clear that China would continue to risk solidifying ASEAN against it. At the ASEAN Regional Forum meeting in Brunei in 1995, China made conciliatory moves toward ASEAN over the Spratlys; by acknowledging the Law of the Sea as a basis for resolving the dispute, the Chinese especially pleased Indonesia.

Yet these qualifications do not upset the basic point: partly because of the shift in focus from Cambodia to the Spratlys, IM&S did emerge in the 1990s as a recognizable if reversible regional security core inside ASEAN.

Overview: Reasons for Resilience

During ASEAN's long preoccupation with Indochina—from Saigon's fall in 1975 to the Paris peace conference on Cambodia in 1991—IM&S were not bystanders on regional security. On the contrary, most of the security-related undertakings over this period could be traced to or centrally involved IM&S: holding ASEAN's first summit in Bali, planning the Kuala Lumpur Declaration, issuing the Kuantan principle, putting together the CGDK, pursuing ZOPFAN and SEANWFZ, setting up Sijori, organizing multilateral workshops among claimants to the Spratly Islands. . . . The list is long, and could be lengthened by recalling Indonesia's own Cambodian initiatives: its role as ASEAN's interlocutor with Vietnam, its "cocktail party diplomacy" and the resulting Jakarta Informal Meetings, and its effort with France to co-manage a settlement enabling outsiders to disengage. Nevertheless, in the 1980s the prominence of IM&S on regional security was still largely upstaged by the sense in which Thailand and its circumstances defined ASEAN policy toward Indochina—then the site of the Association's most serious security concern.

The 1990s did not suddenly activate Indonesian, Malaysian, or Singaporean diplomacy. Rather the reconfiguring of ASEAN's anxiety away from an inward-looking Vietnam and toward an outwardly more assertive China highlighted maritime Southeast Asia and gave greater ASEAN-wide legitimacy to Indonesian and Malaysian worries over China. Jakarta and Kuala Lumpur contributed to this legitimation by reducing the distance between their visions and Singapore's. In the 1990s, by and large, Indonesian and Malaysian diplomatic moves and statements on regional security favored, implied, or were compatible with the idea of nesting ZOPFAN constructively in a check-and-balance pattern of involvement by outsiders.

This reorienting of ZOPFAN outward called for ASEAN to take the lead in tackling security problems in the wider neighborhood. Two new and highly inclusive security frameworks, CSCAP and ARF, involving as they did the United States, China, Japan, Russia, and even the European Union, illustrated the scope of this new priority. These innovations owed much to the creativity and cooperation of IM&S, first at the private level among think tanks and later officially among governments. I have mentioned in this context Jakarta's initiative to host the Spratly workshops involving Taipei and Beijing, among other claimants. Noteworthy too was Singapore's initiative to host a meeting in 1993 between unofficial representatives from Taipei and Beijing in the hope of alleviating the arguably greater danger to regional security posed by the unresolved future status of Taiwan.

In 1995 IM&S were not a triumvirate inside ASEAN. They were not a vanguard explicitly leading the Association. They did not offer its other members a united front with a common position. Trilateral cooperation among them had not been institutionalized, and there was little evidence that it would be. Yet the three states had proven themselves sufficiently central, stable, and active on regional security to resemble a kind of diplomatic kitchen for the house of ASEAN. The cooks might squabble over recipes, but there was less disagreement about the menu: keeping the region secure from external or internal hegemony by trying to fashion mutually supporting external and internal balances of power.

The reasons for this development are many. Among those discussed in this chapter are: the winding down of the Cambodian war, the disengagement of Beijing and Moscow from Indochina, and the ending of Thailand's status as a "front-line state"; Manila's preoccupation with domestic events; tiny Brunei's unwillingness if not demographic incapacity to play a major regional security role; the American military's farewell to the Philippines; fears of a "power vacuum" in Southeast Asia and the rise of China as a candidate to fill it; and the shifting of ASEAN's attention from Vietnam-in-Cambodia to China-in-the-Spratlys and the reaccenting of ZOPFAN to accommodate a more "Singaporean" emphasis on accommodating outsiders in ways that might discourage, or at least postpone, Chinese hegemony.

Still other reasons cited above for considering IM&S as a plausible though frangible regional security core-in-progress include: the originality and enterprise of IM&S in proposing ideas, hosting meetings, and organizing frameworks to safeguard or improve regional security; the embodiment in IM&S of a stabilizing pattern of balanced disparity; the lack of a destabilizing arms race among IM&S or in ASEAN, thanks in part to Indonesian restraint; the greater longevity in office of IM&S leaders, which enhanced their influence; and finally, at a more structural level underlying all of these contingent events and trends, the sheer geographic, demographic, and economic prominence and centrality of IM&S inside the ASEAN region.

Thus my conclusion: *Indonesia, Malaysia, and Singapore were by the mid-1990s a provisionally emerging regional security core.*

What of the future? If IM&S became enemies, ASEAN would be stymied or sidetracked—or collapse. In this extreme sense, the solidity of IM&S-the-emerging-core is critical to the resilience of ASEAN-the-regime. The IM&S triad has not been formally institutionalized; it is not truly trilateral; and its members often disagree. But in stressing these limitations at the core, I have not meant to be pessimistic about the regime. From the standpoint of ASEAN's survival and effectiveness, a certain fragility or openness at its center is desirable. Were

IM&S to become a solidly closed club, the rest of ASEAN would likely reconsider the benefits of their own devalued membership. But this is not likely to happen, and that is good news for peripheral member states, and for the regime as a whole.

If ASEAN continues to expand, it will become more diverse. In becoming more diverse, it could become more disorganized, its dynamics more centrifugal. Under such conditions a regional security core could become at once more necessary and harder to form—or reform. The trick in IM&S will be to continue trying to manage regional security without appearing to monopolize it.

Notes

1. This definition identifies a subtype of the genus "international regime." International regimes have been defined by Andrew Mack and John Ravenhill as "multilateral arrangements that are created to facilitate international cooperation." In Stephen Krasner's more detailed formulation they are sets of "implicit or explicit principles, norms, rules, and decision-making procedures around which actors' expectations converge." Mack and Ravenhill, "Economic and Security Regimes in the Asia-Pacific Region," in Mack and Ravenhill, eds., *Pacific Cooperation: Building Economic and Security Regimes in the Asia-Pacific Region,* Boulder, CO: Westview, 1995, p. 1; Krasner, "Structural Causes and Regime Consequences: Regimes as Intervening Variables," in Krasner, ed., *International Regimes,* Ithaca, NY: Cornell University Press, 1983, p. 2. While it is more than just a security regime, historically ASEAN has done better at maintaining regional security than at promoting, for example, trade among its members.

2. One may argue that Pol Pot and his henchmen, had they not been toppled by the Vietnamese, would in time have threatened Thailand, and that far from opposing Vietnamese hegemony in Cambodia, ASEAN should have welcomed it as a positive contribution to regional security. But Thai authorities did not see things this way. Their suspicions of Vietnam, reinforced by ASEAN's own commitment to state sovereignty, prevailed in turning the rest of the Association against Hanoi, never mind the abattoir that Pol Pot's Cambodia had become. For more on ASEAN's evolution as a security regime, see my chapter, "From Confrontation to Cooperation in Southeast Asia: Lessons and Prospects," in Barbara K. Bundy, Stephen D. Burns, and Kimberly V. Weichel, eds., *The Future of the Pacific Rim: Scenarios for Regional Cooperation,* Westport, CT: Praeger, 1994.

3. Annually on average in 1980–93 China boosted its gross national product (GNP) per person by 8.2 percent. So did South Korea. "World Development Indicators," *World Development Report 1995,* New York: Oxford University Press for the World Bank, 1995 (henceforth cited as *WDI95*), pp. 162–163; "Regional Performance Figures," *Asia 1995 Yearbook,* Hong Kong: Review Publishing, 1995 (henceforth cited as *RPF95*), p. 14. For lack of adequate data, the economies of Cambodia, Laos, Macao, Myanmar, North Korea, and Vietnam are

excluded from this comparison, but there is no reason to think that any of them outran China over this period.

4. In 2006, under these assumptions, China's accumulated and available military capital stock (taking into account depreciation as well as procurement) could equal Japan's. But it will have only one-third the value of America's. Charles Wolf, K. C. Yeh, Anil Bamezai, Donald P. Henry, and Michael Kennedy, *Long-Term Economic and Military Trends 1994–2015: The United States and Asia,* Santa Monica, CA: RAND, 1995, pp. 9 (GDP), 15 (spending), and 18 (stock); see also p. 19 ff. on methods and caveats.

5. Recalculating exchange-rate-dependent GDPs in terms of purchasing power parity (PPP) typically raises their value in poor countries such as China relative to rich ones such as the U.S. and Japan. This is so because the cost of living is generally lower in the former economies than in the latter. The cross-country ranking itself implies a world economy in which the appropriate yardstick is not an inward-facing variable such as the cost of personal consumption but an outward-oriented one that better approximates each economy's relative impact on other economies through foreign trade and investment. PPP-controlled GDPs are also statistically more problematic and available for fewer economies than are their exchange-rate-based counterparts. For these reasons, the country product values cited in this chapter control for inflation but not purchasing power. Such considerations have led one observer to conclude that "China is *not* going to be the most important or powerful economy in the world in the foreseeable future." Barry Naughton, "China's Economic Future," unpublished paper, Graduate School of International Relations and Pacific Studies, University of California–San Diego, La Jolla, CA, August 1995, p. 1.

6. In *Books in Print 1994–95: Titles,* New Providence, NJ: R. R. Bowker, 1994, for example, works starting with the word "China" filled seventeen columns, compared with one column for "ASEAN" and one column for "Southeast Asia" as title beginnings. In the latter two listings, only two books imputed increasing significance to their subjects: *ASEAN Today—Your Partner of Tomorrow* (1981) and *Southeast Asia Emerges* (1987). In contrast, books in the first listing pictured China not just "awakening" or "emerging" but "taking off" and "rising" too, arguably on its way to becoming "Asia's next economic giant." Also see William H. Overholt, *The Rise of China: How Economic Reform Is Creating a New Superpower,* New York: Norton, 1993. Western and (official) Chinese reactions to China's prospects may be compared, respectively, in "Containing China," the cover editorial in *The Economist,* July 29, 1995, p. 23, and "China's Rise: Threat or Not?" *Beijing Review,* 38 (January 30, 1995), pp. 23–25.

7. See, for example, former Indonesian foreign minister Mochtar Kusumaatmadja, "Some Thoughts on ASEAN Security Co-operation: An Indonesian Perspective," *Contemporary Southeast Asia,* 12:3 (December 1990), pp. 162–163.

8. "Human Development Indicators," *Human Development Report 1995,* New York: Oxford University Press for the UN Development Programme, 1995 (henceforth cited as *HDI95*), pp. 186–187, 194–195, 208, and 213.

9. For more on this topic, see "The Case for a Maritime Perspective on Southeast Asia" that I made in the *Journal of Southeast Asian Studies,* 11:1 (March 1980), pp. 139–145.

10. If contiguity on land is also defined as a distance between countries of fifty miles or less, IM&S become even more central, as the proximity of Brunei to Indonesia increases the latter's neighbors from three to four. (The nearness of Indonesia in turn lifts Brunei's neighbors from one to two.)

11. These estimates rely on data for 1993 in *WDI95*, pp. 162–163 and 228. In that year almost nine-tenths of all 462 million Southeast Asians lived in ASEAN countries, while ASEAN included more than three-fourths of all Southeast Asian land.

12. Average annual percentage rates of growth in GDP in 1970–80 and 1980–93 were: 7.2 and 5.8 in Indonesia, 7.9 and 6.2 in Malaysia, and 8.3 and 6.9 in Singapore—compared with 3.6 and 2.9 for all documented countries. *WDI95*, pp. 164–165.

13. These estimates reflect data in *WDI95*, pp. 186–187, supplemented by figures from "Countries of the World," *1995 Information Please Almanac*, Boston, MA: Houghton Mifflin, 1994 (henceforth *COW94*), pp. 143–296 for Brunei (1992) and Cambodia (1991), and from "Nations of the World," *The World Almanac and Book of Facts 1995*, Mahwah, NJ: Funk and Wagnalls, 1994, pp. 740–839 for Myanmar (1992).

14. Based on *WDI95*, pp. 186–187, supplemented by *COW94*, pp. 143–296 for Brunei (1992), Cambodia (1990), Laos (1993), Myanmar (1991), and Vietnam (1992). According to these figures, ASEAN's members, including Vietnam, shipped 99.6 percent of all Southeast Asian exports.

15. In 1991 the value of Singapore's foreign trade (exports plus imports) equaled 312 percent of the city-state's GDP. In the same year Hong Kong's trade dependence was 192 and Malaysia's 148. IM&S's closest rival for Southeast Asian security leadership based on trading prowess, Thailand, scored only 40 percent on this index, seven points below Indonesia despite the latter's vast internal market. "Human Development Indicators," *Human Development Report 1994*, New York: Oxford University Press for the UN Development Programme, 1994, pp. 168–169 and 198. I would have used data for 1992 but for the omission of trade dependence figures for developing countries from *HDI95*.

16. These estimates reflect data obtained from the International Monetary Fund and other sources and kindly supplied to me by the Information Resource Unit of the Institute of Policy Studies in Singapore.

17. On a seven-point scale from "freest" (1.0) to "least free" (7.0), Freedom House rated the Philippines and Thailand at 3.5 and 4.0, respectively, in 1994, compared with Malaysia at 4.5, Singapore at 5.0, and Indonesia at 6.5. "Tables and Ratings," *Freedom in the World: The Annual Survey of Political Rights and Civil Liberties, 1994–1995*, New York: Freedom House, 1995, p. 683.

18. British prime ministers Benjamin Disraeli, William Gladstone, and Winston Churchill all substantially influenced European security while holding office for long periods. Yet the sum of all their terms does not equal Lee's tenure. Also, among the four, only Lee served all of his years as premier consecutively.

19. For more on balanced disparity, including evidence for it from 1985, see my "ASEAN as an International Regime," *Journal of International Affairs*, 41:1 (Summer/Fall 1987), pp. 1–16.

20. *WDI95*, pp. 166–167. Indonesian, Singaporean, and Philippine GDPs stood at U.S. $144.7, $55.1, and $54.1 billion, respectively.

21. *HDI95*, p. 182.

22. Data in this and the next paragraph are drawn from *HDI95,* pp. 182–183.

23. On these plans and their implications, see Dana R. Dillon, "A Scenario for Southeast Asia," *Military Review* (September 1994), pp. 55–60. See also Tim Huxley, "Singapore and Malaysia: A Precarious Balance," *The Pacific Review,* 4:3 (1991), pp. 208–211.

24. The year 1994 was the latest for which data were readily available in 1995. Also, I wanted to describe the situation in ASEAN prior to Vietnam's accession. Conveniently, 1984 came a decade earlier and was the first year of Brunei's membership. I chose 1977 because it was the first year after ASEAN's first summit, in Bali, where the watershed Treaty of Amity and Cooperation was adopted. The treaty's principles underlay the subsequent evolution of the Association as a more formal regional security regime and served as norms to which subsequent Southeast Asian states could—and did—accede en route to full membership in the regime. Table 3.2 thus covers combat aircraft acquisition within a maturing regional security regime. For an overview of ASEAN arms acquisitions that includes naval and army procurement as well, see J. N. Mak, *ASEAN Defence Reorientation 1975–1992: The Dynamics of Modernization and Structural Change,* Canberra: Australian National University, Research School of Pacific Studies, Strategic and Defence Studies Centre, 1993.

25. According to Tim Huxley, the program in Taiwan is the "most extensive and important overseas training operation" Singapore has. Among the facilities and equipment available to Singapore on Taiwan, Huxley lists no planes, but he does mention a detachment of Super Puma helicopters. Huxley, "Singapore Forces Shape Up," *Jane's Defence Weekly,* November 19, 1994, p. 26.

26. J. N. Mak, "The ASEAN Naval Build-up: Implications for the Regional Order," *The Pacific Review,* 8:2 (1995), p. 321; and Mak and B. A. Hamzah, "Navy Blues," *Far Eastern Economic Review,* March 17, 1994, p. 30 (on Thailand).

27. "Zone of Peace, Freedom and Neutrality Declaration," Kuala Lumpur, Malaysia, November 27, 1971, as reproduced in K. S. Sandhu et al., *The ASEAN Reader,* Singapore: Institute of Southeast Asian Studies, 1992, pp. 538–539. "Nuclear-free" in an ASEAN context has referred to weapons, not energy.

28. "The Asean Declaration," Bangkok, Thailand, August 8, 1967, as reproduced in Sandhu et al., *ASEAN Reader,* pp. 536–537. "Freedom" in ASEAN's lexicon has implied sovereignty, not democracy—freedom from foreign intervention, not freedom of speech.

29. Kuala Lumpur and Jakarta were relieved to know that the Indochinese refugees—"boat people"—temporarily housed in Malaysian and Indonesian camps preferred to go on to other destinations. Neither ASEAN host wanted to offer them final asylum.

30. "Singapore," *Asia 1977 Yearbook,* Hong Kong: Far Eastern Economic Review, 1977, p. 283. The minister's ambiguous phrasing could be applied to either of two dangers—external hegemony by, for example, China, or internal hegemony by, say, Indonesia. I have elaborated on this distinction in an essay coauthored with Sheldon W. Simon, "Regional Issues in Southeast Asian Security: Scenarios and Regimes," *NBR Analysis,* Seattle, WA: National Bureau of Asian Research, 4:2 (July 1993), p. 18 ff.

31. See Table 3.1. After Vietnam's accession, Malaysia's population fell further, to one-third of the ASEAN median.

32. Mochtar Kusumaatmadja, "Some Thoughts on ASEAN Security Co-operation: An Indonesian Perspective," *Contemporary Southeast Asia,* 12:3 (December 1990), pp. 167 (on Thailand) and 169 (on the FPDA).

33. Ibid., pp. 170–171.

34. "Malaysia," *Asia 1982 Yearbook,* Hong Kong: Far Eastern Economic Review, 1982, p. 196.

35. "China," *Asia 1993 Yearbook,* Hong Kong: Far Eastern Economic Review, 1993, p. 110.

36. Huxley, "Singapore and Malaysia," pp. 204 (quote) and 213 (arms race). Huxley is right, however, to caution against overoptimism. For example, inaugurating a new Malaysia–Singapore Defense Forum in 1994, Singapore's minister of defense pointed to it as an extension of a record of close military cooperation between the two states dating from 1975. Yet he did not describe the Forum's composition or functions. He did say that multilateral cooperation had a better chance of succeeding once participating countries were "comfortable with each other on a bilateral basis and completely at ease discussing substantive issues in an open and level manner." One might infer from what he did and did not say that these conditions still did not apply to Singapore and Malaysia. Lee Boon Yang, "Asia Pacific Tightens Links: Singapore, Malaysia Set Model for Defense Ties," *Defense News,* February 20–26, 1995, p. 19.

37. For more, see Mak, *ASEAN Defence,* 1993, p. 41, whose source for the reference to "rolling deployment" is the December 1991 *Asian Defence Journal,* pp. 112–113.

38. Interview, November 3, 1995. The conjecture seemed implausible. Contingencies capable of derailing it included a desire by ASEAN or Vietnam not to be seen as taunting China with American power and an American reluctance to stir memories of an unpopular war or raise fears of reinvolvement where it had taken place.

39. Nayan Chanda, "U.S. Maintains Broad Asian Military Pacts," *Asian Wall Street Journal,* April 8, 1992, as cited by Perry L. Wood, "Trends toward Enhanced Defense Cooperation in Southeast Asia," unpublished paper, Midwest Conference on Asian Affairs, Oshkosh, WI, October 1992, p. 42. Apparently Chanda misidentified BITAC as BITEC, which he thought stood for Bilateral Training and Educational Cooperation.

40. "Tightening Security Bonds: A Malaysian View," *Asia-Pacific Defence Reporter,* August 1991, p. 19, as cited in Wood, "Trends," ibid., p. 41.

41. " 'Sensitive' U.S. Policies Urged," *Bernama,* Kuala Lumpur, April 30, 1992, Foreign Broadcast Information Service, *Daily Report: East Asia,* EAS-92–085, May 1, 1992, pp. 1–2.

42. Chandran Jeshurun, "ASEAN as a Source of Security in the Asian-Pacific Region: Some Emerging Trends," in T. B. Millar and James Walter, eds., *Asian-Pacific Security after the Cold War,* St. Leonards, Australia: Allen and Unwin, 1993, p. 86. Among ASEAN states in 1967–95 only Malaysia had border disputes with every other member. Then again, only Malaysia abutted all other members.

43. For more on the two visits, see Michael Leifer, "The Peace Dividend: Israel's Changing Relationship with South-East Asia," *Institute of Jewish Affairs Research Reports* (London), 1 (February 1993).

4

China's Challenge to
Asia-Pacific Regional Stability

Karl W. Eikenberry

Nowhere has the collapse of Soviet power had greater consequences for security issues than in the Asia-Pacific region, and nowhere in the region more than in Southeast Asia.[1] The Cold War witnessed two very different U.S.-led approaches to countering the Soviet Union. In Europe, America was able to forge an enduring collective alliance among nations that shared a commitment to Western liberal political values and open trade regimes. In Asia, however, the potential partners of the United States were divided by historical animosities, dissimilar developmental strategies, incompatible security interests, and fundamentally different philosophies of governing. Consequently, the United States implemented its policy of containment in the western Pacific through a series of bilateral and limited multilateral security treaties and pacts.[2] Thus, even with an abrupt end to the Cold War, we find the North Atlantic Treaty Organization (NATO), although under stress, still cohesive. In East Asia, on the other hand, the implosion of the Soviet Union removed the stimulus that linked the defense concerns of the key players and dampened traditional rivalries.

Pivotal in the post–Cold War security calculations of all of the East Asia regional actors is the People's Republic of China. That such is the case is not surprising. China dominates the Asian landmass with an

---

The opinions, conclusions, and recommendations expressed or implied in this paper are solely those of the author and do not necessarily represent the views of the U.S. Department of Defense.

area slightly greater than that of the United States.[3] It is the most populous nation in the world. Chinese family-oriented Confucian culture, which places high premiums on education and hard work, provides a strong foundation upon which PRC modernization efforts are rapidly proceeding.[4] China's growing economy, by some calculations, is now only surpassed in size by those of the United States and Japan.[5] Additionally, the PRC maintains more soldiers under arms than any other nation.[6] At the same time, most analysts are extremely cautious when estimating the PRC's long-term stability due to the scope of the Chinese people's political disaffection and doubts about the ability of the Chinese Communist Party (CCP) leadership to maintain unity after the passing of Deng Xiaoping.

This conjunction of vast potential power and uncertainty has led to widely varying evaluations of the role the PRC is apt to play in the security of East Asia. A Republic of Korea National Defense College faculty member calls China's defense buildup a "disturbing factor" for Asia-Pacific security.[7] A Russian journalist notes that although his country enjoys neighborly ties with the PRC, "it should not be forgotten that [Chinese] local museums and historical maps show a good part of the Russian land as having been taken from China by force."[8] The *Hindustan Times* warns that Chinese military developments are "causing worries," while a senior Japanese Foreign Ministry official expresses concern that the People's Liberation Army's (PLA)[9] rising budget could trigger "a vicious circle in which Asian countries would strangle themselves in a contest of military might."[10] In contrast, Prime Minister Mohamed Mahathir of Malaysia counsels the countries of the region not to be unduly worried by Chinese defense spending, and PRC defense minister Chi Haotian has decried the "China threat theory" as "ridiculous tales of the Arabian nights."[11] The broad range of views expressed indicates the difficulty of answering the question to which we will turn: Is China a threat to the peace of the Asia-Pacific region through the first decade of the next century?

An understanding of the Chinese expression for "threat" (*weixie*) helps inform our study. The word consists of two characters. The first, *wei,* is defined as "strength" or "power." The second, *xie,* implies "to force" or "to coerce."[12] Combining the root meanings reminds us that the concept of "a threat" entails an awareness of both capabilities and intentions.

Accordingly, the subsequent examination of the PRC's likely impact on the stability of East Asia begins with a discussion of China's capabilities, primarily focusing on its sources of military power. This is followed with a much more problematic inquiry into Beijing's intentions. Based upon a synthesis of the two dimensions of *weixie,* we will then draw some inferences about the nature of the "China threat" to Asia-Pacific stability, and consider the implications of our findings for the foreign policy and military strategy of the United States.

Capabilities

In the field of world politics, power is generally considered to be the capacity of a nation to control the behavior of other states in accordance with its own ends.[13] International relations theorist Kenneth Waltz points out that "an agent is powerful to the extent that he affects others more than they affect him."[14] Such formulations make clear that national capabilities or power resources are usually only meaningful when measured in relative terms. As political scientist Robert Jervis observes: "Knowing how much leverage one state has over another tells statesmen and analysts very little unless they also know how much leverage the other state has."[15]

When appraising the role of power, it is useful to specify scope and domain. The former refers to the effects that matter, and the latter to those actors who can be affected.[16] To illustrate, the statement that the PRC has a great deal of capability tells us little. On the other hand, to assert that China is able to employ its naval and air forces to gain control of the Spratly Islands (a specification of scope) in a conflict with Vietnam (a specification of domain), implies much. We will, therefore, structure our critique of PRC military strength by examining both absolute capabilities (the scope) and relative power (the domain).

Absolute Power

Operationalizing the concept of military power is, of course, a troublesome task. The Chinese define *potential* military power as being determined by a state's political system, level of economic development, military strength, territory, population size, and scope of natural resources.[17] Western thinking is generally similar, with Clausewitz's idea of the "people's share in the great affairs of state" roughly analogous to the Chinese notion of the role of the political system.[18] For sake of economy, we will concentrate our study on three generally robust indicators of military power: (1) defense expenditure; (2) force structure; and (3) national wealth.

(1) Defense expenditure. The PLA's official budget has increased about 190 percent over the past six years, from around 21.8 billion renminbi (Rmb.)[19] in 1988 to 63.1 billion Rmb. in 1995.[20] This sharp rise in military expenditure is often cited by East Asian officials and security specialists as evidence of the threat China presents, or will soon pose, to regional stability.[21] However, the numbers are misleading for two reasons.

First, the selection of 1988 as a baseline year for PLA budget trend analysis heavily biases the outcome. In 1979, the cost of the brief but intense Sino-Vietnamese War drove PRC defense spending up to 22.3 billion Rmb., a sum not surpassed until 1989 as PLA modernization was subordinated to other economic priorities by Beijing's leaders throughout the 1980s.[22] Thus it is equally valid to say either Chinese military expenditures rose 180 percent over the previous sixteen years, or 190 percent over the past six. Moreover, the rather modest size of the 1979 starting point figure must be kept in mind. A linear rise in spending between 1979 and 1995 would equate to only about 2.5 billion Rmb. (about U.S. $290 million) per annum.

Second, official PLA budget figures are nominal and not discounted for the effects of inflation. Consequently, increases in military spending are overstated in real terms. PRC yearly inflation averaged around 5.1 percent during the 1980s, and accelerated significantly in the 1990s.[23] By mid-1994 the urban consumer price index was rising at an annual rate of 23 percent.[24] Lieutenant General Lu Lin, deputy director of the PLA General Logistics Department, commented that over the past ten years price increases due to inflation outstripped the growth of military expenditure (reportedly 130 percent to 116 percent), which undoubtedly reflects some "creative" statistical interpretation, but the fact remains that nominal budget trends do exaggerate the extent of the buildup of the Chinese armed forces.[25] The International Institute for Strategic Studies (IISS), for instance, using a price index controlled for inflation, estimates PRC defense spending to have risen some 44 percent between 1985 and 1992.[26] Thus it seems clear that any meaningful discussion of the recent expansion of PLA budget appropriations must be tempered with explicit recognition of baseline and inflation factors.

Still, it can be argued that PRC official defense budgets, like those of the former Soviet Union, grossly understate actual outlays and are inaccurate gauges of spending levels. Chinese military allocations, as reported to the outside world, do not include the costs of research and development, modernization of defense industry plants and equipment, and various personnel compensation plans.[27] Nor is PLA revenue from its numerous commercial enterprises counted.[28] Conceivably, actual expenditure figures (by Western standards) could be more than double those announced by Beijing.[29]

Nevertheless, there is good reason to speculate that one of the important reasons that official outlays have been increased in recent years is to offset shrinking nonbudget revenues.[30] Most notable has been the precipitous decline in Chinese arms sales, from some $4.7 billion in 1987 to $427 million in 1993.[31]

Two other points need to be made to keep the Chinese military expenditure in proper perspective. First, given the problem of inflation, as well as the Communist Party leadership's anxiety about PLA loyalty, a sizable portion of post–Tiananmen Incident (June 1989) military budget increases has probably been earmarked for improvements in soldier pay and quality of life.[32] Second, with the relatively backward state of the PRC's defense industries, there simply are not many "high payoff" items for the PLA to procure domestically.[33]

(2) Force structure. Since its establishment in 1949, the People's Republic of China has made extraordinary progress in developing a credible defense posture. Despite the constraints of poverty, a large population, intermittent domestic political upheavals, and periodic international isolation, Beijing's leaders over the past forty-five years have generally found the PLA capable of responding to internal and external threats and, when necessary, advancing limited foreign policy objectives by means of force.

China possesses the world's third-largest nuclear weapons arsenal. PLA Second Artillery deployments include some 80–plus IRBMs (intermediate-range ballistic missiles) and 20–plus ICBMs (intercontinental ballistic missiles).[34] Additionally, the PLA Air Force (PLAAF) operates some 180 aircraft capable of delivering nuclear bombs, and the PLA Navy (PLAN) has one SSBN (a ballistic nuclear submarine) armed with 12 ballistic missiles.[35] Considerable resources continue to be committed to the strategic forces. By the end of the century, China will possibly be deploying accurate, mobile, solid fuel ICBMs, perhaps with capabilities on par with the Russian SS-25.[36] It is also anticipated that ICBMs with MIRV (multiple independently targetable reentry vehicle) warheads will be fielded within the next fifteen years.[37]

The PLA's conventional capabilities are also impressive, somewhat enhanced by recent efforts to improve mobility and acquire force projection weapons and equipment. The 2.3 million–strong ground forces have twelve motorized infantry or armored divisions, the PLAN commands a 6,000–man marine brigade, and the PLAAF has an organic airborne corps of three divisions.[38] The PLAAF has improved its aerial combat potential with the 1992 purchase of a squadron of twenty-four SU-27 fighters from Russia;[39] moreover, there is speculation additional SU-27s and possibly other sophisticated attack and command-and-control platforms may be procured by China in the near future.[40] Aircraft range and loiter times have also been extended with the acquisition of midair refueling capabilities from Iran.[41] Finally, the PLAN continues a steady transition from a coastal defense to a blue water force. It has developed its surface warfare, logistic, and communications systems to the point where it can effectively provide muscle to back Beijing's South China Sea territorial claims against regional contenders.[42] And while the much-rumored purchase of an aircraft carrier from Russia or Ukraine has never materialized, the fact that it has been seriously considered a possibility by some East Asian security experts is indicative of the progress Chinese naval forces have made over the past decade.[43]

As with the case of PRC defense expenditure, however, assessments about the quality of the PLA force structure need to be placed in an appropriate context. Neither China's strategic nor conventional capabilities should be considered daunting.

Regarding strategic capabilities, whereas the United States and Russia have a fully integrated "triad" of nuclear forces (bombers, sea-based missiles, and land-based missiles), the PRC, with one SSBN and a fleet of antiquated bombers, possesses only one viable arm.[44] Moreover, the vast disparity in the sizes of the U.S., Russian, and Chinese missile arsenals effectively limits Beijing to a second strike, countervalue doctrine through the foreseeable future.[45] One PRC security expert has said that given such realities, the PLA's approach to developing its nuclear forces is "high in quality, few in number."[46] Thus, although Beijing's strategic arsenal is growing in size and versatility, it is extremely modest by superpower standards and will remain so at least through the first decade of the next century.

Turning to conventional capabilities, it is evident that the PLA's conventional forces can capably operate along or within their nation's borders. But the question of whether or not they pose a threat leads to the issue of power projection, and herein lies a major weakness of China's military.

First of all, while recent PLA inquiries abroad about the purchase of advanced weaponry and military technology have generated much publicity, actual procurements and impact on overall combat effectiveness have been minor. For instance, the one squadron-sized force of 24 SU-27s acquired from Russia hardly compares with the 19 F-15 squadrons (838 F-15s total) fielded by the U.S. Air Force.[47] Additionally, the PLAAF's ability to command and control effectively (the Chinese do not yet have an AWACS, or airborne warning and control system) and maintain a SU-27 squadron is problematic. Simply stated, the numbers are small and the combat power diminished by the PLAAF's inability, as yet, to achieve the important "multiplier" effects that accompany sophisticated supporting C^3I (command, control, communications, and intelligence), training, and logistic systems. Moreover, in contemporary warfare, it is often the synergistic effect that obtains from the simultaneous employment of a broad range of complex weapons systems that proves decisive in battle.[48] The SU-27 represents the only highly capable system in the PLAAF's inventory; full exploitation of synergy remains a somewhat distant goal. Reflecting on this problem, a recent RAND study noted that in the coming decade "there is little hope for the PLAAF to be more than a homeland air defense force with a very limited power-projection capability against a credible foe."[49]

A second constraint on the PLA's capacity for force projection is the PRC's weak indigenous technological and industrial base. Chinese military research and development, production technologies, and weapons systems generally lag ten to twenty years behind the West and Japan.[50] Today's armaments have become so complicated and entail the integration of so many intricate subsystems that China faces enormous challenges in its efforts to reach the cutting edge. The PLAAF's difficulties in designing and producing the Jian-8 II Finback fighter illustrate the magnitude of the tasks ahead. Begun in 1964, the J-8 program has led to the production of over 3,000 aircraft, with a fourth-generation Finback currently under development and projected to be deployed by the end of the decade.[51] Yet the authoritative PRC journal *Modern Weaponry* notes that the "engine and onboard equipment have not advanced [and the] development of the model and major components is uncoordinated."[52] It rates the current model's firepower and control systems fifteen years behind "foreign levels."[53] Such are the nature of the design, test, and validation problems that the PLA confronts as it labors to supply its ground, naval, and air forces with world-class equipment.

Yet a third obstacle to Chinese endeavors to build a power projection capability is presented by the technological and operational demands that are linked to the dramatic ongoing revolution in military affairs. As the major global actors begin to exploit fully the opportunities of the "information age," the PLA finds itself significantly disadvantaged.[54]

China's military officer corps, disconcerted by the results of the Gulf War, seems acutely aware of the problem.[55] PLA National Defense University researchers emphasize that warfare has evolved from a historical stage during which quantity dominated quality, to one in which the reverse is true.[56] They candidly state that PRC weaponry is inferior to that of the developed countries, that its technology lags even further behind, and that the quality of the PLA's personnel is an even more serious handicap.[57] The mouthpiece of the armed forces, *People's Liberation Army Daily,* reported that participants at a military forum in 1993 concluded that whereas the PLA has traditionally looked at tactics from a "strategic angle," it must now do so from a "technological angle"; to downplay the role of science would be to "try to catch a sparrow with blindfolds" (a Chinese proverb meaning to practice self-deception).[58] Whether the PRC can eventually close the technology gap is not in question; the point remains, however, that the process will be a protracted one.

(3) National wealth. The military power a society can generate is dependent not only upon the size of its economy, but on the proportion of wealth that it can allocate to defense expenditure. The former is measured by a nation's GNP, whereas the latter is largely a function of GNP per capita.

However, attempts to derive widely agreed upon estimates of the size of the Chinese economy and per capita wealth inevitably founder upon problems related to currency conversion, purchasing power parity, and statistical data accuracy. Assessments have differed by as much as a factor of ten.[59] Many economists believe the official figures of PRC aggregate and per capita GNP are somewhat, or even grossly, understated.[60] Pending further reforms in price structures, currency exchange mechanisms, and trade policies, the problem of calculating China's wealth will remain formidable. Nevertheless, certain key economic statistics less subject to dispute do indicate that impressive gains have been registered over the past fifteen years. For example, the PRC's economy grew at an average annual rate of 9.4 percent during the 1980s and continues to expand rapidly; China's gross domestic savings stood at a remarkable 39 percent of GDP in 1991; its international trade has more than quadrupled over the past fifteen years; and Beijing's international reserves in late 1993 stood at $22 billion.[61] Moreover, the return of Hong Kong to PRC sovereignty in 1997, along with ever-deepening trade ties with Taiwan, would seem to enhance further China's financial prospects.[62] Barring severe political turmoil (a possibility that cannot be dismissed lightly), it is clear the PLA will be able to modernize at an accelerating pace as a key beneficiary of the PRC's burgeoning economy.

Nevertheless, formidable impediments to development cannot be wished away. The population will grow another 350 million by 2025, creating ever-spiraling demands for jobs, housing, education, and social welfare spending.[63] The shocks of rapid urbanization, market reforms, inflation, and a loosening of political control have led to unemployment and underemployment, corruption, and periodic worker and peasant discontent.[64] The people, despite steady improvements in the standard of living, remain poor, and the government, chary of political unrest and eager to appease, may be inclined to favor consumption-oriented fiscal policies. The energy import bill has escalated sharply in the past few years and will continue to rise, at least in the near term.[65] While the potential of the PRC's human capital is enormous, currently less than 2 percent of the adult population have graduated from universities.[66] And finally, the sector of the national economy that has proven most resistant to market reforms and efficiency drives is precisely the defense industry.[67] Thus, on the one hand, it can be said that if China remains on its current economic growth trajectory, it will be a global superpower by the middle of the next century. On the other hand, conjectures about outcomes five decades hence should be heavily discounted in international affairs. For the next ten to fifteen years the PRC will remain hard-pressed to translate economic gains into significant payoffs for the PLA.

Relative Power

As mentioned earlier, power is only meaningfully discussed in terms of both scope and domain. We now turn to the latter, and judge PRC regional force projection capabilities on a comparative or relative basis.

Two questions are central to an understanding of this issue: First, is there a post–Cold War East Asian "power vacuum" whose existence might prompt Beijing's use of force? Second, are any of the particular regional actors especially vulnerable to a PRC military threat?

(1) Is there a power vacuum in East Asia? As discussed earlier, the United States played a pivotal role in Asia-Pacific security from the end of World War II until the collapse of the Soviet Union. Regional alliances and treaties were primarily oriented toward Washington or Moscow, with Beijing serving as something of a wild card. Have the precipitous decline in Russian power since 1991 and the concurrent significant reduction in the size of the American armed forces led to an unraveling of the complex East Asian security ties that had so effectively checked local historical rivalries?

The idea of an Asian-Pacific power vacuum in the 1990s, of course, evokes images of the region between World Wars I and II, when the erosion of European colonial hegemonism evoked a classical realpolitik response from Tokyo.[68] The absence of strong or domestically legitimated states throughout the theater increased uncertainty, lowered the costs of war, and contributed greatly to the eventual clash between Japan and the United States. Obviously such conditions do not obtain in the Asia-Pacific region of our times. East Asia is, for the most part, comprised of mutually recognized sovereign states. It is economically vibrant with growth rates measurably higher than the global average; by the middle of the next century it is expected to account for 50 percent of world GNP.[69] Moreover, the states of East Asia are relatively stable politically. Although U.S. and Russian military deployments throughout the area have decreased during the 1990s, the effect has been to make more explicit the fundamental strength, not weakness, of the region.

Additionally, the notion that America's role as the "honest broker" or balancer of security interests in the Asia-Pacific arena ended with the Cold War is questionable. Such a hypothesis assumes that U.S. power is rapidly waning in East Asia and that U.S. military forces are hastily being withdrawn. Yet America's aggregate economic strength remains formidable; the collapse of the Soviet Union did nothing to change this fact. It is true that the United States continues to reduce the size of its armed forces, retrenchment having begun in 1991.[70] Within East Asia, the loss of important naval and air bases in the Philippines and the reluctance of regional actors to sponsor forward-based logistic sites have contributed to a decline in the U.S. Pacific Command's operational presence. Yet, again noting that power is relative, it must be remembered that American forces committed to the Asia-Pacific theater during the Cold War were preoccupied with the Soviet Union. Thus the demise of the USSR appreciably increased *comparative* U.S. regional armed strength despite American defense expenditure reductions.[71]

PRC military officers and security experts themselves stress this point in making their own appraisals of the correlation of forces in East Asia. For instance, Guo Zhenyuan of the influential China Centre for International Studies, writes:

> The U.S. is the winner in its confrontation with the Soviet Union and is the only superpower in the world today. Though its strength has been considerably eroded by decades of confrontation with the Soviet Union, it still enjoys superiority in the Asia-Pacific region and throughout the world. By readjusting its security strategy, the U.S. will be able to cut back somewhat while still maintaining its dominant position and leading role in the security structure of the region.[72]

Additionally, the Gulf War demonstrated to PLA commanders that the United States retained a formidable strategic deployment capability that would offset, to a degree, reductions in forward-deployed forces.[73] Finally, Chinese military thinkers openly acknowledge America's continuing influence in the area, especially Northeast Asia, pointing out that "the United States will continue in the future to be an important factor in the maintenance of [Asia-Pacific] regional stability."[74]

(2) Are the regional actors vulnerable? While the overall distribution of military capabilities in the East Asia region can hardly be defined as a power vacuum, one may ask, however, whether there are any particularly lucrative targets in the region for the PRC in the years immediately ahead. Setting aside the issue of Taiwan (to which we will return later) the possibility appears remote. China's geographic ex-

panse, large population, and substantial agricultural and industrial bases combine to make it virtually invincible against a conventional foe bent on occupying the country. However, the picture is quite different for the PRC's use of force beyond its borders. Quite simply, the PLA's punch dissipates exponentially as the distance from the homeland increases and, correspondingly, the relative strength of the potential target states grows. Even during the one-month limited war against Vietnam fought along China's southeast border in 1979, PRC armed forces suffered some 26,000 casualties pushing toward objectives some fifteen kilometers beyond the Sino-Vietnamese frontier; C[3]I and logistic problems proved severe.[75]

The PLA, of course, is much more capable today than it was in the late 1970s; on the other hand, so are its neighbors, at least within the confines of their own territories and littorals. For example, the Japanese Air Self-Defense Force has 158 F-15J and F-15DJ model fighter aircraft.[76] Even the smaller powers, drawing upon the wealth accumulated from sustained economic growth, are generally able to purchase arms that serve as effective conventional deterrents. Malaysia, for instance, recently decided to purchase 18 Russian MiG-29 and eight U.S. McDonnell Douglas F/A-18D Hornet fighters, both world-class aircraft, placing the PLAAF's acquisition of 24 SU-27s in better perspective.[77] Vietnam, the one Asian nation against which the PRC was not reluctant to apply military pressure over the past fifteen years, was mostly distinguished during that time by its degree of international isolation (Moscow being an increasingly unenthusiastic sponsor after 1979). However, with Hanoi's ongoing integration into the East Asian political and economic system, Beijing will likely be required to adjust its means—ends calculations when weighing the use of force against its southern neighbor in the future.

Certainly if the Asia-Pacific region were thrown into political chaos (and there are very plausible scenarios, to be discussed later, that could lead to such an outcome), the prospects of China committing forces beyond its borders would increase. As the national stakes rise, the price of war becomes less of an impediment to action. Yet absent such developments, it appears that the somewhat limited scope and domain of PRC military power, at least over the near term, will mitigate Beijing's inclination to use the PLA as a tool of compellence in its relations with its regional neighbors.

Intentions

A state's military power does not in itself constitute a threat to another nation. As noted earlier, it is power *and* intentions that matter. Canadians do not feel endangered by U.S. military strength, whereas Pakistanis remain vitally concerned with the posture of India's armed forces. The problem, of course, lies in ascertaining what another state's intentions are.

An intention implies a plan or design to promote an actor's interests. However, theorists of world politics differ sharply on the nature of the forces that shape and influence state interests in the domain of security. Neorealists argue that the anarchical, self-help nature of the world political system drives all nations to maintain a core interest in "security maximization."[78] They point out that uncertainties about the future intentions of other nations lead statesmen to pay close attention to capabilities, "the ultimate basis for their security and independence."[79] Thucydides' claim that the Peloponnesian War was made inevitable by "the growth of Athenian power and the fear which this caused in Sparta" is considered by neorealists to be relevant to our times.[80]

Adopting a framework of international politics mostly consistent with structural realism, some scholars have concluded that the history of the world is a story of the continuing rise and decline of states, with upstart challengers going to war with reigning hegemons in order to have the global "rules of the game" rewritten to reflect the actual distribution of power.[81]

Neoliberal institutionalists reject the realist conclusion that humanity is condemned to a world in which states are only concerned with relative gains in power; they maintain that nations are primarily interested in maximizing their wealth in absolute terms and that realists overstate the conflictual nature of the international system. The primary obstacle to cooperation is the absence or failings of institutions that might overcome the "market failure" problem that obtains from the absence of a hierarchical enforcement mechanism in the world system.[82]

Other political scientists find explanations for the security interests of nations in the nature of the state itself. Richard Rosecrance and Arthur Stein write:

> Domestic groups, social ideas, the character of constitutions, economic constraints, historical social tendencies, and domestic political pressures

play an important, indeed, pivotal, role in the selection of grand strategy and, therefore, in the prospects for international conflict and cooperation. Under the present international circumstances, such domestic forces may actually be increasing in scope and importance.[83]

Illustrative of this approach is recent work seeking to explain why democracies do not appear to fight one another.[84]

Some scholars who have focused on the decision-making processes of bureaucracies and statesmen have concluded that the availability and interpretation of information, cognitive limitations, and perceptual biases are critical variables that often profoundly influence the articulation of national interests.[85] Yet others suggest that understanding the role of ideas (explicated by Judith Goldstein and Robert Keohane, in a recent work on this subject, as world views, principled beliefs, and causal beliefs) is frequently essential in explaining a state's preferences and goals.[86]

Drawing upon several of the analytical frameworks described above, we will examine Chinese strategic intentions in two ways: first, by reviewing PRC military doctrine; and second, by speculating on the degree to which China considers maintenance of the international, and especially regional, status quo over the next ten to fifteen years to be in its interests. In both cases, the assumption of the state as a rational unitary actor has been adopted. Such a level of abstraction is appropriate for several reasons. First of all, structural realism, with its focus on the state's efforts to maintain its position within the international system, provides a powerful heuristic in the study of security issues.[87] Second, whereas detailed knowledge of individual leaders, bureaucracies, and state systems is essential in studying crises or short-term outcomes, such information quickly overwhelms attempts to conjecture about broad, long-term trends that a systemic theory of constraints (such as structural realism) might help clarify.[88] Third, in the particular case of China, to search for explanations about PRC intentions within the realms of the leadership or the machinery of the state would be to hopelessly compound the difficulties of the task. To offer a meaningful prediction of the domestic political ideology of Beijing's leaders and the structure of the government apparatus fifteen years hence would require Delphian skills. Thus we will look for answers at the systems level of international politics, while accepting Peter Gourevitch's observation that:

Economic relations and military pressures constrain an entire range of domestic behaviors, from policy decisions to political forms. International relations and domestic politics are therefore so interrelated that they should be analyzed simultaneously, as wholes.[89]

Chinese Military Doctrine

Military doctrine is defined as "authoritative fundamental principles by which military forces guide their actions."[90] It is a set of approved, shared ideas about the conduct of warfare that guides the preparation of armed forces for future wars.[91] Accordingly, military doctrine provides a useful inductive tool that enables the researcher to surmise how a state envisions employing force in the future. In other words, it is generally correlated with the concept of intentions.

The sources of military doctrine evolve from a complex array of geographic, societal, economic, political, and technological factors.[92] It is a state's interpretation of the constraints and opportunities that obtain from its position in the international system, however, that serves as the core unifying element.[93] For example, in the case of the PRC, the PLA doctrine from the mid-1960s through the mid-1980s of "luring the enemy in deep" and "people's war under modern conditions" reflected a very realistic appraisal by Chinese military strategists of the vast disparity between the national power of their country and that of the Soviet Union.[94]

Two aspects of contemporary Chinese military doctrine prove particularly illuminating in analyzing Beijing's intentions regarding the use of military force in the Asia-Pacific region: (1) the internal defense missions of the PLA; and (2) the wide variety of external defense contingencies that Chinese strategists must address.

(1) Internal defense. The People's Liberation Army has played crucial roles in the maintenance of China's domestic stability, and ultimately of Chinese Communist Party control, at several critical junctures in the PRC's relatively brief history. In the late 1940s and 1950s the PLA secured both China's northwest (Xinjiang) and southwest (Tibet), and since then has been periodically called upon to counter local uprisings in those territories. During the late 1960s PLA intervention at the height of the worst excesses of the Cultural Revolution checked the PRC's slide toward self-destruction.[95] More recently,

the CCP's leadership grip on power seemed to hang in the balance until the massive intervention of the Chinese army during the June 1989 Tiananmen Square incident.

PRC military writings quite explicitly emphasize the armed forces' responsibility for maintaining domestic order. A typical PLA General Political Department Mass Work Section article notes that the basic functions of the army are (in the order listed): "1. safeguarding the country's stability; 2. defending state sovereignty and security; and 3. offering a fine, stable environment for the country's reform and construction."[96] Central Military Commission (CMC) vice chairman General Liu Huaqing has underscored (as have all of the PLA's senior leaders) that the Chinese military must be ready to protect the "unity and security of the motherland."[97] The establishment of the 1.2 million–strong paramilitary People's Armed Police in the mid-1980s was intended, in part, to free the PLA to concentrate on external defense missions.[98] The events of June 1989 eliminated most of the progress that had been made to this end.

China's leaders remain committed to market reform and liberalization; any other course of action would consign their country to backwardness and ultimately undermine their claim to rule. They are also aware of the centrifugal forces and trends toward regionalization that will attend such policies. The PLA is viewed, in the final analysis, as the guarantor of domestic stability, and much of its energies are accordingly directed inward.

(2) External defense. The PRC's land boundaries extend over 22,100 kilometers. The climates and terrains across this expanse include tropical rain forests, deserts, glacial barriers, mountain ranges, coniferous forests, and steppes. China's neighbors include three powers with whom it has fought in the past twenty-five years (Russia, India, and Vietnam); the increasingly unstable North Korea; and a host of countries beset with civil strife that has implications for ethnic minorities living within the PRC (Afghanistan, Burma, Kazakstan, Kyrgyzstan, and Tajikistan). Additionally, the PLA must consider the contingencies of instability in Hong Kong after its return to Chinese sovereignty in 1997, and that of an armed clash with Taiwan. The United States, by contrast, has land boundaries about one-half in length (slightly over 12,200 kilometers), and enjoys exceptionally good relations with its only two neighbors, Canada and Mexico.[99]

The point of this comparison is to highlight the extent of China's security dilemma. That the United States has a tremendous amount of power is evident. That it has secure borders, increasing the proportion of power that can be projected outside of North America, should also be clear. PLA military doctrine, at present, reflects the reality that the Chinese armed forces' immediate concerns are located near the PRC's frontiers, not in distant regions.

To be sure, the PLA is emphasizing the creation of highly mobile, elite units, capable of swiftly bringing Chinese military power to bear at potential flash points along its vast borders, which do encompass much of the Asia-Pacific region. After the Gulf War demonstrated the enormous conventional firepower of armed forces equipped with high-technology weaponry and support systems, the *People's Liberation Army Daily* announced that "today's strategy is to first defeat the enemy troops without a war, or [alternatively] to defeat the enemy troops by fighting small battles."[100] The CMC's "principles for strengthening the PLA" emphasize:

> Recent local wars, especially the Gulf War, show that the defeated side was backward in modernization and weak in fighting capacity, although there were other reasons for this failure. . . . We must quicken our pace of modernization in order to keep up with the times and must not slow down.[101]

Consistent with these guidelines, large-scale training exercises have been conducted regularly in recent years in which mechanized, airborne, and marine units were rapidly moved by transport aircraft, helicopters, rail, ship, and other vehicles to hypothetical trouble spots, including the South China Sea region.[102]

However, one must remember the constraints imposed by limited resources and expansive security obligations. General Liu Huaqing has said that the PLA doctrine of "active defense" does not call for the procurement of long-range weapons and the capability to perform global operations, but instead depends on the ability to keep China's territories "free of infringement."[103] Accordingly, PRC military leaders still feel compelled to rely on a large standing army, contending:

> The main threat to the security of our country is limited warfare. However, our country is vast and has varied topography, long coastal and land boundaries, underdeveloped communications, and a low level of

modernization of the Army. It is necessary and appropriate to maintain three million troops at this time.[104]

Thus, in the main, the doctrinal literature and training regimens of the PLA's conventional forces simply do not seem to support assertions that China is intent on fundamentally contesting the regional security order in the near term. Of course, sustained heightened tensions in the Taiwan Strait or the Spratlys might drive the PLA General Staff to place a higher premium on force projection operations. Yet given China's overall resource, technological, and logistical constraints, the art of the possible remains bounded.

In addition, as the only openly declared Asian nuclear power, the PRC has generally displayed a commitment to preventing the spread of weapons of mass destruction, claiming adherence to the Missile Technology Control Regime (MTCR), and signing the Nuclear Non-Proliferation Treaty in 1992 and the Chemical Weapons Convention in 1993.[105] While it has ignored the extended voluntary nuclear testing moratorium being observed by the United States, Russia, and Britain, the PRC has called for a conclusion of the Comprehensive Test Ban Treaty (CTBT) before the end of 1996.[106] China also pledges no first use of nuclear weapons, and argues that all nuclear powers should renounce first use against nonnuclear states.[107] In sum, Beijing's current positions on the control of weapons of mass destruction are, for the most part, not obstructionistic. China definitely seeks to improve its strategic strike capabilities; however, its pace of force development is tempered, not only by the resource limitations noted earlier, but by the PRC's awareness that should it be perceived as opposed to all efforts to limit the size of its nuclear inventories, an uncontrolled regional nuclear arms spiral would likely result.

Is the PRC Dissatisfied with the Status Quo?

A second approach to judging Chinese intentions is to ask whether the PRC is dissatisfied with the international and regional status quo. In responding, we will apply separately theories of structural change in international systems as well as neoliberal and ideational analytical frameworks.

In his work on change in world politics, Robert Gilpin postulates that an international system is stable if no state believes it is profitable to attempt to change the system, and that a state will attempt to change the system if the expected benefits exceed the expected costs.[108] By such criteria, is China prepared to upset the security equilibrium in East Asia?

PRC leaders insist, not surprisingly, that:

> China will not constitute any potential or real threat. Rather it will always be a positive force for peace, stability, and development in the Asia-Pacific region. China's foreign policy of peace is one that can stand the test of time.[109]

Yet the record is not reassuring, and indicates that Beijing clearly has a regional territorial agenda. As Sinologist Samuel Kim points out, China is an irredentist state with more territorial disputes than any other power in the world.[110] It has unresolved land claims against India, Russia, Tajikistan, North Korea, and Vietnam. It also has extensive maritime claims based on the continental shelf principle that involve Japan, the Koreas, Vietnam, Malaysia, the Philippines, and Brunei.[111] Especially disconcerting has been the 1992 passing of a territorial sea law by the Chinese National People's Congress that formally stakes out an extreme negotiating position.[112]

Moreover, Beijing has not been hesitant to use the PLA beyond its borders in pursuit of its foreign policy objectives. John Garver, an expert on PRC security matters, cites fifteen instances of China's international use of force since 1949.[113] The discovery of a Chinese military outpost on Mischief Reef off the Philippines' Palawan Island in early 1995 may be a harbinger of a creeping PRC assertiveness in the South China Sea backed by a willingness to use military power. More worrisome for the future, Beijing has not renounced the possibility of using arms to regain Taiwan, officially declaring:

> Peaceful reunification is a set policy of the Chinese Government. However, any sovereign state is entitled to use any means it deems necessary, including military ones, to uphold its sovereignty and territorial integrity. The Chinese Government is closely following the course of events [that is, efforts to establish two Chinas] and will never condone any maneuver for "Taiwan independence."[114]

Certainly, Chinese military deployments and various missile-firing and amphibious exercises since the May 1995 decision by the United

States government allowing Taiwan President Lee Teng-hui to visit his alma mater, Cornell University, have reminded all parties that the Politburo will not hesitate to call upon the PLA to preserve its claim to one China.

On the other hand, it cannot be argued in any convincing fashion that China is a revolutionary or reformist power. Its era of radical international activism of the 1960s and early 1970s coincided with a period of time when it was weak and played only a marginal role on the world stage. The pursuit of ideological goals in the conduct of foreign policy is a luxury only afforded to those with little power (and little to lose) or with very great power (and much to expend).[115] However, China today is at neither the periphery nor the core; it is a middle-ranking state very much constrained by the distribution of power within the Asia-Pacific region. While on an upward growth path, it is still far from the point at which it might seek to rewrite the rules, in the fashion of, say, Germany or Japan in the 1930s.

Alternatively, adopting neoliberal and ideational frameworks, it still appears the PRC cannot be categorized as a profoundly disaffected nation. Neoliberals believe that trade and economic intercourse are a source of peaceful relations among nations because the mutual benefits of trade and expanding interdependence among national economies will tend to foster cooperative ties.[116] The PRC's rapid integration into the international trade and financial orders over the past fifteen years has been remarkable for a state that had pursued the goal of autarky for the first thirty years of its existence. It is a member of the World Bank Group and Asian Development Bank, and has applied for full membership in the World Trade Organization. China's exports and imports as a percentage of GNP grew from some 10 percent in 1978 to around 30 percent in the 1990s.[117] Foreign direct investment climbed from a negligible level in 1980 to over $221 billion in contracts and $60 billion actually invested by 1993.[118]

In the short run, at least, the pursuit of power and wealth do conflict, and the amassing and exercising of military resources entail costs that can undercut economic efficiency.[119] At present, given the favorable conditions presented by the international economic order, it is still very much in China's self-interest to work within a system from which it has profited so greatly.

Furthermore, the influence of international institutions, norms, and ideas on future PRC behavior regarding security issues should not be discounted. To the extent that there is a "world society" in which there exist broadly shared values that set some limits on the conditions under which one state may use force against another, that emphasize the appropriateness of consultation and collective action, and that induce nations to adhere to widely recognized security and arms control regimes, China may be less inclined to unilaterally project its military power than if the international system were simply a Hobbesian jungle.[120] The PRC has but a forty-five-year history in the community of nations, and its full participation in global and regional political, economic, and security regimes is a relatively recent phenomenon. Its behavior has increasingly reflected a respect for and commitment to world societal practices and standards. This is not to argue that somewhat "fuzzy" terms such as "international norms" constrain nations from employing the means necessary to defend their vital interests. For that matter, so-called global values are often best understood by examining the underlying distribution of state capabilities that give rise to and support these values; power and interest do count greatly.[121] Nevertheless, the employment of force that runs counter to world norms often entails significant reputational costs (witness the efforts of even a superpower, the United States, to lower such costs by building an international coalition in the recent conflict with Iraq). It is likely, therefore, that given its still limited resources, the PRC will be inclined to work strategically "within the system" to resolve less serious regional problems, rather than sacrifice its investment in future credibility for immediate but small payoffs.

Inferences about the "Threat" and Implications for U.S. Policy

We return to the question of whether or not China poses a threat to Asia-Pacific stability in the next ten to fifteen years. Clearly, there are plausible scenarios that could find at least parts of Asia engaged in an arms race, or even in the throes of war. Uncertainty, random events, imperfect information, and miscalculations all play important roles in international affairs and undermine the most sophisticated forecasts. In 1979, for example, none of those commenting on the Soviet invasion of Afghanistan concluded that within fifteen years the Iron Curtain would fall, the USSR disintegrate, and the Moscow-based communist challenge to the West disappear.

What are the scenarios in which Beijing might be at, or near, the epicenter of instability or conflict in East Asia? Externally, five possibilities are most worrisome: (1) a declaration of independence by Taiwan, or PRC preemption of such a possibility; (2) war on the Korean Peninsula arising from either Pyongyang's aggression or internal collapse; (3) accelerated Japanese defense spending and the acquisition of nuclear forces, giving rise, in turn, to a regional arms race and alliance diplomacy; (4) conflict between China and other claimants to islands and resources in the South China Sea; and (5) renewed hostilities between the PRC and Vietnam over oil exploration and production rights.

Internally, the prospects of domestic instability cannot be ignored. The record of communist regimes gracefully handing power over to more democratic successors is discomforting. Moreover, the CCP leadership's predisposition to see Western subterfuge behind domestic demands for political reform (the latest foreign plot being to inflict upon China the evil of "peaceful evolution") bodes ill for PRC external policies in the midst of severe civil unrest.[122]

At the same time, there are important constraints and opportunities China cannot ignore as it advances through the first decade of the twenty-first century. Such factors, stemming from the structure of the international system and East Asia regional subsystem, the imperatives of economic growth, and the limitations on the pace at which the PRC can accumulate relative military power, collectively pose a set of incentives and disincentives that will strongly influence Chinese calculations about the utility of force.

China is a rising power with enormous growth potential. It has a capable but technologically backward military, some years away from significant power projection capability. Rewards from participation in the world's liberal trading order are substantial, and Beijing finds the benefits of the status quo outweighing the costs. Hence neither in terms of capabilities nor of probable intentions can the PRC be regarded as a serious threat in the mid-term to Asia-Pacific stability.

If such a conclusion is correct, what are the implications for U.S. foreign policy and military strategy? The question is a timely one since the post–Cold War era marks the first time in the history of Sino-American relations that the United States has dealt with China for its own sake, and not simply in the context of crises with other major powers (such as with Japan from the 1920s through World War II, and thereafter with the Soviet Union).[123] Building upon the preceding analysis, three recommendations are offered.

First, the United States must maintain a strong military presence in Asia. The reassurance that a credible American force posture provides to the potential mutual antagonists of Northeast Asia, as well as to the many actors concerned about the security of the sea lanes and freedom of navigation through South and Southeast Asia, is crucial to the continued stability of the region. Were a severe crisis to unfold unexpectedly in East Asia, *and* were U.S. military power found lacking for reasons of capability or will, an arms spiral similar to that which consumed the European powers in the years leading to World War I could be set in motion. As PLA security specialist Major General Pan Zhenqiang notes:

> During the cold war years, taking an explicit commitment to a broad engagement in the affairs of the region, [the U.S.] became an indispensable factor in the security pattern of the Asia-Pacific area. To provide extended deterrence to its allies and to maintain the U.S. military presence is part of this security structure.[124]

The current security structure does provide the modicum of certainty necessary to promote continued regional growth and stability. America must not mistakenly apply the "overextended global cop" metaphor to its current commitment of military forces in an Asia-Pacific region so vital to U.S. strategic and economic interests.

Second, the United States must increase the scope of its ties with China and promote PRC interdependence in the international economic system. The evidence seems so overwhelming that modernity begets political liberalization that such a policy is hard to assail on strategic grounds. On the other hand, as Major General Pan points out:

> If Beijing fails in its formidable efforts to reorganize its economic as well as political structures and its modernization programs fall apart, there is a possibility that it will shrink back into a sealed society again; or worse, like what happens in the former Soviet Union, the country falls into a painful process of split, with perhaps millions upon millions of refugees and immigrants flocking to neighboring countries. The impact could really be catastrophic.[125]

Plainly, the United States can ill afford to see Beijing's transition from a command to a market economy fail.

Further, as part of Washington's policy of engagement with Beijing, Sino-American security ties must be increased and regularized. There are important shared strategic concerns that should not be obscured by the contradictions between the two nations. For example, Chen Qimao of the Shanghai Institute for International Studies comments:

> China would not like to see ultranationalism and religious fundamentalism prevail in regions after the Cold War. In this respect, it shares a common interest with many countries, possibly including the United States.[126]

More specifically, within the East Asia region, Washington and Beijing agree on the threat posed by nuclear proliferation, and on the importance of the maintenance of stability on the Korean Peninsula and of upholding the international principles that underpin the liberal trading order.

At the same time, it is very much in America's own long-term security interests to maintain access to the PLA. An enduring aspect of Chinese strategic culture is the emphasis placed on the maxim of Sun Zi that "all warfare is based upon deception."[127] The PLA, by the standards of most armies in the 1990s, remains enshrouded in secrecy. As the PRC becomes more powerful, the United States will require a more precise understanding of Chinese military capabilities and intentions. Routinized bilateral dialogue and exchanges will increase PLA transparency.[128]

A third policy recommendation is that the United States work with China and the other major actors in East Asia to establish subregional or issue-specific forums for consultation and coordination on security issues. For example, China, Japan, Russia, and the United States all hope to reduce tensions on the Korean Peninsula, and an informal mechanism could usefully be established for the exchange of information and opinions. However, at present, the interests of the actors comprising the broader region are simply too diverse to make profitable an Asia-Pacific-wide dialogue based upon a European model. For that matter, there is no reason, a priori, that what is understood to be the Asia-Pacific region logically should be embraced by an overarching security condominium. Chinese leaders, however, do remain receptive to more modest or restricted proposals, and the United States should take advantage of the favorable existing environment and exert the leadership necessary to create appropriate institutions.[129] The ASEAN Regional Forum (ARF) and the Northeast Asia Cooperative Dialogue (NEACD) offer two possible avenues for the establishment of effective subregional multilateral security fora. There have been some tangible positive results—most notably the PRC's apparent concession at the ARF in Brunei on August 1, 1995, concerning its recognition of the United Nations Convention on Law of the Sea (UNCLOS) as a basis for negotiating disputes in the South China Sea. Significantly, the Chinese also agreed to discuss differences with all seven ASEAN nations, whereas previously they had only been willing to negotiate bilaterally with individual states.[130] Nevertheless, overall progress to date in both fora has been slow.

China's leaders envision that the PLA will become "one of the most powerful armies in the world by the mid-twenty-first century." If the PRC continues to grow at its present rate and the country remains unified, this expectation will be realized. Yet, as we have noted, in international affairs the future is highly problematic. In the time frame that does matter in security issues relating to potential challengers (perhaps fifteen years into the future) the PRC is unlikely to disrupt the equilibrium in East Asia. Limits on force projection capabilities continue to constrain the PRC militarily in many potential areas of conflict, especially in the Taiwan Strait and South China Sea. Adventurism is further inhibited by the risk of galvanizing regional and even international opposition at a time when Chinese national power is still relatively weak compared to the other major global actors. Nevertheless, U.S. policy must be consistent with the assumptions upon which such an analysis is based; that is, it must continue to be actively engaged in regional security issues. To do so is both to promote Asia-Pacific stability and to hedge against the unforeseen.

Notes

1. The terms "Asia-Pacific" and "East Asian" regions are used interchangeably throughout this paper. Unless otherwise noted, both terms will refer to China, its contiguous areas, the island states of East and Southeast Asia, and the surrounding oceans and seas. As a global, and more specifically, Pacific power, the United States is also assumed to be a member of the region.

2. Among the most important U.S. security relationships in Asia during the Cold War were the 1951 tripartite security treaty with Australia and New Zealand (ANZUS) and bilateral treaties with Japan and the Philippines; the 1953 bilateral

treaty with the Republic of Korea; the 1954 bilateral treaty with the Republic of China (abrogated in 1979 with the establishment of diplomatic ties between Washington and Beijing); and the creation in 1954 of the Southeast Asia Treaty Organization (SEATO) consisting of the United States, United Kingdom, Australia, New Zealand, France, Pakistan, the Philippines, and Thailand. See Amos A. Jordan, William J. Taylor, Jr., and Lawrence J. Korb, *American National Security: Policy and Process,* Baltimore, MD: The Johns Hopkins University Press, 1993, pp. 33–34, 356–383.

3. China's land area is 9.33 million square kilometers while that of the United States is 9.17 million square kilometers. From the U.S. Central Intelligence Agency, *The World Factbook,* Washington, DC: U.S. Government Printing Office, 1992, pp. 71, 358.

4. The "economic miracles" of Taiwan, Hong Kong, and Singapore, as well as the extraordinary performances of overseas Chinese around the world, are excellent indicators of the enormous potential of China's population of some 1.2 billion.

5. Asra Q. Nomani and Robert S. Greenberger, "China's Economy World's No. 3, IMF Calculates," *The Wall Street Journal,* May 21, 1993, p. A-6.

6. The International Institute for Strategic Studies (IISS), *The Military Balance 1993–1994,* London: Brassey's, 1993, p. 152.

7. Hwang Pong-mu, *Wolgan Chungang,* July 1993, pp. 518–529, Foreign Broadcast Information Service (FBIS) *Daily Report: East Asia* (hereafter *FBIS-EAS*), September 29, 1993, p. 33.

8. Vladimir Skosyrev, "China Increases Defense Expenditure," *Izvestiya,* March 20, 1993, p. 33, FBIS *Daily Report: Central Eurasia,* March 30, 1993, pp. 26–27.

9. The term PLA refers to all of the armed forces of China: the ground forces, the navy (PLAN), the air force (PLAAF), and the strategic rocket forces or Second Artillery.

10. M. K. Dhar, *The Hindustan Times,* March 10, 1993, p. 12, FBIS *Daily Report: Near East and South Asia,* March 18, 1993, p. 46; and Kyodo News Service, Tokyo, March 17, 1993, *FBIS-EAS,* March 17, 1993, p. 3.

11. Voice of Malaysia, Kuala Lumpur, August 21, 1993, *FBIS-EAS,* August 24, 1994, p. 54; and Li Wei, Beijing Zhongguo Xinwenshe, FBIS *Daily Report: China* (hereafter *FBIS-CHI*), October 22, 1993, p. 23.

12. Beijing Waiguoyu Xueyuan Yingyuxi, *Hanying Cidian,* Beijing: Shangwu Yinshuguan, 1982, pp. 713, 763.

13. A. F. K. Organski and Jacek Kugler, *The War Ledger,* Chicago: University of Chicago Press, 1980, p. 30.

14. Kenneth N. Waltz, *Theory of International Politics,* New York: McGraw Hill, 1979, p. 192.

15. Robert Jervis, "Realism, Game Theory, and Cooperation," *World Politics,* April 1988, p. 334.

16. David A. Baldwin, "Neoliberalism, Neorealism, and World Politics," in *Neorealism and Neoliberalism: The Contemporary Debate,* David A. Baldwin, ed., New York: Columbia University Press, 1993, pp. 16–17, 25.

17. *Cihai: Junshi Fence,* Shanghai: Shanghai Cishu Chubanshe, 1980, p. 3.

18. Carl Von Clausewitz, *On War,* translated and edited by Michael Howard

and Peter Paret, Princeton, NJ: Princeton University Press, 1976, pp. 585–594. Two excellent studies of the interrelationship between economic development and military potential include Robert S. Gilpin, *War and Change in World Politics,* New York: Cambridge University Press, 1990; and Paul Kennedy, *The Rise and Fall of the Great Powers,* New York: Random House, 1987. For the influence of geography on military power see Harold and Margaret Sprout, *The Rise of American Naval Power,* Princeton, NJ: Princeton University Press, 1939.

19. The renminbi (Rmb.) is the PRC's basic currency unit. In May 1994, Rmb. 8.6664 = U.S. $1. All figures are in nominal prices unless otherwise stated.

20. Sandra Deger, "World Military Expenditure," *SIPRI Yearbook 1993: World Armaments and Disarmament,* New York: Oxford University Press, 1993, p. 387; Lincoln Kaye, "Pre-Emptive Cringe," *Far Eastern Economic Review* (hereafter *FEER*), March 24, 1994, pp. 48, 50; and "Jiang Zemin Zhishi Jiefangjun Bixu Guojin Rizi," *Shijie Ribao,* January 1, 1996, p. A-5.

21. See, for example, Jim Mann and David Holley, "China Builds Military; Neighbors, U.S. Uneasy," *The Los Angeles Times,* September 13, 1992, pp. A-1, A-26; Nicholas D. Kristoff, "China Builds Its Military Muscle, Making Some Neighbors Nervous," *The New York Times,* January 11, 1993, pp. A-1, A-11; and William Branigin, "As China Builds Arsenal and Bases, Asia Fears a 'Rogue in the Region,' " *The Washington Post,* March 31, 1993, pp. A-21, A-27.

22. Paul Humes Folta, *From Swords to Plowshares?: Defense Industry Reform in the PRC,* Boulder, CO: Westview Press, 1992, pp. 19–20, 216–219.

23. The World Bank, *World Development Report 1993: Investing in Health,* New York: Oxford University Press, 1993, p. 262.

24. "Prices and Trends," *FEER,* May 19, 1994, p. 60.

25. Beijing Zhongguo Xinwenshe, March 20, 1993, *FBIS-CHI,* March 23, 1993, p. 68.

26. IISS, *The Military Balance 1993–1994,* p. 226, and *The Military Balance 1995–1996,* p. 176. IISS estimates 1985 spending of U.S. $19.8 billion and 1994 spending of U.S. $28.5 billion.

27. Deger, "World Military Expenditure," 1993, pp. 387–388; and CIA, Directorate of Intelligence, *The Chinese Economy in 1991 and 1992: Pressure to Revisit Reforms Mounts,* Washington, DC: CIA, 1992, p. 12.

28. One report indicated that the PLA may back or actually control up to 20,000 companies. See Tai Ming Cheung, "Serve the People," *FEER,* October 14, 1993, pp. 64–66.

29. Deger, "World Military Expenditure," 1993, p. 387; and CIA, Directorate of Intelligence, *The Chinese Economy in 1991 and 1992,* 1992, p. 12.

30. CIA, Directorate of Intelligence, *The Chinese Economy in 1991 and 1992,* 1992, p. 12.

31. Stockholm International Peace Research Institute, *SIPRI Yearbook 1994: World Armaments and Disarmament,* New York: Oxford University Press, 1994, p. 484.

32. Paul H. B. Godwin, "Force and Diplomacy: Chinese Security Policy in the Post–Cold War Era," in *China and the World: Chinese Foreign Relations in the Post–Cold War Era,* Samuel S. Kim, ed., Boulder, CO: Westview Press, 1994, p. 178.

33. Economist Dwight Perkins convincingly makes this point. Incurring high production opportunity costs to field obsolete weapon systems is an approach that

China abandoned when it launched its modernization drive in the late 1970s. See Perkins, "The Economic Background and Implications for China," *The Sino-Soviet Conflict: A Global Perspective,* Herbert J. Ellison, ed., Seattle, WA: University of Washington Press, 1982, p. 110.

34. Dunbar Lockwood and Jon Brook Wolfsthal, "Nuclear Weapon Developments and Proliferation," *SIPRI Yearbook 1993: World Armaments and Disarmament,* New York: Oxford University Press, 1993, p. 239. IRBMs include the CSS-2 and -6 (ranges 2,800 km. and 1,800 km.), while the ICBM force consists of the CSS-3 and -4 (ranges 4,750 km. and 13,000 km.).

35. Lockwood and Wolfsthal, "Nuclear Weapon Developments and Proliferation," 1993, p. 239; and IISS, 1993–94, p. 244. The SLBMs are classified CSS-N-3 and have ranges of between 2,200 and 3,000 km.

36. Jim Mann, "China Upgrading Nuclear Arms, Experts Say," *The Los Angeles Times,* November 9, 1993, p. H-2; and Lockwood and Wolfsthal, "Nuclear Weapon Developments and Proliferation," 1993, p. 239. The SS-25 has a range of 10,500 km., CEP (a measure of accuracy) of 200 meters, and a throw-weight of 10,000 kilograms (see IISS, 1993–94, p. 241).

37. Mann, "China Upgrading Nuclear Arms, Experts Say," 1993, p. H-2; and Lockwood and Wolfsthal, "Nuclear Weapon Developments and Proliferation," 1993, p. 239.

38. IISS, *The Military Balance 1993–94,* pp. 152, 155.

39. The Russian SU-27 Flanker fighter is roughly equivalent in performance capabilities to the U.S. F-15 Eagle, although American avionics and fire-control systems are superior.

40. Patrick Tyler, "Russia and China Sign a Military Agreement," *The New York Times,* November 10, 1993, p. A-15; and Lincoln Kaye, "Courtship Dance," *FEER,* May 26, 1994, p. 24. For a thorough account of Sino-Russian military ties, see Bin Yu, "Sino-Russian Military Relations: Implications for Asian-Pacific Security," *Asian Survey,* March 1993, pp. 302–316.

41. Godwin, "Force and Diplomacy: Chinese Security Policy in the Post–Cold War Era," 1994, p. 181.

42. See John W. Garver, "China's Push Through the South China Sea: The Interaction of Bureaucratic and National Interests," *The China Quarterly,* December 1992, pp. 999–1,028, for an excellent account of the PLAN's progress in developing a power projection capability that can extend to the South China Sea area. The PLA's recent expansion of a landing strip on Woody Island in the Paracels has further boosted the scope of air cover available to PLA naval and marine forces operating in the area. See Tai Ming Cheung and Nayan Chanda, "Exercising Caution," *FEER,* September 2, 1993, p. 20.

43. Yu, "Sino-Russian Military Relations: Implications for Asian-Pacific Security," 1993, p. 302; and Godwin, "Force and Diplomacy: Chinese Security Policy in the Post–Cold War Era," 1994, p. 179.

44. The two PLAAF bombers with nuclear delivery capabilities, the H-5 and H-6, are adaptations of two Soviet bombers, the IL-28 Beagle and TU-16 Badger, first flown by the Russians in 1947 and 1954, respectively. See Harlan W. Jencks, *From Muskets to Missiles: Politics and Professionalism in the Chinese Army, 1945–1981,* Boulder, CO: Westview Press, 1982, p. 288.

45. To illustrate, the United States currently has some 6,000 strategic nuclear

warheads in its arsenal. Under START (the Strategic Arms Reduction Talks) II, the number will be reduced to 2,228. China, on the other hand, has some 280 strategic warheads, 170 of which would have to be launched from highly vulnerable air- and sea-based platforms. See IISS, 1993–94, p. 235; and Lockwood and Wolfsthal, "Nuclear Weapon Developments and Proliferation," 1993, p. 239.

46. Song Jiuguang, *START and China's Policy on Nuclear Weapons and Disarmament in the 1990's,* Stanford, CA: Stanford University Center for International Security and Arms Control, 1991, p. 14.

47. IISS, *The Military Balance 1992–1993,* London: Brassey's, 1992, pp. 24–25.

48. The United States Army key doctrinal manual, for instance, notes: "Arms and services *complement* each other by posing a dilemma for the enemy. As he [the enemy] evades the effects of one weapon, arm, or service, he exposes himself to attack by another." United States Department of the Army, *FM 100–5, Operations,* Washington, DC: U.S. Government Printing Office, 1987, p. 25.

49. Kenneth W. Allen, Glen Krumel, and Jonathan D. Pollack, *China's Air Force Enters the 21st Century,* Santa Monica, CA.: RAND, 1995, p. 179.

50. Richard A. Bitzinger, *Chinese Arms Production and Sales to the Third World,* Santa Monica, CA: RAND, 1991, pp. 20–29.

51. Zhong Yongqian, "Brief Look at China's Fighter Aircraft Development Level," *Xiandai Bingqi,* October 1993, pp. 2–4, *Joint Publications Research Service, China Report,* January 31, 1994, pp. 20–21; and Richard J. Latham and Kenneth W. Allen, "Defense Reform in China: The PLA Air Force," *Problems of Communism,* May–June 1991, p. 46.

52. Zhang Yongqian, "Brief Look at China's Fighter Aircraft Development Level," p. 21.

53. Ibid., p. 21.

54. For a discussion of the impact of information technology on military affairs, see General Gordon R. Sullivan and Colonel James M. Dubik, "War in the Information Age," *Military Review,* April 1994, pp. 46–62.

55. Chinese Communist Party Secretary and Chairman of the Central Military Commission Jiang Zemin, summing up the U.S.-led coalition's impressive application of high technology in the 1991 campaign against Iraq, reportedly said, "To fall behind [technologically] means to get thrashed." See Mann and Holley, "China Builds Military; Neighbors, U.S. Uneasy," 1992, p. A-26.

56. Zhou Tao and Ren Yanjun, "Rally under the Banner of Modernization," *Jiefangjun Bao,* August 22, 1993, p. 1, *FBIS-CHI,* September 1, 1993, p. 25.

57. Ibid.

58. Yang Wei, Zhang Guoyu, Guo Zhengping, and Hu Siyuan, "Military Forum Column–Sponsored Pen Meeting on Tactical Studies," *Jiefangjun Bao,* May 28, 1993, pp. 22–26, *FBIS-CHI,* July 2, 1993, p. 24.

59. See CIA, Directorate of Intelligence, *The Chinese Economy in 1990 and 1991: Uncertain Recovery,* Washington, DC: CIA, 1991, for a discussion of PRC GNP calculation problems. Three methods commonly used are exchange-rate conversion, physical indicators, and purchasing power parity. All have significant disadvantages.

60. In 1991 China's official GDP was estimated to be U.S. $370 billion and per capita GNP about U.S. $370. See The World Bank, *World Development*

Report 1993: Investing in Health, 1993, pp. 238, 242. Given the continued rapid PRC economic growth since that time, per capita GNP by mid-1994 is around U.S. $450.

61. The World Bank, *World Development Report 1993: Investing in Health,* 1993, pp. 240, 254; "Prices and Trends," *FEER,* May 19, 1994, p. 60; and Samuel S. Kim, "China and the Third World in the Changing World Order," *China and the World: Chinese Relations in the Post–Cold War Era,* Samuel S. Kim, ed., Boulder, CO: Westview Press, 1994, pp. 156–157.

62. For a series of essays on the prospects for Mainland–Taiwan–Hong Kong (the so-called "Greater China") cooperative development, see "The Emergence of Greater China," *Chinese Economic Studies,* Winter 1993–94.

63. The World Bank, *World Development Report 1993: Investing in Health,* 1993, p. 288.

64. Barber B. Conable, Jr., et al., *United States and China Relations at a Crossroads,* Washington, DC: The Atlantic Council of the United States, 1993, pp. 20–27.

65. Carl Goldstein, "Not So Slick," *FEER,* April 7, 1994, pp. 66–67; and William Branigin, "Oil-Hungry Asia Relying More on Middle East," *The Washington Post,* April 18, 1993, pp. A-33, A-36.

66. Jin Ling, "China's Comprehensive National Strength," *Beijing Review,* August 16–22, 1993, p. 24.

67. Tai Ming Cheung, "Elusive Plowshares," *FEER,* October 14, 1993, pp. 70–71.

. 68. James B. Crowley, "A New Deal for Japan and Asia: One Road to Pearl Harbor," *Modern East Asia,* James B. Crowley, ed., New York: Harcourt, Brace, and World, 1970, pp. 235–63; and Kennedy, *The Rise and Fall of the Great Powers, 1987,* pp. 275–343.

69. Daniel K. Okimoto, "The Asian Perimeter, Moving·Front and Center," The Aspen Strategy Group, *Facing the Future: American Strategy in the 1990's,* Lanham, MD: University Press of America, 1990, p. 146.

70. In 1995 the U.S. Department of Defense announced a commitment to maintain "a stable forward presence" in the Asia-Pacific region at the existing level of about 100,000 troops for "the foreseeable future." *United States Security Strategy for the East Asia-Pacific Region,* Office of International Security Affairs, U.S. Department of Defense, February 1995, pp. i, 24.

71. The Russian military has suffered not only by demobilization and severe budget cuts, but by tremendous personnel turbulence as well, threatening to make it a "hollow force." See Konstantin E. Sorokin, *Russia's Security in a Rapidly Changing World,* Stanford, CA: Stanford University Center for International Security and Arms Control, 1994, pp. 39–46.

72. Guo Zhenyuan, "Changes in the Security Situation of the Asia-Pacific Region and Establishment of a Regional Security Mechanism," *Foreign Affairs Journal* (Beijing), September 1993, p. 40.

73. Author's conversation with Major General Wang Pufeng, Director of the Department of Strategy, PLA Academy of Military Sciences, in Beijing, July 3, 1993.

74. Tian Xinjian, "Dongya Anquande Fenxi Yu Zhanwang," *Zhanlue Yu Guanli,* November 1993, p. 22.

75. John W. Garver, *Foreign Relations of the People's Republic of China,* Englewood Cliffs, NJ: Prentice-Hall, 1993, pp. 315–316.

76. IISS, *The Military Balance 1993–94,* p. 159.

77. Barbara Opall, "Europeans Court Asia with Tech Transfers," *Defense News,* December 13–19, 1993, p. 36; Michael Vatikiotis, "Wings of Change," *FEER,* June 16, 1994, p. 20; and IISS, *The Military Balance 1993–94,* p. 148.

78. Waltz, *Theory of International Politics,* 1979, p. 126.

79. Joseph M. Grieco, "Anarchy and the Limits of Cooperation: A Realist Critique of the Newest Liberal Institutionalism," *International Organization,* August 1988, pp. 498, 500.

80. Thucydides, *History of the Peloponnesian War,* R. Warner, trans., New York: Penguin Books, 1988, p. 49.

81. See Gilpin, *War and Change in World Politics,* 1990; Organski and Kugler, *The War Ledger,* 1980; and George Modelski, "The Long Cycle of Global Politics and the Nation-State," *Comparative Studies in Society and History,* April 1978, pp. 214–235.

82. See, for instance, Robert O. Keohane, *After Hegemony: Cooperation and Discord in the World Political Economy,* Princeton, NJ: Princeton University Press, 1984, pp. 1–132; Charles Lipson, "The Transformation of Trade: The Sources and Effects of Regime Change," *International Regimes,* Ithaca, NY: Cornell University Press, 1993, pp. 233–271; and Robert Axelrod and Robert O. Keohane, "Achieving Cooperation under Anarchy: Strategies and Institutions," *Neorealism and Neoliberalism: The Contemporary Debate,* David A. Baldwin, ed., New York: Columbia University Press, 1993, pp. 85–115.

83. Richard Rosecrance and Arthur A. Stein, "Beyond Realism: The Study of Grand Strategy," *The Domestic Bases of Grand Strategy,* Ithaca, NY: Cornell University Press, 1993, p. 5.

84. See Bruce Bueno de Mesquita and David Lalman, *War and Reason: Domestic and International Imperatives,* New Haven, CT: Yale University Press, 1992, pp. 95–177; Ze'ev Maoz and Bruce Russett, "The Normative and Structural Causes of the Democratic Peace," *American Political Science Review,* September 1993, pp. 624–638; Bruce Russett, *Grasping the Democratic Peace,* Princeton, NJ: Princeton University Press, 1993; and Jack Levy, "Domestic Politics and War," *Journal of Interdisciplinary History,* Spring 1988, pp. 653–673.

85. See, for example, Alexander L. George, *Presidential Decisionmaking in Foreign Policy: The Effective Use of Advice and Information,* Boulder, CO: Westview Press, 1980; Alexander L. George and Richard Smoke, *Deterrence in American Foreign Policy: Theory and Practice,* New York: Columbia University Press, 1974; Robert Jervis, *Perception and Misperception in International Politics,* Princeton, NJ: Princeton University Press, 1976; and Ole Holsti, *Crisis, Escalation, War,* Montreal: McGill-Queens University Press, 1972.

86. Judith Goldstein and Robert O. Keohane, "Ideas and Foreign Policy: An Analytical Framework," *Ideas and Foreign Policy: Beliefs, Institutions, and Political Change,* Judith Goldstein and Robert O. Keohane, eds., Ithaca, NY: Cornell University Press, 1993, pp. 3–26. Two interesting analytical studies on the role of ideas in Chinese foreign and domestic economic policies are: J. D. Armstrong, *Revolutionary Diplomacy: Chinese Foreign Policy and the United Front Doctrine,* Berkeley, CA: University of California Press, 1980; and Nina P. Halpern,

"Creating Socialist Economies: Stalinist Political Economy and the Impact of Ideas," in *Ideas and Foreign Policy,* pp. 87–110.

87. Charles Lipson, "International Cooperation in Economic and Security Affairs," *Neorealism and Neoliberalism: The Contemporary Debate,* David A. Baldwin, ed., New York: Columbia University Press, 1993, pp. 70–76; and Arthur A. Stein, *Why Nations Cooperate: Circumstance and Choice in International Relations,* Ithaca, NY: Cornell University Press, 1990, pp. 87–111.

88. For a lucid discussion of the "forest for the trees" problem in the study of international relations, see Waltz, *Theory of International Politics,* 1979, pp. 116–123.

89. Peter Gourevitch, "The Second Image Reversed: The International Sources of Domestic Politics," *International Organization,* Autumn 1978, p. 911.

90. Major Paul H. Herbert, *Deciding What Has to Be Done: General William E. DePuy and the 1976 Edition of FM 100–5, Operations,* U.S. Government Printing Office: U.S. Army Combat Studies Institute, 1988, p. 3.

91. Ibid.

92. Peter Paret, "Introduction," *Makers of Modern Strategy: From Machiavelli to the Nuclear Age,* Peter Paret, ed., Princeton, NJ: Princeton University Press, 1986; and Stephen P. Rosen, *Winning the Next War: Innovation and the Modern Military,* Ithaca, NY: Cornell University Press, 1991, pp. 185–220.

93. See, for example, Barry R. Posen, *The Sources of Military Doctrine: France, Britain, and Germany Between the World Wars,* Ithaca, NY: Cornell University Press, 1984, pp. 220–236.

94. Paul H. B. Godwin, "Changing Concepts of Doctrine, Strategy and Operations in the Chinese People's Liberation Army, 1978–1987," *The China Quarterly,* December 1987, pp. 572–590, and "Mao Zedong Revisited: Deterrence and Defense in the 1980's," *The Chinese Defense Establishment: Continuity and Change in the 1980s,* Paul H. B. Godwin, ed., Boulder, CO: Westview Press, 1983, pp. 21–40. See also Jonathan D. Pollack, "China's Agonizing Reappraisal," *The Sino-Soviet Conflict: A Global Perspective,* Herbert J. Ellison, ed., Seattle, WA: University of Washington Press, 1982, pp. 50–73.

95. See Jencks, *From Muskets to Missiles,* 1982, pp. 103–107.

96. PLA General Political Department Mass Work Section, "Do Good Jobs of Supporting the Government and Cherishing the People in the New Situation of Reform, Opening Up," *Qiushi,* August 1, 1992, pp. 2–5, *FBIS-CHI,* September 4, 1992, p. 36.

97. Liu Huaqing, "Unswervingly Advance along the Road Building a Modern Army with Chinese Characteristics," *Jiefangjun Bao,* August 6, 1993, pp. 1–2, *FBIS-CHI,* August 18, 1993, p. 17.

98. IISS, *The Military Balance 1993–94,* p. 155. PAP's missions include, among others, border and internal security, antiterrorism, and fire fighting. Author's discussion with General Wang Guozhong, Director of the Logistics Department, People's Armed Police, in Beijing, September 18, 1987.

99. CIA, *The World Factbook 1992,* pp. 71, 358.

100. "Turn to Science, Technology for Troop Quality," *Jiefangjun Bao,* September 27, 1991, p. 3, *FBIS-CHI,* October 11, 1991, p. 27.

101. Shi Genxing, "Unswervingly Deepen Reform of the Army," *Jiefangjun Bao,* July 31, 1992, p. 3, *FBIS-CHI,* August 27, 1992, p. 33.

102. See, for example, Chen Hui and Zhang Zhongshun, Beijing Xinhua Do-

mestic Service, August 27, 1993, *FBIS-CHI,* August 30, 1993, p. 40; Sun Mao-qing, Beijing Xinhua Domestic Service, January 6, 1993, *FBIS-CHI,* January 11, 1993, p. 23; and Tai Ming Cheung and Nayan Chanda, 1993, p. 20.

103. Liu Huaqing, "Unswervingly Advance along the Road Building a Modern Army with Chinese Characteristics," 1993, p. 19.

104. Ibid., p. 20.

105. IISS, *The Military Balance 1993–94,* pp. 249–51; and Ragnild Fern, "Annex A. Major Multilateral Arms Control Agreements," *SIPRI Yearbook 1993: World Armaments and Disarmament,* New York: Oxford University Press, 1993, p. 768. PRC adherence to MTCR had been brought into question by alleged Chinese sales of M11 missiles and missile technology to Pakistan. See Nayan Chanda, "Red Rockets' Glare," *FEER,* September 9, 1993, pp. 10–11.

106. "China Airs Stand on Nuclear Testing," *Beijing Review,* October 18–24, 1993, p. 4; Shen Dingli, "Toward a Nuclear-Weapon-Free World: A Chinese Perspective," *The Bulletin of the Atomic Scientists,* March/April 1994, pp. 51–54; "Bomb Test in China Upsets U.S.," *San Jose Mercury News,* June 11, 1994, p. A-10; "Regional Briefing," *FEER,* June 23, 1994, p. 13. PRC officials emphasize that while the United States has conducted some 1,050 nuclear tests, Russia (the former Soviet Union) 700, and France 200, China has only tested some 40 times since it exploded its first nuclear device in 1964. As such, they say that the PRC must continue limited testing for reasons of safety and reliability (see Shen, "Toward a Nuclear-Weapon-Free World: A Chinese Perspective," 1994, pp. 51–52). Although Beijing claims to support a CTBT conclusion by the end of 1996, it is ambiguous on whether it will stop nuclear testing at that time or until a CTBT is put into force.

107. "China Airs Stand on Nuclear Testing," 1993, p. 4.

108. Gilpin, *War and Change in World Politics,* 1990, p. 50.

109. "China Never Seeks Hegemony" (address by Vice Premier and Foreign Minister Qian Qichen to the ASEAN Foreign Ministers' Meeting July 23, 1993), *Beijing Review,* August 2–8, 1993, p. 11.

110. Samuel S. Kim, "China as a Regional Power," *Current History,* September 1992, p. 248.

111. CIA, *The World Factbook 1992,* p. 71.

112. Robert G. Sutter, *East Asia: Disputed Islands and Offshore Claims, Issues for U.S. Policy,* Washington, DC: Congressional Research Service, 1992, pp. CRS-6, CRS-7.

113. John W. Garver, *Foreign Relations of the People's Republic of China,* 1993, p. 251.

114. Taiwan Affairs Office and Information Office of the State Council of the People's Republic of China, Beijing, August 1993, *Beijing Review,* September 6–12, 1993, pp. vi–vii.

115. Stephen D. Krasner, *Defending the National Interest: Raw Materials Investment Policy and U.S. Foreign Policy,* Princeton, NJ: Princeton University Press, 1978, pp. 329–352. Krasner cites the U.S. war in Vietnam as an example of a very great power applying its vast resources in pursuit of ideological goals. States with fewer capabilities are constrained to focus on the preservation of their positions within the international system.

116. Robert Gilpin, *The Political Economy of International Relations,* Princeton, NJ: Princeton University Press, 1987, p. 31.

117. Thomas W. Robinson, "Interdependence in China's Foreign Relations," *China and the World: Chinese Foreign Relations in the Post–Cold War Era,* Samuel S. Kim, ed., Boulder, CO: Westview Press, 1994, p. 193.

118. Ding Jingping, *China's Domestic Economy in Regional Context,* Washington, DC: The Center for Strategic and International Studies, 1995, p. 36.

119. Gilpin, *The Political Economy of International Relations,* 1983, p. 47.

120. The concept of a world society that promotes norms, principles, and ideas that are important determinants of state behavior has been articulated by Hedley Bull in *The Anarchical Society: A Study of Order in World Politics,* New York: Columbia University Press, 1977. The importance of ideas in ensuring compliance to rules in the absence of enforcement mechanisms is also argued effectively by Douglass C. North, *Structure and Change in Economic History,* New York: W.W. Norton, 1981, pp. 33–68.

121. See Susan Strange, *"Cave! Hic Dragones:* A Critique of Regime Analysis," *International Regimes,* Stephen D. Krasner, ed., Ithaca, NY: Cornell University Press, 1983, pp. 337–354; and Stephen D. Krasner, "Global Communications and National Power: Life on the Pareto Frontier," *World Politics,* April 1991, pp. 337–366.

122. See Kenneth Lieberthal, "Domestic Politics and Foreign Policy," *China's Foreign Relations in the 1980's,* Harry Harding, ed., New Haven, CT: Yale University Press, 1984, pp. 43–70; and James D. Seymour, "Human Rights in Chinese Foreign Relations," *China and the World: Chinese Foreign Relations in the Post–Cold War,* Boulder, CO: Westview Press, 1994, pp. 202–225.

123. Nancy Bernkopf Tucker, "China and America: 1941–1991," *Foreign Affairs,* Winter 1991–92, pp. 75–92.

124. Pan Zhenqiang, "Future Security Needs of the Asian-Pacific Area and Their Implication for the U.S. Defense Policy," paper presented at the 1993 United States National Defense University and United States Pacific Command Pacific Symposium, Honolulu, Hawaii, March 4, 1993, p. 16.

125. Ibid., pp. 14–15.

126. Chen Qimao, "New Approaches in China's Foreign Policy," *Asian Survey,* March 1993, p. 248.

127. Sun Zi, *Sun Zi Bingfa Qianshuo,* ed. and trans. (into modern Chinese) Wu Rusong, Beijing: Jiefangjun Chubanshe, 1985, pp. 29–40.

128. For an elaboration of the United States' security policy objectives in its strategy of bilateral military engagement with China, see Secretary of Defense William H. Perry's remarks to the Washington State–China Relations Council in Seattle, October 30, 1995 (Dr. William H. Perry, "U.S. Strategy: Engage China, Not Contain It," Washington, DC: *Defense News,* Volume 10, Number 109).

129. Qian Qichen, "China Never Seeks Hegemony," 1993, pp. 10–11.

130. *Far Eastern Economic Review,* August 10, 1995, pp. 14–16.

5

Japan's Emerging Strategy in Asia

Kenneth B. Pyle

Major historical forces are today leading Japan toward a new Asian strategy. Together these forces are creating one of the important turning points in Japanese history. It is already clear that in many ways the Japanese people are unprepared for this new era, and its challenges are likely to be especially painful and demanding. We cannot yet see all the important implications of this new Asian policy, but this essay will show the trajectory of change, analyze its dynamics, and examine the effort of Japanese leaders to shape new policies toward Asia.

One major new force fundamentally changing the dynamics of Japanese policy toward Asia is economic. By the 1980s Japan had achieved the century-long goal of catching up with the world's advanced industrial nations. As Japan emerged as an economic superpower, the world's largest creditor nation, and largest donor of official aid, an international agreement to increase sharply the yen's value against the dollar (the Plaza Accord of 1985) led to a Japanese economic surge into Asia. Quite suddenly, Japanese contacts and interests, as well as foreign direct investment (FDI), in Asia dramatically increased.

The other major historical force leading Japan toward a new Asian policy is the transformation of the international environment following the end of the Cold War. Japan's post–World War II foreign policy and its domestic political system were shaped by the Cold War, and its ending inevitably had far-reaching consequences for Japan. Perhaps no other country has been more sensitive to changes in the international environment than Japan. Japanese foreign policy has long been based on pragmatic adaptation to international circumstances and trends. One of the Foreign Ministry's leading thinkers recently responded to an American journalist's inquiry regarding the place of fixed principles in Japanese foreign policy with the riposte, "The histories of our two countries are different. Your country was built on principles. Japan was built on an archipelago."[1] Japan, he seemed to be saying, could not afford to take its stand on principle; its economy and geopolitical position made it too vulnerable. Pragmatic nationalism, that is, an opportunistic adaptation to international conditions in order to enhance the power of the Japanese state, has been the guiding philosophy of the ruling elite since Japan entered the international state system in the mid-nineteenth century. The transformation of the international system in the post–Cold War era is, not surprisingly, leading Japan to a fundamental reassessment of its foreign policy and particularly its role in Asia.

Postwar Foreign Policy Toward Asia:
The Yoshida Strategy

In the first four decades of the postwar period, Japan's relations with the rest of Asia were distant and largely limited to trade. The former empire had left a legacy of bitterness toward and hatred of Japan in Asia. The American occupation required the Japanese to make reparations, but on the whole Japan withdrew from close political ties and concentrated on rebuilding its own national livelihood.

The postwar national purpose was guided by a shrewd economic nationalism shaped by Prime Minister Shigeru Yoshida. Yoshida, who served as prime minister during most of the first postwar decade (1946–54), dominated the postwar scene by ensconcing his followers in the bureaucracy and in conservative party politics and by formulating pragmatic nationalist principles that would restore Japanese power in the new international circumstances.

On the surface, Japan was committed to rebuilding its national livelihood on the basis of a new democratic order and in line with the role that its pacifist constitution envisioned for Japan in the world. However, as a former vice minister of international trade and industry wrote in 1988, "Postwar Japan defined itself as a cultural state holding the principles of liberalism, democracy, and peace, but these were only superficial principles. The fundamental objective was the pouring of all our strength into economic growth."[2] Yoshida resisted U.S. efforts at the outbreak of the Cold War to engage Japan in collective security agreements with other Asian nations. He was determined to use the circumstances of the Cold War to Japan's maximum advantage and to pursue a narrowly defined sense of economic self-interest. Yoshida contrived to keep Japan lightly armed, and to trade bases on Japanese soil for a U.S. guarantee of Japanese security.

Avoiding any collective security commitments in Asia became an *idée fixe* of postwar Japanese diplomacy. Yoshida and his successors resisted an American effort to create an Asian counterpart to the North Atlantic Treaty Organization, or NATO. They built an elaborate set of policies to prevent Japan's being drawn into any overseas commitments whatsoever. When the Japanese Self-Defense Forces (SDF) were organized in 1954, the upper house of the Diet passed a unanimous resolution opposing their overseas dispatch. Subsequent prime ministers maintained the position that any collective security agreement would be unconstitutional. Other subsequent, complementary policies included the "three nonnuclear principles," the three principles proscribing arms and military technology exports, and the limitation of 1 percent of GNP for defense spending.

By maintaining a narrow interpretation of its constitution, Japan's conservative leaders were able to limit positive commitments to the Cold War effort in Asia. In this regard, former foreign minister Sunao Sonoda recalled, "The Americans were always asking us to do this and do that, to take over part of the burden of their Far Eastern policies. But all their efforts were sabotaged by one Japanese cabinet after another."[3] As Masataka Kosaka, a leading theorist of the ruling Liberal Democratic Party's mainline conservatism, candidly admitted in 1991, Japan shrewdly "evaded" the American demand for an active role in the Cold War and "took refuge behind Article Nine of its American-made constitution, which renounces war as an instrument of the state. This may have been cynical, but the ploy was effective nonetheless."[4] Thus able to rely on its alliance with the United States to guarantee its security and maintain the international free trade order, Tokyo was free to follow policies of economic nationalism.

As a consequence, for most of the first four postwar decades, Japan's contacts with Asia were distant and largely limited to trade. Yoshida's firmness allowed Japan to avoid involvement in the Korean War and instead to profit enormously from procurement orders. Similarly, in the case of the Vietnam conflict, while South Korea dispatched more than 300,000 troops to fight alongside the Americans, the Japanese were spared direct military involvement. At the same time the Japanese procurements industry reaped immense profits. Moreover, Tokyo avoided accepting refugees from Indochina. As of the end of 1994, Japan had permanently resettled less than 10,000 of the nearly 1.3 million refugees. Even distant Germany, a slightly smaller country, had accepted more than twice the number of refugees from Indochina as Japan.[5]

An interesting contrast can be drawn between postwar Japan and postwar West Germany. The latter, under Chancellor Konrad Adenauer's leadership, sought entry into NATO as a way of integrating itself with the rest of Europe, of anchoring the Federal Republic to the West, and of diminishing concern over "the German question." Adenauer anguished over issues of German war guilt and pressed for reparations to Israel. Yoshida, in contrast, shunned collective security ties with the rest of Asia; he resisted reparations unless they seemed to offer the prospect of markets; and he dismissed issues of war guilt, believing that there was nothing fundamentally wrong with the prewar Japanese system. The war, he said, was "an historic stumble," the result of blunders by inept leaders.[6] As a result of this shunning of ties with other Asian nations and avoidance of the issues of war guilt, the legacy of war responsibility was left for a later generation of Japanese leaders to face.

Yoshida's strategy of concentrating on economic growth and avoiding issues of political-military involvement, what I have called the Yoshida Doctrine, not only set Japan's foreign policy course for forty years, it also shaped the domestic political system. It kept the domestic peace. By concentrating on economic growth and avoiding active involvement in the Cold War, this strategy accommodated the foreign policy concerns of the left wing. In fact, many observers perceived a tacit agreement between mainstream conservatives and opposition socialist and pacifist groups that divisive issues of constitutional revision and substantial military spending would be moderated and priority given to economic growth and social welfare. The powerful Liberal Democratic Party (LDP) tactician and former prime minister (1988–89), Noboru Takeshita, candidly admitted this tacit understanding in an interview with James Sterngold in *The New York Times* on September 14, 1994. Sterngold wondered whether the coalition government established in 1994 between the Socialists and the conservative LDP, erstwhile mortal enemies throughout the Cold War, was not implausible:

> Mr. Takeshita emphasized that the composition of the new coalition was not as contradictory as may have seemed. Throughout the cold war, he said, the Liberal Democrats had used the possibility of criticism by the Socialists to avoid unpleasant demands by the United States, such as taking a more active role internationally.
>
> "In that sense there was a sort of burden sharing between us," Mr. Takeshita said. "If I were to use a pejorative adjective, I'd call it a cunning diplomacy."

The Yoshida Doctrine proved to be a finely tuned and brilliant strategy for pursuing policies designed to aid Japan's recovery and to allow its economy to catch up with the West. It allowed Japan to concentrate its energies and resources on productive investments and growth strategies that facilitated its emergence as an economic superpower. Only rarely in history had a nation captured so substantial a share of international trade in such a short period as Japan did from 1960 to 1990. In his memoirs, Henry Kissinger credits postwar Japanese foreign policy decisions with being "the most farsighted and intelligent of any major nation of the postwar era."[7] Yet in the long run the Yoshida Doctrine also had major drawbacks. It created a political-economic system in which the economic bureaucrats in the Ministry of International Trade and Industry (MITI), the Ministry of Finance (MoF), and the Economic Planning Agency (EPA), working cooperatively with conservative interests in business, guided the country's fortunes smoothly and shrewdly to achieve long-term goals; but it left the country unprepared to deal with the political consequences of this newly acquired economic power. Moreover, it ignored latent issues of wounded national pride caused by the subordinate role Japan adopted in the American world system. Political issues of war responsibility were left to fester, and international respect and trust were never fully restored.

It was not until the 1980s that the failures and shortcomings of the Yoshida Doctrine began to be addressed by important groups. A combination of forces and trends was responsible for eroding support for the foreign policy that had served Japan so well in the postwar period.[8]

Japan's Economic Surge into Asia

In the 1980s Japan had clearly achieved the goal of the Yoshida strategy. The nation had emerged as an economic power. By many measures the Japanese economy and the level of technology had reached overall parity with the West. Powerful economic forces propelled the Japanese nation toward a new global involvement for which little in its 2,000–year history had prepared it. Year after year, in this decade, Japan amassed trade and current account surpluses. Surplus savings so great that they could no longer be absorbed at home were exported to the world. Financial deregulation and yen appreciation likewise helped propel Japan into greater export of capital. Japan now needed to define a new strategy to replace the policies and institutions that had been established in the postwar period and earlier to achieve the long-held goal of becoming a "first rank" country. The first Japanese to recognize this need were the advisors to Prime Minister Yasuhiro Nakasone during his administration from 1982 to 1987. These so-called neoconservative intellectuals, confident that Japan had at last caught up with the Western industrial economies, began to define a broader conception of Japanese national interest than that represented by the Yoshida strategy. As Japanese economic power burgeoned in the 1980s and overseas investments and interests mounted, these neoconservatives became acutely aware that Japan's own interests would no longer be best served by mercantilist policies and a reactive and passive foreign policy. So great had Japan's stake grown in the international political-economic order, due to its export of goods and capital, that a fundamental revision of Japanese strategy was required.

A remarkable confluence of developments in the mid-1980s, testifying to Japan's emergence as an economic superpower and constituting one of the most momentous changes in modern Japanese history, led to Japan's economic surge into Asia. Heretofore, Japan had kept its manufacturing base at home, but the new economic fundamentals made a dramatic change necessary. The most important development that provided the opportunity to establish a strong new economic role in the Asia-Pacific region was the Plaza Hotel Accord of 1985 and the sharp rise in the value of the yen. At the Plaza summit, the Group of Seven nations agreed to increase the value of the yen from 260 to 180 yen to the dollar. This international agreement made it profitable to shift production and assembly of many Japanese manufactures to other Asian countries which had lower wage scales. Thereafter the yen continued to rise, making offshore manufacturing increasingly attractive. In addition, foreign direct investment was made more attractive by rising production costs at home, Japan's tightening labor market, the change in comparative advantage, and the proximity of Asia's booming markets. Other significant developments at the same time included Japan's emergence as the world's largest creditor and donor of official development assistance (ODA), liberalization of the Japanese capital market, and foreign pressure to restructure the Japanese economy so as to reduce its trade surpluses and increase its import of manufactured goods.

North America and Europe absorbed much of Japanese FDI, but Asia's share grew rapidly. By 1991 Japan had become the largest foreign investor in Singapore, Hong Kong, the Philippines, and Thailand, and the second largest in Taiwan, Indonesia, and Malaysia. By 1992 Japan had invested $19.6 billion in Asian newly industrialized economies (NIEs) and $35 billion in the countries of the Association of Southeast Asian Nations (ASEAN). Asian nations offered a growing market for Japanese goods. From 1986 to 1993 Japan's trade surplus with Asian countries rose from $16.4 billion to $55.6 billion, exceeding its surplus with the United States for the first time.[9] Hisahiko Okazaki, Japan's ambassador to Thailand and a brilliant strategic thinker, in a long and thoughtful essay in 1992, advocated investment in Southeast Asia and the Chinese coast as "a springboard for future economic expansion." Okazaki saw that the rise in the value of the yen after the Plaza Accord offered Japan an extraordinary opportunity to use FDI to create the basis for international leadership:

> If Japanese overseas investment in the manufacturing industry continues unabated for another ten years, or even until the end of this century, this country is likely to find itself in a position comparable to that of Britain in the nineteenth century or the United States during the middle of the twentieth, racking up long-term trade surpluses and freely investing its excess capital overseas. This means Japan's influence will be felt in some way or another in every major area of world economic activity. Even after its competitiveness declines, Japan, like Britain and the United States today, will have enough accumulated assets abroad to sustain future generations. Thus, overseas investment is also a good strategy for an aging society like Japan's.[10]

It was around these new economic interests that a coherent Japanese strategy in Asia began to take shape. This strategy was wholly driven by economic considerations. A half century of single-minded attention to promoting economic growth ensured that the principal motive forces of national life were the economic dynamism of Japanese firms, the institutional framework within which they operated, and the values of economic rationality that supported and motivated them. While the institutional legacies of the postwar experience continued to limit severely its competence in foreign policy, Japan moved swiftly and adeptly to seize a leadership role in Asia's economic dynamism once domestic and international structural change made it attractive. The task of formulating a comprehensive and coordinated approach to Asia in terms of economic policies fit the postwar inclination of the Japanese state, with its strength in economic institutions, capacity for bureaucratic planning and coordination, and ability to fine-tune policies to enhance market forces.

In the late 1980s Japanese bureaucrats began to devote their attention to the coordination of these new sources of economic influence within the region. Given Japan's reservoir of private capital for investment, its commitment to provide massive official aid, and its stores of transferable technologies, the bureaucrats could use a mix of government and private resources to promote Japanese influence and power. In addition to FDI, Japan was prepared to offer other Asian countries a persuasive set of economic inducements to follow its leadership: foreign aid, commercial loans, technology transfer, and preferential access to the Japanese market. The Ministry of Finance, MITI, the Economic Planning Agency, and the Ministry of Foreign Affairs undertook extensive studies to examine Japan's relations within the region and the ways in which Japan might promote its role in the region's economic integration. A 1988 EPA study recommended a comprehensive integration of the economies of Asia, with the Japanese bureaucracy serving as the "Asian brain" that would mastermind the region's economy, determining its development through investment and technology.[11]

In 1987 MITI announced its New Asian Industries Development Plan, or New AID Plan, designed to push Japanese industry into lower-cost Asian countries, which was happening anyway because of ineluctable economic forces. This New AID Plan gave MITI a tool to guide the market forces and thereby to assert its influence over the process of restructuring the economy, easing trade frictions, and promoting commercial advantage. Private investment, trade, and ODA should be coordinated so they serve as a "trinity" or "three sides of one body (*sanmi-ittai*)."[12]

What began to emerge was a series of policies to promote a regional division of labor under quiet Japanese leadership—a strategy that sought to lay the basis for a soft, regionwide integration of economies under Japanese leadership. The favorite metaphor of planners for this pattern of development was the "flying geese" formation, a phrase coined by Kaname Akamatsu, a prewar Japanese economist. This analogy envisioned a vertical division of labor, not wholly unlike Japan's prewar pan-Asian economic thinking. It prescribed a lead economy with others ranked behind in order of their economic strength and technical sophistication.

Aid became a powerful instrument in the new strategy. By the early 1990s nearly two-thirds of Japanese aid went to Asia, amounting to six or seven times the sum of annual American ODA to the region. As most observers agree, this Japanese ODA was targeted for strategic commercial purposes. Instead of focusing on single infrastructure projects—a dam, a harbor development, or a highway—the strategy of the Japanese government became more proactive and comprehensive, more attentive to the development of structural complementarities with the Japanese economy.

In assessing the Japanese economic strategy in Asia, it is important to stress that much analysis has missed the mark. As Kozo Yamamura points out, "Japan is not building an inward-looking trade bloc or a yen bloc but vertically integrated production networks with increasing market power."[13] Since the mid-1980s Japanese multinationals and their *keiretsu* firms have been making huge investments to establish production networks across the Asian NIEs and ASEAN nations. The interfirm relations that proliferated during the high-growth period at home are being replicated in Asia. That is, the small and medium-sized firms belonging to vertical *keiretsu* at home are following their parent firms abroad. In addition, majority-owned subsidiaries and local Asian firms are drawn into these networks. As Yamamura observes, "in both the automobile and electronics industries, a large and growing number of these 'local' suppliers used by Japanese manufacturers in Asia actually are Japanese firms."[14] For example, a Matsushita television plant in Malaysia depends on local suppliers for 55 percent of its parts, but over 90 percent of these parts are produced by Japanese-affiliated firms in Malaysia.[15] As the Foreign Ministry's Okazaki wrote in 1992, by establishing offshore production networks in Southeast Asia it would not be necessary to worry about protectionism, nor would it make sense to seek an inward-looking trade bloc:

> When the bulk of trade consists of captive imports from factories built through direct investment and the captive export of machinery and materials needed to produce such merchandise, there is little need to worry about protectionism. Indeed, current investment patterns are more likely to cause friction with areas outside the region than within it, as Western nations begin to suspect Japan of exporting its system of vertically integrated corporate groups, or *keiretsu,* and shutting other industrial countries out of the market.[16]

The implication of this strategy was that as long as Japan maintained control of the move to offshore production networks and the process of captive imports and exports was maintained this would work to Japan's advantage. In contrast to what had happened in the United States, wrote Yuji Masuda of Tokyo University in 1994, "this is not a 'hollowing-out' of the structure of the Japanese economy but positioning Japanese industries and firms at the core of the networks that are now covering all of the Asian economies."[17]

The new strategy required sensitivity and finesse. Suspicion and resentment of Japan throughout Asia left no room for the self-confident bombast of political nationalism or the narrowly self-interested methods of economic nationalism. Sophisticated leaders of the bureaucracy and big business recognized that a more accommodative approach and a broader sense of the national interest were required. They were coming to realize that what Nakasone and his advisors had been saying was true, namely, that Japan's economic interests required a much more proactive engagement with the world.

Japan's net external assets rose from $10.9 billion in 1981 to $383 billion a decade later. By 1990 Japan had become the largest net creditor in the world—as Edward Lincoln has written, "the greatest creditor nation the world has ever known." In 1970 the cumulative value of Japanese overseas investments was $3.6 billion; in 1980, $160 billion; and in 1991, $2.0 trillion.[18]

As a consequence, Japan was drawn into international affairs in a way unprecedented in Japanese experience. Earlier Japanese contact with the world through trade allowed foreigners to be kept at arm's length. Imports and exports were most often handled through large general trading companies, requiring relatively little real contact. But the new investment patterns required genuine economic intimacy with other peoples. As Lincoln has observed, "Successful direct investments require an understanding of foreign cultures, legal systems, idiosyncratic conditions in local financial and real estate markets, political systems, labor supply conditions, labor law or customary work conditions, and a tolerance and acceptance of diverse ethnic and racial groups."[19]

The implications for the Japanese people were awesome. Such investment led to a rapid growth in the number of Japanese managers and their families living abroad. In 1970, 267,000 Japanese lived abroad; in 1980, 445,000; in 1990, 620,000. In 1985, 23,830 Japanese went abroad for education or training; in 1990 the figure was 121,645. This new human interaction with foreign peoples led the Japanese to think of the new era as one of *kokusaika,* or internationalization. Achieving a closer relationship with Asia was one of the significant challenges of this period of internationalization. For four decades Japan had remained aloof from Asia, concentrating on investment and production at home. But the new economic forces radically changed this situation, and Japanese interest in the development of other Asian economies dramatically increased.

At the same time, it was difficult for Japan to exert political leadership in Asia because of the legacy of World War II. Japan's postwar conservative leaders had not dealt forthrightly with the Japanese role in Asia during the war. While many Japanese were severely self-critical in assessing Japan's wartime role, mainstream conservative leaders were not. A series of episodes confirmed the persistence of this conservative view. Only grudgingly and after international outcry did education bureaucrats permit high school social studies texts to mention the Japanese invasion of China. Repeatedly, international protests forced the dismissal of cabinet ministers who argued that the colonization of Korea had been legitimate or that the rape of Nanjing was a fabrication. Only reluctantly, when confronted with evidence, did the government admit that tens of thousands of Asian women had been compelled to serve as "comfort women," providing sexual favors for the Japanese army. Such continuing episodes made the formal, carefully scripted apologies that Japanese leaders periodically offered seem inadequate and incomplete.

The internationalists who advised Prime Minister Nakasone tried unsuccessfully to deal with these issues. They argued that with such great new overseas involvement it was in Japan's national interest to abandon the Yoshida Doctrine and adopt a new role abroad. Nakasone and his advisors argued that Japan had to develop a more liberal nationalism, which would understand the need for a broader national purpose and would provide popular support for a more active and responsible role in the United Nations and other international organizations. In particular, they argued that the Japanese must develop new and friendly relationships with other Asians to provide legitimacy for Japanese political-economic leadership in the region. Nakasone advocated the internationalization of Japanese education, which would introduce foreign area studies into the school curriculum, bring foreign instructors, and set a goal of attracting 100,000 foreign students to Japanese colleges and universities by the year 2000.

Nakasone left office in 1987 disappointed with the failure to reorient Japan's national purpose. The balance of power was still with the policies of the past. Nakasone was attacked on all sides: by the bureaucracy, for overriding its prerogatives in trying to revise its narrow policies of self-interest; by the mainline conservatives, who wished to hold to the successful Yoshida policies; by left-wing parties, which saw him undermining the constitutional limits on Japanese foreign policy. As the Cold War abruptly ended at the close of the 1980s, Japan was still divided, adrift, and reactive in its foreign policy. The dominant impulse was to favor an extension of the Yoshida Doctrine.[20]

The Gulf War, the Cambodian Adventure, and the End of the Yoshida Strategy

The purposeful and well-coordinated advance of Japanese economic interests into Asia at the end of the 1980s provided a sharp contrast with the political immobilism that characterized Japan's response to the Persian Gulf War and the confused and inept Japanese participation in Cambodian peacekeeping operations. The Gulf War was the first international crisis of the post–Cold War era, and Japanese leaders were wholly unprepared to deal with the new context of its foreign policy. The storm of international criticism that greeted the grudging support that Japan gave the UN-sanctioned coalition stunned Japanese politicians. Protestations of constitutional inhibitions were no longer persuasive for a country of such economic power and prominence. Although Japan eventually contributed $13 billion to the coalition, the failure to provide personnel in any form was widely criticized.

In the face of this international criticism, the political consensus that had supported the Yoshida Doctrine throughout the Cold War began to buckle. A new generation of assertive political leadership in the LDP demanded a reinterpretation of the constitution. The most prominent of these younger leaders were Ichiro Ozawa and Ryutaro Hashimoto. Ozawa dismissed the government's long-standing constitutional interpretation prohibiting overseas deployment of troops as a "subterfuge" (*gomakashi*) of the Yoshida School, which he said had made Japan selfish and money-grubbing, ignoring the cost of maintaining the international freedom and peace upon which the Japanese economy depended.[21] Ozawa, whose thinking closely resembled Nakasone's, although the two were not close, headed an LDP study group on Japan's international role. In early 1992 the group recommended a reinterpretation of the constitution. "Japan," the report said, "is being asked to shift from a passive stance of mainly enjoying the benefits of a global system to an active stance of assisting in the building of a new order."[22] The commission recommended a revision of the Self-Defense Forces Law so as to provide an explicit legal foundation for what it called "international security," that is, collective security efforts sanctioned by the United Nations, such as participation in UN peacekeeping operations, a UN army, and UN-sanctioned multinational forces. The report did not, however, approve the concept of collective self-defense, which would allow the U.S.–Japan Security Treaty to be reciprocal. Nonetheless, the reinterpretation of Article Nine, the no-war clause of the Japanese Constitution, was a departure from the Yoshida Doctrine, whose foundations began to erode.

Following intense debate the Diet passed the UN Peacekeeping Operations (PKO) Cooperation Bill on June 15, 1992, which ended the ban on dispatching SDF troops abroad. It limited troop deployment, however, to logistical and humanitarian support, monitoring elections, and providing aid in civil administration. Under a compromise required to gain the support of small opposition parties, a section of the law entailing SDF involvement in armed UN missions, such as monitoring cease-fires, disarming combatants, and patrolling buffer zones, was frozen for the time being.

Passage of this legislation, as limited and constrained as it was, marked a significant step in the decline of "Yoshida politics." One sign of the erosion of the national consensus that the Yoshida strategy had held together throughout the Cold War was the diehard opposition to the PKO bill of the Socialist Party, whose lower-house members in symbolic protest submitted their resignations before the vote. It was the first major challenge to the foreign policy consensus since ratification of the U.S.–Japan Mutual Security Treaty in 1960, which had led to the largest mass demonstrations in Japanese history. In this case, however, the left-wing opposition failed. With the Cold War over, public opinion was unresponsive to the left's protests. It was a sign of the changed times that a plaintive appeal for the defeat of the PKO legislation by postwar Japan's leading progressives fell on deaf ears. "We cannot blithely overlook this 'superpower nationalism' that is motivating the bill's supporters," they wrote in a public manifesto. "All their fine talk about 'international responsibility' and 'human contributions' has from the very beginning been aimed at meeting an American demand. . . . When we consider the international and domestic circumstances lying behind this proposal, moreover, we must conclude that it represents the first step toward a reversal of Japan's precious postwar heritage as a peaceful state."[23] There was a conspicuous lack of signatures to this manifesto from the younger generation. One might take this failure of the left-wing opposition as the final death knell of postwar progressivism.

After passage of the PKO legislation, the Japanese government dispatched an SDF engineering battalion of about 600 troops, eight ceasefire monitors, and a contingent of civilian police officers to join the UN peacekeeping mission in Cambodia in September 1992. Participation in the UN's 22,000–member peacekeeping operation intended to end Cambodia's long civil war was a test case for the Japanese. It was a departure, albeit limited and tentative, from the Yoshida Doctrine, and it marked the first direct postwar involvement in military-strategic affairs in Asia. It was the first time since World War II that Japanese ground forces were dispatched to foreign soil.

Public support for participation in the Cambodian operation was fragile. The Japanese public tended to justify the dispatch of SDF troops largely in terms of satisfying foreign criticism of Japan's failure to make personnel available to international peacekeeping. Typically, Japanese public discussion held that it was necessary for Japan to make a symbolic "contribution" to satisfy this criticism. A prominent

Japanese writer on defense affairs, Tadae Takubo, was in a minority when he observed, "We should not focus solely on the danger of being criticized by other countries and lose sight of the fact that making such contributions is in our own interest."[24]

Self-Defense Forces and election monitors, together with civilian police officers, served under the United Nations Transitional Authority in Cambodia (UNTAC). Along with the Japanese peacekeepers came hundreds of Japanese reporters and cameramen intent on assessing the venture. It was fortunate that UNTAC was headed by a veteran Japanese diplomat, Yasushi Akashi, who understood the exceptional nature of the Japanese operation. The Japanese forces were housed in "homey surroundings" far from dangerous areas, in luxurious air-conditioned quarters with satellite televisions and Japanese-style bath houses with computerized temperature controls. They operated under a bewildering set of rules of engagement. Unlike other UN peacekeeping forces, the Japanese could use their weapons only in self-defense. They could not use them if they were obstructed in their duties or to protect other nationals. As one former Japanese general explained, "For the SDF to fire on the Khmer Rouge to protect non-Japanese would represent an exercise of the right of collective self-defense which the government has ruled out."[25]

UN officials were reportedly bitter over the special circumstances under which the Japanese peacekeepers operated. Even Akashi compared them to "maidens" because they were "rather timid and tentative." He described the Japanese participation as "teething experiences."[26] In fact, when a Japanese volunteer, not part of the official mission, and a Japanese policeman were killed in the spring of 1993, the Japanese media went into a "feeding frenzy," pandering to the public's shock at this first loss of Japanese life. Leading Japanese newspapers leaned toward withdrawal from UNTAC; a member of the cabinet also favored withdrawal; and the government dispatched a mission to seek relocation of Japanese participants to even safer areas. According to UN records, more than twenty Japanese policemen, nearly one-third of the total, fled their assignments, taking their UN vehicles back to the safety of Phnom Penh. Four Japanese peacekeepers deserted the country and drove their UN vehicles across the border to Thailand, taking refuge in the Japanese embassy in Bangkok. A senior UN official remarked that "the only time the Japanese were tested by fire, they abandoned us. We understand the special constitutional restrictions on the Japanese, but in a situation of undeniable danger, how can we repeatedly ask people of one nationality, but not another, to take risks?"[27] In the end the Cambodian elections came off smoothly, and the Khmer Rouge, for whatever reason, did not attack other Japanese. Had more Japanese been killed it almost certainly would have disrupted the mission. Ozawa expressed surprise and relief to a foreign scholar that the Japanese had not been targeted.[28] Successful completion of the Cambodian operation was an important point in the slow evolution of reorienting Japan's international role.

Groping for a Political Strategy in Asia

The sharply increased economic importance of Asian economies to Japan had to be supported by a new long-term political strategy. To underwrite its economic interests, the strategy that began to emerge had four parts: (1) to reassure Asians that Japan would not translate its economic strength into military power; (2) to maintain a strong public commitment to the U.S. alliance to demonstrate Japan's intention of not becoming an independent military power; (3) to develop cultural policies that would strengthen Japan's identity as an Asian nation; and (4) to pursue an increased political role in Asia by working through multilateral institutions and fora.

Suspicion and concern over Japanese intentions were still high when the Cold War came to an end. The ruling conservative elite, as we have seen, made little effort in the postwar period to restore international trust. When Japanese minesweepers were dispatched to the Persian Gulf in May 1991 to aid in the cleanup operation after the Gulf War, former Singapore prime minister Lee Kuan Yew worried that allowing the Japanese defense forces to participate in overseas operations was like "giving liquor chocolates to an alcoholic."[29] It was not only memories of World War II that had to be overcome. Japan's subsequent aloofness from the Asia-Pacific region and the narrow pursuit of its economic self-interest during the Cold War also deferred the task of restoring trust. The Yoshida strategy was a shrewd way to pursue Japan's postwar interests and to restore Japan's position of power and importance, but "what would have happened," Hisahiko Okazaki recently mused, "if Japan had pursued a normal military policy within the context of its postwar foreign policy framework, including the Japan–U.S. Security Treaty?" Okazaki speculated that Japan's active participation in the Cold War effort in Asia and in the Gulf War would have engendered "a relationship of trust and a sense of camaraderie" with other Asian nations: "A country wins the confidence of other nations through the repetition of such acts. Foreign peoples and governments have no way of knowing whether Japan is really the sane and responsible country it claims to have become until they have had a chance to observe it in action." Owing to the pursuit of the Yoshida strategy for the past forty years, "Japan forfeited its chance to build up a record as a country deserving of international trust." Economic aid also failed to win confidence in Asia as "the widespread perception of Japan as a country driven purely by economic motives makes this difficult."[30]

To reassure Asians, it became almost a mantra repeated by Japanese officials that Japan would never again become an independent military power. As a Ministry of Finance report in 1990 emphasized, Japan, "learning from the lessons of history," would remain a "non-military economic power," a "non-ideological nation," and a "new-style peace-loving and cultural nation."[31]

Similar themes were repeated throughout the early 1990s. In 1992 Prime Minister Kiichi Miyazawa appointed a "Roundtable on Japan and the Asia-Pacific Region in the Twenty-first Century," chaired by the president of Keio University, Tadao Ishikawa, a scholar of modern Chinese affairs. Characterized by extreme caution and circumspection, the panel's final report, issued just prior to Miyazawa's tour of Southeast Asia at the beginning of 1993, emphasized that Japan could no longer remain aloof from the problems of Asia but rather must take a more active political role in the region. But the meaning of this emphasis was left vague, and the entire tenor of the report, on the contrary, implied a continued low profile. The report's final section, entitled "Toward a Japan that the World Trusts," concluded that "much room remains for the Japanese to make a humble response to foreign criticism and to take the initiative in reforming themselves. Talking of the relationship between the Asia-Pacific region and Japan in the 21st century, the Japanese must first reflect on their own agenda. . . . Rather than working hard solely at building up the peace and prosperity of one nation, rather than smugly advocating our particular ideals, we must work to create a future Japan recognized as a true partner."[32]

Miyazawa made a tour of Southeast Asia in January 1993, hard on the heels of this report. His speeches, which were supposed to enunciate a "Miyazawa Doctrine" by announcing a greater political profile for Japan in Asia, were even more bland than the report. Commenting on the prime minister's speech in Bangkok, in which he assured Asia that Japan would "never again become a military power" and would "always think and act together" with Asian peoples, the *Nikkei Weekly* derided Miyazawa for his blandness and said his speech raised questions about the purpose served by organizing this study group in the first place.[33]

Part of the effort to reassure Asians of Japan's intentions entailed dealing with the questions of war responsibility which had been largely ignored by postwar leaders. Miyazawa's successor, the reformist head of the Japan New Party, Morihiro Hosokawa, seized the nettle at his first press conference on August 10, 1993. He stated in the clearest terms of any prime minister that Japan had engaged in "a war of aggression and it was a mistake." Less than a week later, at ceremonies attended by the emperor and empress to honor Japan's war dead on the anniversary of surrender, Hosokawa expressed "humble condolences to victims of the war and their families in the neighboring countries of Asia." At this same ceremony, Takako Doi, speaker of the lower house, observed that "we still have not achieved reconciliation with Asian peoples who were forced to undergo horrible sacrifices because of our nation's errors."[34] Unfortunately for the strategy of reassuring Asia, Japanese were still not of one mind on these issues. The frank admission and apology from Hosokawa, whose grandfather had led Japan into the Pacific War, created a great stir in Japan because many, perhaps most, conservatives believed that while Germany had fought a war of aggression, Japan's had been a war of self-defense on behalf of Asia against Western imperialism. The notion of war responsibility was widely rejected by conservatives, and the outspoken nationalist Shintaro Ishihara said that a leader who distorts his country's history "deserves certain death."[35] A subsequent proposal to have the Diet issue a formal apology for the war on the fiftieth anniversary of surrender also foundered on mounting controversy. Although the Socialist prime minister made a formal apology, the Diet after protracted debate could only agree on a bland resolution to "reflect" on Japan's past relations with Asia.

Apologies and frank admissions of aggression were not the only legacies to stir furor; the issue of tens of thousands of Asians commandeered as "comfort women" for the Japanese imperial army emerged as another incendiary issue. Initial official denials had to give way to reluctant admission when Japanese historians produced documentary evidence of the widespread practice of compelling Asian women to serve the army in this fashion. Further apologies, hand-wringing, debates over the legal obligations, avowals of wishes to make restitution, and avowals that Japan would never again become a military power ensued.

Given the evidence of Asia's new economic dynamism and Japan's deeper economic ties to the region, some Japanese leaders were prepared to abandon a defensive stance and assert closer identification with Asia. They advocated policies that would enhance awareness of common cultural traditions that Japan shared with Asia. One such effort that drew considerable attention was a 1993 essay by a high-level Foreign Ministry official, Kazuo Ogura, subsequently appointed ambassador to Vietnam. Ogura asserted that "Western-style modernization and industrialization [have reached] a dead end."[36] It was necessary to abandon seeing Asia in the negative light of the Western world view as stagnant, passive, authoritarian. Asia at the end of the twentieth century was becoming dynamic, active, and the new source of universal values. An "Asian restoration" must begin by overcoming past animosities among Asian countries:

> It will be difficult for Asia to take off and soar again unless it can get over the legacy of ill will caused by past invasions and strife. . . . Japanese awareness and contrition alone will not suffice. . . . The countries that were injured will have to refrain from being prisoners of the past and adopt a future-minded position.

Another step important to the rise of Asia, Ogura wrote, was overcoming the influence of the Western-trained Asian elites who were tied to a Western mind-set:

> As we prepare for the twenty-first century, we must seriously reexamine the role of these Western-oriented intellectuals and leaders . . . [who] are using their links with the West to maintain the legitimacy of their superior position. What we see is in a sense a survival, although under a different guise, of the old colonial arrangement by which natives with Western learning could skillfully develop ties with the rulers and thereby dominate the un-Westernized general populace. Under these circumstances, members of the political elite have been hesitant to

stress Asian values lest they undermine the legitimacy of their own power.

To remedy this situation, Asia must begin to train its own leaders. Asia could produce universal values to transmit to the world by developing a "theory of Asian capitalism."

> What Asia has treasured is the view of society and human beings that underlies such areas as Japanese-style management, lifelong education, and family upbringing, and it has also treasured the economic and social systems that are built on this view.

Although he paid tribute to "China's cuisine and calligraphy, and Korea's songs and dances," Ogura clearly had in mind the Japanese economic system when he spoke of Asian ideals that had universal significance. When he spoke of a "theory of Asian capitalism" he left no doubt that Japan was the model. To spread these Asian values, to bring about an "Asian restoration," it was necessary to set up study centers as alternatives to the traditional Western centers of learning where Asian students had been going.

Ogura's views were representative of a growing belief in mainstream thought that Japan's international role in the post–Cold War era must be defined in terms of regional leadership and a stronger identification with Asia. Another example of this view is found in the recent writings of Yasusuke Murakami, Japan's leading social scientist who died of cancer in the summer of 1993. Murakami, who has been called "the Max Weber of Japan," was the theoretician of the neoconservative thought that underlay Yasuhiro Nakasone's policy positions during his prime ministership from 1982 to 1987. Murakami and Nakasone in fact coauthored a prescription for the post–Cold War order in 1992. The same year, months before his death, he published a magisterial work, *Hankoten no seiji keizaigaku* (An anticlassical theory of political economy), which expressed a strong belief that Western values were losing relevance to the future course of history. In a 1988 essay he went beyond the common view that the West was experiencing a relative weakening of its economic and political power: "The very ideals sustaining modern Western society are being shaken to their roots. . . . The fact is that the Western tradition of philosophy has long since reached a dead end." Murakami wrote in this article that it was "the Japanese challenge, a development of global historical significance," that demonstrated the decline of the West:

> Japan has probably outdone Western Europe and North America in the guarantee of liberties. Based on objective national indicators, Japan also achieved greater equality than almost any country in the West. Most important, the secret of Japan's success relates at least in part to non-Western organization principles. In this sense, Japan's achievements represent a severe blow to modern Western ideals. Furthermore, the same phenomenon is occurring in Hong Kong, Singapore, South Korea, and Taiwan; what we seem to be witnessing is not simply a Japanese challenge but an Asian challenge, a development that cannot but call into question the very basis of the Pax Americana.[37]

The New Context of Defense Strategy

Even the strongest advocates of a closer identification with Asia have affirmed the essential nature of the U.S. alliance and support the continued U.S. presence in Asia. In fact, across the spectrum of Japanese opinion, there is now near unanimity in supporting the Mutual Security Treaty. When the Socialist Party joined in coalition with the LDP to form a government in June 1994, the new Socialist prime minister, Tomiichi Murayama, explicitly abandoned the fundamentals of his party's postwar foreign policy. For forty years the Socialists had opposed the Self-Defense Forces as unconstitutional; they had supported unarmed neutrality, opposed American military bases and the U.S.–Japan alliance, and opposed recognition of South Korea. They had opposed the PKO Cooperation Bill of 1992, which allowed the SDF to be dispatched abroad. Murayama, the first Socialist prime minister in nearly half a century, abruptly reversed the party's policies on all these issues. Probably the most parochial of all postwar prime ministers, utterly lacking in foreign policy experience, scarcely having traveled abroad, he dismissed the previous policies as outdated. Initially opposition Diet members derided his *volte face,* but Murayama plunged ahead with more reversals, sanctioning the flying of the Rising Sun flag in schools, the singing of the national anthem, visits by cabinet ministers to the Yasukuni Shrine, defense of the sea lanes, close ties with South Korea, purchasing of AWACS planes, and the use of nuclear power for domestic energy needs. The Socialist Party in a subsequent meeting approved these changes. With this sudden opportunistic reversal, the principal foreign policies of the Japanese left wing were swept away; the postwar left–right axis in foreign policy virtually disappeared.

With the collapse of the left-wing foreign policy position, the resistance to constitutional revision was weakened. In November 1994 Japan's largest daily newspaper, the *Yomiuri Shimbun,* with a circulation of over 10 million, published a draft proposal for revising the constitution. The draft proposal came out of a two-and-a-half-year study led by Masamichi Inoki, a widely respected scholar of national defense issues. The draft proposed replacing Article Nine, the no-war clause, with a provision permitting "an organization for self-defense, to maintain the peace, independence, and security of Japan."[38] At the same time, in order to reassure foreign concerns, it included the "three nonnuclear principles"—not to produce, possess, or permit the introduction of nuclear weapons in Japan—and prohibited a military draft. A December 1994 *New York Times*–CBS–Tokyo Broadcasting System poll for the first time found that a majority of Japanese—53 percent—said Japan should consider constitutional revision.[39]

The cumulative changes in Japan's foreign policy position since the end of the Cold War required a fundamental review of national defense strategy and the consolidation of a national consensus. In February 1994 Prime Minister Hosokawa appointed an advisory panel of bureaucrats, business leaders, and intellectuals to recommend revisions in what had been the nation's Cold War defense strategy, the so-called National Defense Program Outline of 1976. The report of the advisory panel on August 12, 1994, was characteristically cautious.[40] It strongly reaffirmed a defensive military posture and dependence on the security alliance with the United States. The report expressed readiness to do more to underwrite the American military bases in Japan. It called for further improvements in host-nation support and agreement to provide supplies (including fuel) and logistical service for U.S.–Japanese military exercises. Beyond the provisions recommended to make the alliance more reciprocal by increasing financial support, greater interoperability, and further steps to enhance joint military exercises, the most significant change the advisory panel recommended in the National Defense Program Outline was a more forward-looking stance on multilateral security activities. The report recommended revision of the Self-Defense Force Law to provide for participation in United

Nations peacekeeping activities as a primary duty. The activities would include monitoring of cease-fires, patrolling buffer zones, and others not presently permitted.

As it moves away from the Yoshida strategy under the impetus of economic interests and the post–Cold War environment, Japan is exploring the approaches of multilateralism in both economic and security fields. Multilateralism has many advantages for Japan. While bilateral relations with the United States remain critical both to the Japanese foreign policy position as well as to the domestic political structure, we have seen how relations with Asia have grown dramatically in importance since 1985. Japanese trade with Asia now exceeds trade with the United States. Japanese FDI in Asia is growing much more rapidly than Japanese FDI in North America. Nearly two-thirds of Japan's massive ODA goes to Asia. Japan's economic surge into Asia since 1985 requires more involvement in the region to protect its increased interests. Multilateralism provides some moving away and softening of the dominance of U.S.–Japan relations. While the historic legacy of the Pacific War is still not overcome, multilateralism provides a cover, a quiet approach to the region, one that will help to restore Japan's legitimacy and claims to leadership. Engagement in multilateral organizations not only offers a way to respond to foreign suspicions as well as criticisms of its self-absorption, but also a way of overcoming domestic resistance to a more active international role. Without question one of the motivations of Ozawa, Nakasone, and other Japanese advocates of a "normal country" in seeking a Japanese permanent seat on the United Nations Security Council has been to wean a substantial portion of the Japanese population of its residual "one-country pacifism" (*ikkoku heiwa-shugi*), or what is really isolationism. The UN's prestige has always been high with the old left wing of the political spectrum, and a UN Security Council seat would offer an avenue for increasing Japan's international engagement.

For all of these reasons, Japan has begun probing and exploring opportunities in multilateral fora and other organizations. It has encouraged the creation of the ASEAN Regional Forum (ARF) and the Council for Security Cooperation in the Asia Pacific (CSCAP), but characteristically has reserved its greatest efforts for the Asia-Pacific Economic Cooperation (APEC) forum. With its loose, deliberative, informal nature, its concentration on economics, and its inclusion of the United States, APEC offers a multilateral organization with which the Japanese feel relatively comfortable. Japan has tried to position itself to serve as a bridge between Asia and the West. On the one hand, despite the urgings of many business leaders, Japan has resisted Malaysia's proposed East Asia Economic Caucus (EAEC), which would exclude the United States, Australia, Canada, and other non-Asian states. A blue ribbon committee of the Japan Forum on International Relations, always reflective of the establishment's thinking, in a recent study stressed pursuit of a "constructive and open regionalism."[41] On the other hand, Tokyo has also resisted American efforts to move swiftly toward rules and regulations to establish trade and investment liberalization. Representing Asian apprehension that the United States will demand common rules of economic behavior, Japan has argued for respect of Asia's diversity and a gradualist approach—what the Japan Forum study called "organic economic integration guided by market mechanisms."

Driven by its economic interests but handicapped by its historic constraints, Japan is thus pursuing a cautious, low-key strategy in post–Cold War Asia. As Okazaki acknowledges, the legacy of the Yoshida strategy will be with Japan for some time: "If Japan had behaved in a conventional manner during the decades since the end of World War II, it could have undergone a smooth transition, taking its place in the world as a country with sufficiently good judgment to be trusted with normal military capabilities. But the opportunity to become a normal country has repeatedly eluded Japan." The Japan–U.S. alliance remains of the greatest consequence to Japan's future. Asia alone is no substitute. The policy of using East Asia as "a springboard" for economic expansion, which Okazaki advocates, cannot be pursued successfully "in the next 10 or 15 years" without the alliance. Asia alone is also not sufficient to sustain Japan's growth for the foreseeable future. "Moreover," Okazaki notes, "the ASEAN countries welcome Japanese expansion into the region as long as Tokyo maintains friendly relations with Washington." A rift with the United States would not only undermine Japan's Asia strategy. Okazaki acknowledges that he, in common with other Japanese elite strategists, believes that it would also result in domestic political upheaval. He therefore cautions against an "impetuous Asianism" or any harm to the health of the alliance: "It is vital not to damage the bedrock of the bilateral alliance, on which the fate of this nation rests."[42]

Notes

1. Hisahiko Okazaki, "Ajia Chōtaiken' e no shinsenryaku," in *This Is Yomiuri*, August 1992, pp. 42–90; translated as "Southeast Asia in Japan's National Strategy" in *Japan Echo*, vol. 20 (special issue 1993), p. 61.

2. Naohiro Amaya, *Nippon wa doko e iku no ka* [Where Is Japan headed?], Tokyo: PHP, 1989, p. 189.

3. Quoted in John Welfield, *Empire in Eclipse*, London: Athalone Press, 1988, p. 251.

4. Kosaka Masataka, "Reisengo no shinsekai-chitsujō to Nihon" [Japan and the Post–Cold War New World Order], *Kokusai Mondai*, October 1991.

5. Figures cited in the *Japan Times*, December 13, 1994.

6. J. W. Dower, *Empire and Aftermath: Yoshida Shigeru and the Japanese Experience, 1878–1954*, Cambridge, MA: Harvard University Press, 1979, p. 277.

7. Henry Kissinger, *White House Years*, Boston: Little, Brown, 1979, p. 324.

8. In my book, Kenneth B. Pyle, *The Japanese Question: Power and Purpose in a New Era*, I have discussed the Yoshida Doctrine and its legacy at some length (AEI Press, 1992).

9. See Kozo Yamamura, "Japan's Production Network in Asia: Regionalization by *Keiretsu?*" unpublished paper, University of Washington, March 1994.

10. Okazaki, "Ajia Chōtaiken' e no shinsenryaku" ["Southeast Asia in Japan's National Strategy"], 1992, p. 53.

11. See David Arase, "U.S. and ASEAN Perceptions of Japan's Role in the Asia-Pacific Region," and Steven C. M. Wong, "Japan in Search of a Global Economic Role," in Harry H. Kendall and Clara Joewono, eds., *Japan, ASEAN, and the United States*, Berkeley, CA: Institute of East Asian Studies, 1991, pp. 275, 296–297.

12. Ibid., p. 273.

13. Yamamura, "Japan's Production Network in Asia: Regionalization by *Keiretsu?*" 1994.

14. Ibid.

15. Ibid.

16. Okazaki, "Ajia Chōtaiken' e no shinsenryaku" ["Southeast Asia in Japan's National Strategy"], 1992, p. 54.

17. Quoted in Yamamura, "Japan's Production Network in Asia: Regionalization by *Keiretsu?*" 1994.

18. Edward J. Lincoln, *Japan's New Global Role*, Washington, DC: Brookings, 1993, pp. 59–62; also Lincoln, "Japanese Trade and Investment Issues," 1993, in Danny Unger and Paul Blackburn, eds., *Japan's Emerging Global Role*, Boulder, CO: Lynne Rienner, 1993, p. 135.

19. Lincoln, *Japan's New Global Role*, 1993, p. 58.

20. For an elaboration of Nakasone's policies see Pyle, *The Japanese Question: Power and Purpose in a New Era*, 1992, ch. 6.

21. *Asahi shimbun*, November 29, 1991.

22. *Asahi shimbun*, February 21, 1992.

23. "Kinkyū apīru: PKO hōan ni tsuite" ["Urgent appeal: Concerning the PKO Law"], *Sekai*, July 1992; translation in *Japan Echo*, vol. 19, no. 3 (Autumn 1992), pp. 57–58.

24. Tadae Takubo, "Kokuren wa bannō de wa nai" ["The UN Is Not Al-mighty"], *Shokun*, July 1993; translation, slightly modified, from *Japan Echo*, vol. 20, no. 3 (Autumn 1993), p. 15.

25. Sachio Genkawa and Akihiko Ushiba, "Nakata Atsuhito-shi no 'ikun,' " *Shokun*, June 1993; translated as "The Peculiar Constraints on Japan's Peacekeep-ers" in *Japan Echo*, vol. 20, no. 3 (Autumn 1993), p. 9.

26. *The New York Times*, October 24, 1993.

27. Ibid.

28. Personal interview with Ozawa, May 1993.

29. *International Herald Tribune*, May 4, 1991.

30. Okazaki, "Ajia Chōtaiken' e no shinsenryaku" ["Southeast Asia in Japan's National Strategy"], 1992, p. 56.

31. Foundation for Advanced Information and Research, *Interim Report of Asia-Pacific Economic Research*, Tokyo: FAIR, 1990, pp. 217, 226.

32. Roundtable on Japan and the Asia-Pacific Region in the Twenty-first Cen-tury, unofficial translation of final report, December 25, 1992.

33. *Nikkei Weekly*, January 25, 1993.

34. *Japan Times*, August 17, 1993.

35. *Japan Times*, October 23, 1993.

36. Kazuo Ogura, " 'Ajia no fukken' no tame ni," *Chūō Kōron*, July 1993; translated as "A Call for a New Concept of Asia" in *Japan Echo*, vol. 20, no. 3 (Autumn 1993), pp. 37–44.

37. Yasusuke Murakami, "Daigaku to iu na no shinsei kigeki," *Chūō Kōron*, July 1988; translated as "The Debt Comes Due for Mass Higher Education" in *Japan Echo*, vol. 15, no. 3 (Autumn 1988), pp. 71–80.

38. *Yomiuri shimbun*, "A Proposal for the Revision of the Text of the Consti-tution of Japan," Tokyo, November 3, 1994.

39. *The New York Times*, December 30, 1994.

40. Advisory Group on Defense Issues, *The Modality of the Security and Defense Capacity of Japan: The Outlook for the 21st Century*, August 12, 1994.

41. The Japan Forum on International Relations, *The Future of Regionalism and Japan*, Tokyo, June 1994.

42. Okazaki, "Ajia Chōtaiken' e no shinsenryaku" ["Southeast Asia in Japan's National Strategy"], 1992, pp. 62–63.

6

Post–Cold War Security Issues in Thailand and the Philippines

Clark D. Neher

Shape of Global and Regional Power

Virtually all analyses of global security issues now begin with explanations of the fundamental transformation of the international arena. Indeed, qualitative changes in the past several years have had a remarkable impact on how the world's nations relate to one another. Although much of the transformation and its impact on Southeast Asian security has been unpredictable, with scholars and diplomats scarcely able to foresee the direction or scope of rapidly changing forces, some patterns emerge.

After World War II, nearly all the conflicts in Southeast Asia were related to Cold War politics, but by the early 1990s, the Cold War no longer was the driving force. Today no communist power threatens the sovereignty of any Southeast Asian nation. The demise of the communist empire has created different security concerns and needs. Russia is no longer a major player in Southeast Asian politics, as shown by its disengagement from Vietnam and Cambodia. China is more concerned with trade ties with the nations of the Association of Southeast Asian Nations (ASEAN) than with supporting insurgent forces in the Philippines or Thailand. Even conflict among the communist nations has decreased since former Soviet president Mikhail Gorbachev's retreat from Vietnam. Beijing and Hanoi have normalized ties, and the UN–brokered Cambodian settlement will further reduce Vietnamese-Chinese tensions.

The end of communist threats to Southeast Asia corresponds to a reduced role for the United States in the region. In the 1990s U.S. foreign policy priorities have focused on the European Community, the Commonwealth of Independent States, Japan, China, the Middle East, and Latin America. Southeast Asia has become a secondary priority, largely because U.S. interests in that area have been met and there are no crises threatening those interests. Conditions in Southeast Asia now reflect the goals of the United States during the Vietnam War: ASEAN nations (except the Philippines) are flourishing economically as dynamic models of development; the communist nations of Vietnam, Laos, and Cambodia have become militarily impotent; and enemy superpowers have withdrawn from the region.

This period of non-crisis (the Cambodian and South China Sea imbroglios are the obvious exceptions) stems from the fact that the historical flashpoints in Southeast Asia—the struggle against colonialism, the threat from communist superpowers, communist-supported insurgency, and the Vietnam War—are no longer volatile. These crises have been relegated to history, and are no longer central considerations for Southeast Asian governments. Instead, Southeast Asia's security, both externally and internally, has never been more assured.

As international bipolarity between the United States and the Soviet Union gives way to multipolarity (and, temporarily, to unipolarity, with the United States dominant), Southeast Asian regionalism has expanded, with the ASEAN nations moving toward new trade alliances. This regionalism will eventually expand to include Laos and Cambodia (Vietnam became a member of ASEAN in 1995) as they adopt liberalized economic policies. Indeed, Thailand has already initiated a rapprochement with Indochina, as illustrated by the concept of *Suvanaphum* (Golden Land), in which Thailand is to take a leading role in the economic opening of Vietnam, Laos, Cambodia, and Burma. The Philippines has not yet played a major role in these new ties.

Enhanced regionalism in Southeast Asia reflects the fact that economics is now in command and ideology is in decline. Security issues have taken a back seat to trade and aid issues, such as the role of the World Trade Organization (WTO), intellectual property rights, economic growth triangles, and the like. Economic relations are at the forefront of the new diplomacy, necessitating a new breed of foreign policy specialists that knows the unique language of economics rather than military security. However, to assure continued budgetary and policy clout, military leaders note that the new emphasis on trade, far from making security matters obsolete, requires an expanded notion of security, including protecting access to needed resources. The new 200–mile exclusive economic zones (EEZs), for example, have brought some 2.6 million square miles under state jurisdiction among the ASEAN nations alone, thereby creating new responsibilities for the national navies.[1]

Central to understanding the post–Cold War era is the worldwide movement toward democratization. Both Thailand and the Philippines have been greatly influenced by the trend, with citizens of both nations demonstrating in favor of the end of authoritarian rule and the advent of democracy. Today, in both countries, leaders must consider the views of a wide array of groups: media, dissident leaders, ethnic associations, nongovernmental organizations (NGOs), members of parliament, political party leaders, and the military. Foreign policy formulation is no longer the exclusive prerogative of the military in Thailand, or of Ferdinand Marcos' cronies in the Philippines.

Although these changes are breathtaking and for the most part reflective of U.S. interests, Southeast Asia continues to be a crucial area of security concerns. Despite the end of the Cold War, Asia is rearming faster than any other region in the world. Asiawide weapons purchases constitute 40 percent of the world total. This rearmament stems in part from the perceived pullback by the United States from Asia as a result of the closing of military bases in the Philippines and the desire of U.S. leaders to have Japan and South Korea play larger defense roles in the region. The rearmament also stems from the perceived threat of China's moves in the Spratly Islands in the South China Sea, where Vietnam, the Philippines, Malaysia, Brunei, and Taiwan also assert claims.

In 1992 Taiwan purchased advanced fighter jets from France and the United States to counter a weapons buying program by China. As Singapore, Malaysia, Thailand, and Indonesia have prospered through economic development, they have also increased their weapon purchases. No longer concerned about internal insurgency or communist aggression, these ASEAN nations look to their shared oceans and waterways as potential trouble areas. The Malacca Straits, connecting the South China Sea and the Indian Ocean, are crucial shipping lanes, and the fishing waters of the region are a critical economic resource. The nations of Southeast Asia are building up their air forces and navies in particular as part of a forward defense strategy to resist aggression at the outer limits rather than within their boundaries.

Fluid capital and weaponry at cheap prices, the decline of American influence in the area, the growing military strength of China and Japan, and a desire to ensure security are the obvious reasons for the arms race in Southeast Asia. The Persian Gulf War, which illustrated the importance of high-tech military hardware in modern warfare, has also contributed to the recent arms buildup. For the Philippines, the issue is also the obsolescence of its armed forces, in particular its navy, which is the oldest in Southeast Asia. Because Southeast Asia's armed forces have traditionally been oriented toward preserving domestic security, new expenditures are focused on those external problems currently at the forefront of the governments' security agendas. The decline of a strong U.S. presence has already exacerbated historical animosities and regional ambitions among China, Russia, Japan, North and South Korea, and the nations making claims in the South China Sea. All the nations of East and Southeast Asia have increased their defense budgets and weapons purchases in the past two years as the American defense shield has been lowered.

Because regional and international policies are closely interwoven in Southeast Asia, both merit discussion. The most important external event affecting the perceptions of Southeast Asian (including Thai and Philippine) officials was the Gulf War, which confirmed for many that the end of the Cold War did not mean the end of conflict in the world. On the contrary, security analysts wondered if the new international order, characterized by the decline of superpower involvement in world affairs, could actually increase the risk of local-level conflict as local and regional leaders took advantage of a vacuum to assert their ambitions. Southeast Asia's leaders are asking, "Who will guard Asia?"[2]

The collapse of the Soviet Union and the reluctance of the United States to be the dominant military force in Southeast Asia could lead to larger security roles for Asia's major powers: India, China, and Japan. This potential change in Southeast Asia's international relations is an important reason why the ASEAN nations are strengthening their military capabilities and why they are considering regional defense structures. Nevertheless, because the governments of Southeast Asia cannot agree on probable adversaries, the likelihood of a formal regional defense alliance is very small.

Regional security concerns also focus on Japan, the area's economic superpower. Although memories of Japan's depredations in Southeast Asia during World War II are waning, an increased Japanese military capability frightens Southeast Asia's citizens. Clearly Japan is compelled to protect its oil and trade routes in the South China Sea, since its survival depends on Middle East oil. Nevertheless Japan's government has stated unequivocally that Japan will play no military role in Southeast Asia.

There is irony in the fact that in 1992 ASEAN diplomats visited Russia to encourage a more visible Russian role in Asia. Moreover, ASEAN diplomats were eager for Russia to invite foreign investment. Because of internal difficulties, Russia has focused on domestic issues and on relations with Europe and the United States. There is evidence that Russia has transferred significant amounts of weaponry to its eastern borders, and this transfer and upgrading of weapons systems is the primary concern of Asian defense planners, despite the fact that there is no evidence of preparation for an attack. Nevertheless, the Russian buildup is one reason why ASEAN diplomats consider a continued U.S. presence to be a stabilizing force.[3]

Patterns of Stability and Instability in Thailand and the Philippines

Generally, periods of noncrisis lead to noncharismatic, pragmatic, and technocratic leadership. Vietnam has moved from the charismatic Ho Chi Minh to the colorless Nguyen Van Linh, and then to the equally bland Do Muoi; Indonesia from the flamboyant Sukarno to the administrator Soeharto; Singapore from the brilliant Lee Kuan Yew to the pragmatic Goh Chok Tong; the Philippines from the egocentric Ferdinand Marcos to the phlegmatic Fidel Ramos; and Thailand from the nationalist dictators Phibun Songkram and Sarit Thanarat to the quiet, all but unknown Chuan Leekpai, and then to the rural and obscure Banharn Silpa-archa. These new pragmatists are concerned mostly with domestic economic issues, keeping the military and ideologists constrained, feathering their own nests, and negotiating with other world powers on trade and aid.

Periods of noncrisis also bring new groups into the political sphere. In the Philippines and Thailand, business-oriented members of parliament increasingly dominate both the political and economic debates. Technocrats run the bureaucracies while generals seek to professionalize their forces and retain their budget prerogatives. Leaders in both countries must consider the views of more than the traditional elites.

Thailand

Politics in Thailand has long been characterized by stability—that is, the continuing capacity of the authorities to cope with changing domestic and international demands and to foster and sustain a high degree of legitimacy. Indeed, Thai authorities have usually had the prescience to foresee the needs of their citizens and to have met or contained those needs before they became discordant demands that could undermine the regime's legitimacy.

Certainly the fact that Thailand was never formally colonized has enhanced the leadership's ability to cope. The Thais have been able to pick and choose those aspects of Westernization they deem compatible with their traditional culture. In their international relations they have "bent with the wind," keeping their options open and making accommodations after they assessed the power configurations surrounding them.

In addition, the congruency between the general attitudes, values, and beliefs of the Thais toward politics and the actual structure of the political system has led to political stability. The political culture is compatible with the hierarchical, status-oriented, patron–client structures that are the foundation of Thai politics. The network of patron–client relationships, the heart of Thai politics, is also congruent with the personalistic nature of Thai political structures.

Moreover, societal homogeneity and the assimilative and cooptive policies of successive Thai governments have contributed to political stability. This is in contrast to the severe ethnic conflicts in Thailand's neighbors, Malaysia and Burma. Thailand has no dissident ethnic group that threatens the tranquility of the kingdom. Thus the political system "fits" Thai culture.

Also crucial for understanding Thai political stability is the role of the king. Traditionally above politics and universally venerated by Thais, the king became involved in political affairs in the 1980s, when he supported the government of Prime Minister Prem Tinsulanond against military coups. The king's strong resistance to the coups helped to defuse the crises. Having reigned longer than any previous monarch, King Bhumipol Adulyadej brings legitimacy to the present government.

Political stability has also been related to economic conditions. Indeed, Thailand has experienced some of the highest economic growth rates in the world. Exports have grown at least 24 percent each year for the past five years. Manufacturing is now responsible for a larger share of the gross domestic product than is agriculture.

Although 70 percent of the Thai people are in the agricultural economy, the number in rice farming is decreasing. Thai farmers have diversified into such crops as vegetables, fruits, maize, tapioca, coffee, flowers, sugar, rubber, and livestock. The standard of living in the countryside has improved substantially since the 1970s.

The factors responsible for the kingdom's economic successes include a commitment to free-market, export-driven policies by highly trained and generally conservative technocrats. These new officials are not as steeped in personalistic, clientelist politics as their counterparts in the Philippines are.

The vital involvement of Thailand's Chinese minority cannot be overestimated as a factor explaining the vibrancy of the economy. This dynamic minority has provided leadership in banking, trade, manufacturing, industrialization, monetary policy, foreign investment, and diversification. Because Thai society has provided autonomy to the Chinese to run their economic enterprises without government interference, the Chinese have reinvested their profits, with comparatively little capital fleeing overseas. Philippine society, on the other hand, has interfered with Chinese entrepreneurship, resulting in large amounts of capital moving out of the Philippines to nations deemed safer.

In just one generation Thailand has managed to lower its population growth rate from 3.0 percent to 1.6 percent. The decrease resulted from a massive government-sponsored education program that has changed attitudes about the optimum family size and made birth control devices available throughout the country. This has resulted in a higher standard of living for families, higher educational attainment and literacy, and lower poverty rates.

These economic and societal achievements have buttressed Thailand's political stability. However, Thailand faces severe difficulties that could undermine its stability. The greatest obstacle to continued economic growth is the poor state of infrastructure, as exemplified by Bangkok's infamous traffic gridlock, inefficient port facilities, and unreliable electricity and telecommunications. Given the close relationship between economic growth and overall stability, the potential for economic decline as a result of infrastructure overload threatens stability.

A second problem is the depletion of Thailand's natural resources, especially its forests. Recent legislation has banned logging, but the government has failed to implement the law. As a result, floods, soil erosion, and droughts have led to increasing devastation.

The AIDS crisis also has the potential to undermine Thailand's economic growth. Depending on prevention practices and changes in behavior, some 2 to 4 million Thais will be diagnosed as HIV positive by the year 2000. Between 1991 and 2000, the direct and indirect costs of the projected AIDS cases will total between $7.3 billion and $8.7 billion. AIDS deaths during the decade could reach 500,000. AIDS is likely to have an even broader impact on the Thai economy, particularly on tourism, direct foreign investment, and remittances from abroad.[4]

The total number of youths matriculating from Thai high schools is lower than in most of the other Southeast Asia countries, leading to a dearth of trained persons for Thailand's new industries. Compared to other Asian newly industrializing economies, Thailand has too few trained engineers and scientists to move the economy smoothly into industrialization.

It is also possible that a monarchical succession crisis could undermine governmental stability. The heir apparent to the throne is Crown Prince Vachiralongkorn, who does not enjoy his father's revered position. On the contrary, the prince is often criticized for his lack of commitment and discipline. He is the object of much negative gossip, although lèse majesté laws assure that he is not criticized publicly. The king has promoted his daughter, Princess Sirindhorn, to the rank of *Maha Chakri* (crown princess), thereby placing her in the line of succession along with her brother, the crown prince.

No female has ever succeeded to the throne in Thailand. At present it appears as if the crown prince has become more involved in ceremonial duties and is being trained to ascend to the throne. At worst, Thai citizens will denounce the inheritance and insist that the crown princess become the monarch. More likely, the Thais will acquiesce to the prince's ascension and simply ignore the monarchy or reduce their veneration. In either case, the Thai monarchy may no longer be the bedrock of stability and legitimacy in the kingdom.

Western and Thai scholars who had emphasized Thai stability

failed to predict the military coup of February 23, 1991. Most analysts had asserted the conventional wisdom that coups were an anachronistic part of the nation's past, no longer pertinent to the new democratic kingdom. The quelling of the communist insurgency, which had plagued Thailand in the 1960s and 1970s, and the absence of an external security threat were thought to have removed the major rationale for military intervention into governmental affairs. Moreover, the strengthened role of political parties and the parliament, as well as a general attitudinal change more favorable to democratic, civilian rule, were said to have reduced the military's influence. In addition, the remarkable economic growth of 11 percent per year (highest in the world for three years) was thought to have provided an insurmountable bulwark against intervention by military leaders who, after all, benefited from the enormous profits that came from the rapid transformation of the Thai economy and thus had a stake in the status quo. Finally, the king's determination to oppose a military coup was thought to lessen the chance that one would succeed.

Nevertheless, on February 23, 1991, military leaders abrogated the constitution, dismissed the elected government and established martial law—a superb example of why it is impossible to predict "stability." Thai and foreign scholars failed to foresee the coup, although in retrospect the causes were clear. Democratization had not ended the personalism, corruption, and factionalism that have long been a part of Thai politics. Certain military factions believed that because the civilian administration had seemed to undermine their traditional sources of power, a coup was necessary to protect access to political, social, and economic resources.

The coup temporarily ended Thailand's steady progress toward democracy. General Suchinda Kraprayoon appointed a respected civilian, Anand Panyarachun as interim prime minister, and backed a constitution designed to keep the military dominant. Elections were held in March 1992, but they were characterized by fraud, candidate-buying, and vote-buying. Pro-military parties, which enjoyed the advantage of unlimited funds, forged a coalition and named General Suchinda prime minister.

To express their dismay, citizens took to the streets to demonstrate against the "second coup" and the "illegitimate" Suchinda administration. Led by educated and middle-class Thais, the demonstrations culminated on May 18, when a confrontation with the military turned violent, and hundreds of demonstrators were killed or injured.

Suchinda had underestimated the depth of commitment educated Thais had to the notions of democracy and civilian dominance. His claim that the demonstrators were pawns of "communist" elements who desired the end of the monarchy was vintage rhetoric from the 1960s, irrelevant to 1992 realities. He also underestimated the response of the king, who stepped in to force the resignation of Suchinda and to place the immense prestige of the monarchy on the side of democratic rule.

Elections were held once again, this time in September 1992. "Watchdog" committees lessened the degree of fraud considerably, compared to the elections six months prior. This time a coalition of pro-democracy parties succeeded in forming the new government with Democratic Party leader Chuan Leekpai as prime minister. Chuan, who was Thailand's first truly civilian prime minister, was soft-spoken, fair-minded, unpretentious, and honest.

The struggle between state officials, led by the military, and politicians and business elites remains center stage in Thai political activity. The 1991 military coup and the subsequent debate on how to fashion a new government exemplified the attempt and the failure to resolve this struggle. The public explanations for the coup—corruption and parliamentary dictatorship—were rationalizations by a segment of the military to secure prerogatives thought threatened by civilian leadership.

The rise of a middle class, far more educated and aware than any previous generation, suggests that the battles for political power in Thailand in the near future will be between this new civilian force and the formerly entrenched military. The military is now on notice that future coup attempts will lead to an outpouring of protest from hundreds of thousands of citizens.[5]

The immediate crises faced by the Chuan Leekpai government were important for assessing both short- and long-term political stability in Thailand. The coalition was made up of rival parties inexperienced in cooperating on policy formulation. Personal rivalries were more significant than party loyalty, thereby threatening gridlock and presenting the military with an excuse for intervention. The coalition's bare majority in the parliament did not bode well for the long-term stability of the administration. For example, in mid-1993 the Social Action Party left the coalition to join the opposition, thereby reducing the coalition's majority. The coalition existed more for political reasons than for shared ideological or policy views. To keep the coalition together, Chuan had to meet each party's demands for cabinet positions and financial resources. There was a constant threat that the coalition would break up, forcing another parliamentary election and undermining the government's capacity to govern.

The Chuan Leekpai administration also had to cope with the decision of the constitutional tribunal that the generals who oversaw the violence of May 1992 were to remain protected by the amnesty decreed by former prime minister Suchinda. Support for the amnesty undermined campaign promises that the generals would be prosecuted, while opposition to it tempted the military to intervene to protect its honor. Other significant issues concerned the widening gap between the urban rich and the rural poor, traffic gridlock and pollution in Bangkok, ecological destruction, AIDS, child labor, and prostitution.

About to lose his parliamentary majority when another coalition party defected, Prime Minister Chuan called for new elections to be held July 2, 1995. The campaign featured twelve political parties, 2,300 candidates vying for the 391 parliamentary seats, and about 40 million voters. Campaign issues were vague because political parties generally do not present platforms. Nevertheless, the candidates focused on the voters' concern about the buying and selling of candidates and votes, rural poverty, Bangkok's notorious traffic, land reform, and bureaucratic inefficiencies.

The political party that won the most seats was *Chart Thai* (Thai Nation), and its leader, Banharn Silpa-archa, became Thailand's twenty-first prime minister after mobilizing a coalition of seven parties into a parliamentary majority. The Democrats, led by Chuan, became the major opposition party. Banharn had vast experience as a six-term member of parliament, a billionaire business executive, and former cabinet minister. His opponents campaigned that Banharn was corrupt, and a close associate of rural "godfathers." His admirers argued that Banharn was most experienced in meeting the needs of his local constituents, and could use that same strength nationally as prime minister.

Rather than moving the nation toward a more progressive democracy, the 1995 election was viewed by Thai intellectuals as a backward move with the reemergence of old-style politicians with their money interests. At the same time, the military played no role in the election, a sign that elections were accepted as the appropriate way to change leaders.

The reasons for optimism about continued movement toward stable, democratic rule and away from military-dominated, highly authoritarian, self-serving centralized government are many. First, Thailand has successfully ended internal insurgency. Second, the country is free from serious outside threats to its security. Third, with one of the highest economic growth rates in the world and a reputation for conservative fiscal management, the prospects for continued development are excellent. The fourth reason for optimism about future stability is the professionalization of the armed forces and the embarrassment of army generals about the 1991 coup. The international movement toward democratization has penetrated most of the major elements of Thai society, including the military.

Finally, the rise of an educated, more cosmopolitan, middle class is often viewed as the sine qua non for stable government. In Thailand, that class has become more and more a focal point of economic and political decision making. Supporting the middle class are new interest groups, including NGOs, that are demanding rights and resources formerly thought available only to the elites. Along with political parties and parliament, these new institutions are taking on the functions formerly carried out by patron–client networks.

In contrast to the Philippines, the Thai economy is flourishing and acts as a support for the present democratic government. Virtually all economic classes have improved their standard of living, even though the gap between rich and poor has increased over the last decade.

Barnhan's challenge is to find the proper balance between stability and democracy, between the requirements of order and the desire for civil liberties, between respect for authority and empathy for the demands of the people, and between the role of the military as the guarantor of security and the desire for civilian dominance. The kingdom's tradition of treading the "Middle Path" through these balances augers well for Thailand's future stability.

The Philippines

The Philippines is in striking contrast to Thailand. Whereas the Thai government has worked assiduously and successfully to promote stability and economic growth, Philippine authorities have failed miserably. Without fundamental change in the structure of the Philippine state, the prospects for stability are dismal. At present, the Philippine government is incapable of providing the necessary underpinnings and incentives for resolving the nation's overwhelming problems.[6]

The overriding, unmet challenge is to fashion a stable political structure that is predictable enough for the development of external economic ties and domestic entrepreneurship. Instead, the Philippines continues to be ruled by an oligarchy intent primarily on self-aggrandizement rather than the public good.

Unlike Thailand, foreign aid and investment in the Philippines has not appreciably or positively altered the nation's political economy. In the words of one observer:

> The impact of external resources on the Thai bureaucratic polity was to help fuel an economic growth that has created new social forces; these social forces, in turn, provide a clear basis for major change in the political sphere. In the Philippines, on the other hand, external resources merely financed the perpetuation of the hothouse within which patrimonial features have flourished. The economic growth that these resources fueled did not lead to the creation of new social forces, and the result has been little change in the political sphere.[7]

If Thailand has been a favorite model for the successful economic development of rural societies, the Philippines has become the model for what *not* to do. On a par with Thailand in the mid-1970s, when each nation had an annual per capita GNP of just over $300, the Philippines by 1992 had achieved only $820, compared to Thailand's $1,800. GNP growth in the Philippines has been negligible for almost two decades. In 1991 the GNP growth was 1 percent in the Philippines, compared to 8 percent in Thailand. The nation's high population growth (2.6 percent per year compared to Thailand's 1.6 percent) also limited real economic growth. Although the picture has improved immeasurably, the Philippines remains decades behind ASEAN's dynamos.

Economic problems in the Philippines begin with its traditional land policies. Whereas in Thailand the majority of farmers own their own land, farmers in the Philippines are mostly tenant renters. No administration has ever set forth a meaningful land reform program, so that bare subsistence farming dominates and radical political movements flourish.

The Marcos economy was characterized by crony capitalism, with coveted contracts given to incompetent presidential clients rather than to effective contractors. Marcos had given his best friends monopoly control over the sugar and coconut sectors, which led to their amassing fabulous riches stashed in Swiss and U.S. bank accounts. The flight of capital subverted the economy and brought it to the brink of disaster.

Foreign investment never took off, in contrast to Thailand, where Japanese, Taiwanese, South Korean, and U.S. capital has stimulated and sustained economic growth. Seven military coup attempts against President Corazon Aquino from 1986 to 1992 frightened away trade, aid, and investment. Hence, even after the fall of Marcos, the democratic Aquino administration was not able to solve the nation's problems: great economic inequality, land disputes, monopolistic industries, corruption, and self-interested elites. President Aquino did not exert sufficient leadership to transform the democratic (but misleading) facade of Philippine government. Today, it appears that this goal can be attained only through fundamental changes by political leaders who are willing to undercut their own privileged positions.

Adding to the economic and political morass are the natural calamities, including floods, hurricanes, and volcanic eruptions, that have devastated the islands and hampered efforts to build needed infrastructure. The government's inefficient response to the crises has also undermined citizen support for the system.

The Philippines is an example of a state that intervened in the economic system with ruinous results. In contrast to Thailand, the Philippine state has critically hurt the economy through its corrupt intervention and its subservience to the economic dynasties that have dominated the nation since the days of Spanish colonialism. The dynasties, with their power bases in the provinces, are often at odds with state authorities. The prospects for improving these conditions are slim, unless fundamental changes are carried out by leaders who are sincerely concerned with the public welfare. The experience of the past decades offers little reason for hope, although President Ramos has succeeded in ending the disastrous consequences of the Marcos years.

Domestic insurgency is one of many problems subverting Philippine political stability. Although there is evidence of a decline in the number of New People's Army (NPA) insurgents, the dire economic conditions suggest that the decline may be only temporary and that a resurgence is possible. Key leaders of the NPA have been captured or co-opted, and the armed forces have become more professional in their counterinsurgency activities. The decision to remove U.S. troops from Subic and Clark military bases also foiled a principal propaganda point of the insurgents that the Philippine government was a lackey of "imperialist America." Nonetheless, economic decline and administrative incompetence could reinvigorate insurgency.

Another contributing factor to the Philippines' domestic instability is the excessive administrative centralization of government, which crushes entrepreneurial and creative efforts by the citizenry. The oversized bureaucracy has strangled every area it controls, including such basic services as electricity, water, garbage collection, telecommunications, police protection, and education.[8]

President Ramos also faces ubiquitous corruption, which has undercut the legitimacy of every post-independence government. Despite the formally democratic structures of government, the Philippines remains ruled by cronyism and feudalism, dominated by dynastic families who govern in their own self-interest. Waiting for the propitious moment to intervene is the army, whose commitment to professionalism and civilian rule is merely nominal.

In his 1992 campaign against six other major candidates for president, Ramos won only 24 percent of the vote; 76 percent of the population voted for other candidates, and a large number of supporters of losing candidates believe that Ramos was elected through fraud. Six weeks elapsed before a final vote tabulation was announced, providing numerous opportunities for cheating. Moreover, because Ramos' party supporters in the national legislature constitute a small minority, the chances that a coherent program will be enacted are few. The president lacks the charisma and extraordinary character that could lift the spirit of Filipinos and mobilize them to enact fundamental changes, and he does not have the loyal backing of the factionalized armed forces.

Hence the chances for needed reform are not good. Nevertheless, Ramos has begun to pull the Philippines out of its predicament by opening the country to foreign investment (as in Thailand), reducing cronyism by basing economic decisions on merit, limiting corruption, and creating a workable tax system.[9] The nation's infrastructure, especially the production of electric power, has been overhauled in an effort to end the constant brownouts that sap industrial output. State-owned enterprises are being privatized.

Politically, Ramos must modernize the bureaucracy, decentralize decision making, and find ways to make the dynastic families contribute to the nation's best interests. He will need to reinvigorate ties with the United States because a period of deterioration has followed the

1991 rejection of the Military Base Agreement by the Philippine Senate. U.S. aid programs have been greatly reduced, and only a midranking official (the director of the Peace Corps) was sent to the Ramos inauguration. President Clinton's visit to Manila in November 1994 went far to improve economic ties despite student protests against "American imperialism," which were featured on news reports in the United States.

Long-term leadership evolution is difficult to predict. Clearly Filipinos have a commitment to democracy (in the abstract) and will resist coups. The NPA is largely a spent force, factionalized and deprived of leadership. Only a total economic breakdown would lead to a communist-led revolution. More likely is a military takeover by officers who present themselves as noncorrupt saviors willing to move the Philippines in dramatic new directions. A military move would be based on the initially successful Marcos model in 1972 when the overwhelming majority of Filipinos were willing to accept his declaration of martial law as being "for the greater good."

In the short run, Ramos will undoubtedly complete his six-year tenure as president. His major strengths are: (1) his personal reputation as an honest person; (2) his willingness to open the country to foreign investment, to eliminate corruption, and to create a workable tax system (although the chances for real tax reform for the rich are negligible); (3) his endeavors to woo the Philippine Congress; (4) his success in 1994 in forming a coalition between his party and the main opposition parties, thereby providing enough strength in the Congress to assure passage of his economic reforms; (5) his support from the business community, important factions of the military, and the U.S. government; and (6) Filipino commitment to democratic institutions.

Ramos' weaknesses are: (1) his lack of charisma and his unwillingness to make the dramatic decisions needed to move the nation economically; (2) his inability to break up the dynastic-controlled economies in the provinces; (3) his impotence in dealing with the horrible natural disasters that continue to devastate the islands; and (4) his lack of a mandate, after receiving less than one-fourth of the presidential vote.

Ramos has focused on political stability since becoming president in June 1992. Economic growth was about 2 percent in 1993. In 1994 the growth rate increased to 4.5 percent, respectable by any standards except in Asia, where gross domestic product growth rates have averaged about 7 percent. Interest payments consume almost one-third of budget expenditures. At 2.5 percent, the Philippines' population growth is the highest in Southeast Asia. Jaime Cardinal Sin, the leader of the Catholic Church in the Philippines, has fiercely criticized Ramos for the president's moderate suggestions for ending rapid population growth. And the Philippines has one of Southeast Asia's worst records of environmental abuse. The forests are largely denuded, rivers are dead, fish have been depleted from the seas, and pollution is at dangerous levels in Manila.

Favorable conditions include low interest rates (about 9 percent in 1994) and inflation (7 percent in 1994) and liberalized foreign investment procedures. Deregulation has provided an incentive for foreign investment. A new law gives foreign investors the right to 100 percent ownership. Ramos' focus on political stability could have long-term positive results by increasing both domestic and foreign confidence. Trade has improved, with exports increasing (although imports have grown at a higher rate). Subic Bay, the former U.S. naval base, has been transformed into an enterprise zone complete with new U.S. and other foreign companies, including Reebok and Federal Express.

To ease the economic difficulties faced by the central government, President Ramos privatized numerous state enterprises, including Philippine Airlines. Most importantly, he also pushed through a fast-track system to privatize power companies, a decision that has helped solve the ubiquitous problem of electrical shortages.

President Ramos became increasingly popular as his term of office progressed, largely because of the turnaround in the economy which provided renewed hope to Filipinos. As economic growth approached 5 percent and foreign investment grew dramatically, Philippine leaders began referring to the nation as "tiger cub," a clear reference to the fast-growing Asian tigers. These high performance levels led to support for Ramos' coalition during the May 8, 1995, elections, when candidates loyal to him won a clear majority of seats in the bicameral parliament.

More than any country of Southeast Asia, the Philippines has been known as the "showcase of democracy." That acknowledgement is a source of pride to Filipinos. Moreover, memories of the Marcos years are still fresh, and, for most Filipinos, humiliating. (The return of Marcos' body to the Philippines led to embarrassment for the Marcos family when few persons came to pay their respects.) Structurally the

Philippines meets the major criteria for democracy, but a Filipino's loyalty is directed first to family, then to close friends, then to the local community, then to personally known political leaders, and finally to distant, impersonal governmental agencies. Patron–client ties are at the heart of Philippine politics. Filipino elites are often alienated from their roots and from the masses of the people, most of whom they scorn. The elites' first value is to take care of themselves and not to concern themselves with the public good. Such values are antithetical to democratic rule, a form of government that requires mutual trust.

On May 8, 1995, Filipinos voted for 12 vacant Senate seats, 202 seats in the House of Representatives, 76 governorships, and 17,000 municipal offices. Despite complaints about voting fraud, the elections resulted in support for the coalition led by President Ramos. Most of the Senate was made up of members of dynastic families who ruled their provinces for generations. Winning a house seat in Leyte Province was Imelda Marcos, despite her conviction of corruption and her twenty-year sentence to prison. (She campaigned while free, pending an appeal.) Less fortunate was Marcos' son, Ferdinand Jr., who lost his bid for a Senate seat. (In August 1995 he was found guilty of tax evasion and sentenced to prison.)

For true democratization to take root in the Philippines, the formal institutions of government must become more than facades for oligarchical rule. Inasmuch as the great majority of newly elected senators and representatives are members of dynastic families, the prospects for meaningful democracy are bleak.

Foreign Policy Issues for the Philippines and Thailand

Thailand

For Thailand, the Spratly issue is secondary because the kingdom makes no claim to these islands. Far more important to Thai security are relations with Vietnam, Laos, and Cambodia. Since Prime Minister Chatichai Choonhavan announced in 1988 that Thailand desired to turn the fighting fields of Indochina into a marketplace, Thailand has served as a channel for finance and investment there. Indeed, Thailand has wanted to transform itself into the economic center of a resurgent mainland Southeast Asia, a *Suvanaphum* with Thailand as the centerpiece.

Chatichai's initiatives were a stunning rebuke to Thai Foreign Ministry officials, who had long viewed Vietnam as the major threat, and a vindication for the prime minister's academic advisors, who opposed the "conservative inflexibility" of the Foreign Ministry's policy. The ministry quickly reversed itself in 1989 and moved toward a constructive relationship with Vietnam, Cambodia, and Laos. The thrust of the new policy was clearly economic: Thailand saw a unique opportunity to "become a funnel for foreign assistance; a bridge linking the Indochinese states and the global economy, and a gateway and springboard for interested foreign investors."[10]

Under Chatichai and ever since, economics has been in command in Thai foreign policy. Business interests now have more say in foreign policy formulation, as shown by approval of the first bridge over the Mekong River, linking Laos with Thailand and facilitating the transport of trade items, and also by the negative Thai response to UN sanctions to pressure Cambodia's Khmer Rouge into complying with the 1991 Paris peace agreements. Thailand's negative response was an indirect function of the lucrative cross-border trade between Thailand and Cambodia, including the Khmer Rouge.

For Thailand, the problem was reluctance, then inability, to control business arrangements worth tens of millions of dollars. Gems (mostly rubies), arms, and logging are in the hands of well-connected Thai businessmen, military leaders, and rebel forces who have operated in the area for generations. Thai officials claim that it is impossible to control the 800–kilometer border.

Thai economic interests also focus on the Gulf of Thailand, where there are offshore oil and gas deposits, and on the Andaman Sea, where a Southern Seaboard Development Project is to be built. The plan is to build a land bridge of road, rail, and oil pipeline to connect the Andaman Sea and the Gulf of Thailand.[11] The project will give Thailand control over an alternate transportation route between the Indian and Pacific oceans, avoiding reliance on the Straits of Malacca.

Thailand's economy-driven foreign policy is manifested in its leadership within ASEAN of the effort to create a free trade area to enhance security. By extending its domestic economic growth programs from the national to the regional level, Thai officials hope to improve their domestic economy and strengthen the capacity to meet external threats.[12]

The January 1992 agreement to create an ASEAN Free Trade Area (AFTA) is a cooperative effort to compete with the European Community and North American Free Trade Agreement, and to respond to concern about economic dependence on Asian superpowers, namely Japan. AFTA, which will comprise a market of 320 million people in a rapidly growing region, is based on the principle of open trade, with participating nations lowering trade tariffs on one another's goods. Thus far the rhetoric of free trade is greater than the actuality because the ASEAN nations have little to trade with each other. They export similar products: trade within the six countries constituted only $32 billion in 1991, about one-fifth of their total trade. ASEAN nations compete economically with each other more than they complement each other. The AFTA could encourage more investment in ASEAN, however, as it moved toward a single market.

Altogether, Thailand has responded effectively to issues characterizing the new international era, with initiatives toward a "new nationalism," toward normalization of relations with the Indochinese nations, and toward economic rather than security relations. The new nationalism has taken the form of relating to the United States as an equal rather than as a client. Under Prime Ministers Chatichai Choonhavan, Anand Panyarachun, and Chuan Leekpai, Thai foreign policy reduced security dependence on the United States, asserted a policy of equidistance in its relations with allies and adversaries, and launched a new Indochina policy without seeking U.S. concurrence.

Until the Chatichai government, the Thai military dominated foreign policy. More recently, foreign relations have required expert knowledge of trade, intellectual property rights, protectionism, the GATT, and the Generalized System of Preferences. As Thailand's economy is integrated into the world capitalist system, the nation's leaders must be correspondingly better informed about economics. Thai stability is increasingly vulnerable to external economic pressures and fluctuations. Moreover, as Cold War considerations ebb, the importance of the United States to Thai security decreases. Thailand's integration into the world trading system, the end of the Cold War, and Thailand's new nationalism have diminished the importance of U.S. security guarantees and contributed to the intensification of Thai efforts to forge closer ties with China, Indochina, Japan, Russia, and its ASEAN neighbors.

The Philippines

A significant change in Philippine domestic and foreign policy was the decision to remove the United States from military bases at Clark Air

Base and Subic Bay. After months of negotiations, in September 1991 the Philippine Senate rejected the Military Base Agreement and requested that the Americans leave Subic. Prior to this decision, the United States, as a result of the destruction from Mount Pinatubo, had begun its withdrawal from Clark Air Base.

The Philippine Senate's determination was based on the desire to move from a dependency relationship with the United States to a more nationalistic posture. The decision led to tensions and challenges in the U.S.–Philippine relationship as the nation substituted its traditional reliance for security on the United States to a broader, more complex security arrangement. While the Philippines remained under the American "nuclear umbrella," and while there was no clear threat from abroad to Philippine security, there was the luxury of time to carry out the transformation.

In the short run, the decision to oust the Americans reduced foreign confidence in Philippine stability, thereby worsening the already desperate economy. However, the long-term effect could be an important boost to the country's psyche: it could mean that Filipinos will take responsibility for their nation's ills rather than blame "American dominance" for every difficulty, and it undermines NPA propaganda about "American neoimperialism." One reason for such hope is the fact that the relationship with the United States was not an issue in the 1992 presidential campaign.

In his June 1992 inauguration speech, Fidel Ramos stressed his broad view of security, which includes military, political, economic, societal, and environmental factors. He spoke about the importance of political stability, access to resources, societal unity in the context of cultural autonomy, and protection of the nation's resources as the new, crucial variables that measure security. He stressed that a strong economy guarantees security as well as autonomy. Ramos argued that the major security problems are massive poverty, communist insurgency, Muslim secession movements, military rebellion, and urban unrest. He did not list external threats.

Ramos' litany of domestic ills was an apt reflection of security concerns. The absence of an external threat to Philippine security was fortunate, since its armed forces were incapable of defending the country from external aggression. Training and expenditures had focused primarily on internal defense, to control communist insurgency and Muslim separatism. By 1992 the twenty-four-year-old Communist

Party of the Philippines had stalled, beset by internal differences and government penetration. Nevertheless, precisely because of its domestic problems, the Philippines was the only ASEAN nation with a viable communist party and a Muslim separatist force.

In an attempt to find a compromise between the short-run disadvantages and the long-run advantages of the American withdrawal from Subic and Clark, President Ramos announced in November 1992 that American ships, aircraft, and troops could continue to have access to military installations in the Philippines. The policy to give Americans a lease on part of Subic was designed to reduce defense expenditures by the Philippines, undercut the military's insistence on a bigger budget, assure American involvement in case of an attack on the Philippines, recoup rental payments, and improve ties with the United States. The disadvantages of the policy were the potential for revived furor over a continuing U.S. presence and the delays such access could bring about in turning Subic into a commercial, privatized, economic zone.

Shortly after Ramos' announcement, some Filipino senators questioned the effectiveness of the Mutual Defense Treaty between the United States and the Philippines, which commits the two countries to mutual support in the event of external aggression. U.S. diplomats responded with frustration that the Philippines could end up as the only ASEAN country that does not allow U.S. ships refueling and visiting rights.

For the Philippines, the Spratly Islands imbroglio is now considered the flashpoint crisis. Although it is not clear which of the interested nations could be the aggressor, China is viewed as the greatest threat by both Thai and Philippine officials because of its huge population and growing military strength. Although Thailand does not have any territorial interest in the South China Sea, Thai officials have expressed concerns about China's claims to the Spratly Islands. Because the Philippines is one of the claimants, Filipinos see China's claims as more ominous. Philippine officials believe that there are vast, untapped resources, including oil and natural gas, in the South China Sea. The sea is a strategic waterway for the vital trade routes linking the Persian Gulf with Japan, Taiwan, and South Korea, all of which rely on free passage for their oil imports.

Philippine interest in the South China Sea involves its claims to eight of the islands and to maritime jurisdiction over a wide expanse of ocean resources. Philippine officials have defined the problem in terms of respect for Philippine territorial rights and sovereignty. The military, in particular, has made the dispute over the Spratlys a matter of national prestige and overall security, thereby precluding compromise with the other claimants such as Malaysia, China, Taiwan, and Vietnam.

The Philippine government has not made the dispute a national issue, probably because the prospects that the controversy will be resolved in favor of the Philippines, either legally or militarily, are low. Philippine garrisons in the area are neglected and incapable of effective fighting. Malaysia, for example, has a navy with far greater capability in the South China Sea. President Ramos' administration prefers to rely on diplomatic negotiation for a favorable settlement.

The ambiguous status of the Mutual Defense Treaty has raised questions about American assistance to the Philippines if the islands claimed by the Philippines are threatened. Caught in the contradiction between the desire for autonomy from the United States and the desire to have American support for Philippine claims, both Filipinos and Americans have presented a series of conflicting statements as the two nations negotiate about the meaning of the Mutual Defense Treaty. The major debate centers on American obligations to come to the Philippines' aid, particularly in the Spratlys, in the event of aggression.[13] For example, Foreign Minister Roberto Romulo stated in December 1992 that if the Philippines should come under attack in the Spratlys, the United States is obliged to come to its aid. However, at the same forum, Philippine senators reminded the foreign minister that without American military bases, the Philippines is no longer of primary interest to the United States.

Implications for U.S. Foreign Policy

The transformation of the international system has brought about a period in which there is no clear conceptual framework for a U.S. security role in Southeast Asia. The historical rationale for U.S. engagement in the region—that is, containment of Soviet aggression—is no longer valid. Nevertheless, there are three important American interests in Southeast Asia and, more specifically, in Thailand and the Philippines:

- First, to preserve political stability in Southeast Asia. To a great extent, the goals of the United States in the Vietnam War era have been reached. ASEAN nations are stable (the Philippines is still the exception) and flourishing economically. The communist Indochinese nations are overwhelmed by domestic crises that preclude aggressive policies. Vietnam and Laos have chosen to liberalize their economies and to cooperate with, rather than confront, their ASEAN neighbors. Cambodia, too, is moving toward economic and political association with ASEAN by the end of the decade.

- Second, to encourage economic development through capitalism. Virtually all of Southeast Asia has moved toward free-enterprise, export-oriented economic policies. Trade in goods and services between the United States and Southeast Asia has grown every year for two decades. Two-way trade between the United States and all of Asia is larger than the amount of trade between the United States and Europe. As long as U.S. security interests in Southeast Asia depend on the continuing vibrancy of that region's economies, Washington should encourage these trends with free-trade and development-oriented policies. Protectionism and precipitous military withdrawal will subvert Thailand's ability to sustain its economic growth, and the Philippines' ability to initiate such growth.

- Third, to preserve access. There is no adversarial regional power in Southeast Asia that today threatens U.S. interests. ASEAN nations have built and sustained an alliance and have offered the United States needed military bases. At present, American armed forces have complete access to Southeast Asia and freedom of movement throughout the region.[14] After the loss of the Philippine bases, U.S. policy planners determined that a home base is no longer vital to American interests in the region. Instead, American forces are dispersed among existing facilities, from the north Pacific to Singapore, for training, supply, repair, refueling, and storage. In addition, Washington has developed new military ties with ASEAN nations, and has engaged in joint military exercises with Malaysia, Indonesia, Thailand, and Singapore. Thailand, in particular, has allowed U.S. military aircraft to use its airports and ports for refueling and maintenance. Thailand's security treaty with the United States has supported annual exercises (called "Cobra Gold") involving air, naval, and ground forces. This dispersal has provided flexibility of movement and freedom from reliance on a single unstable ally.

Despite the favorable security environment in Southeast Asia, major questions and issues still exist. Is the post–Cold War condition in Southeast Asia more stable than the Cold War environment? It is difficult to imagine a negative response when the present time is compared to the earlier period of economic stagnation, communist insurgencies, periodic aggressions, and volatile leadership. Those problems have been largely resolved, and few comparable crises have arisen. Nevertheless, for the Philippines, the post–Cold War era remains unstable because of the inability of the government to meet the needs of its citizens. While there is no external threat to the Philippines, there are perennial domestic threats.

Inasmuch as Thailand is no longer a front-line state, it can place more emphasis on domestic ills. Keeping the military at bay, lessening the gap between the few rich and the many poor, protecting the environment, building an infrastructure, and ending the spread of AIDS are the major problems faced by the new civilian administration. Thailand's traditionally astute leadership and its flourishing economy suggest optimism about meeting these challenges.

The second question is whether ASEAN can be sustained without an outside enemy. The Association is not necessary for protection against outside aggressors; it is now primarily an economic alliance, with little security purpose. In the event of outside aggression, ASEAN members still benefit from forward-deployed American forces. The loss of military bases in the Philippines did not significantly reduce U.S. military capability in the region. ASEAN leaders do not look toward the transformation of ASEAN into a military alliance, although the new ASEAN Regional Forum institutionalizes Asia-Pacific security discussions. At most, increased security cooperation through joint military exercises is contemplated. More than that would undermine the new nationalism and new resilience of the separate ASEAN nations, each of which proclaims autonomy as a key to its foreign policy.

Certainly the American security umbrella has allowed allied governments to maintain lower defense budgets and to concentrate on economic development. ASEAN leaders continue to prefer an American presence as a balance wheel in the area. Furthermore, a U.S. withdrawal could lead to increased military activity in Southeast Asia by Japan (despite denials by the Japanese government), China, and India, a circumstance deemed threatening by Southeast Asia officials and citizens. There is universal approval (including by the Indochinese states) in the region for the United States to continue to play a preeminent role in the 1990s.

Hence the dramatic transformation of the international arena has not led to a fundamental change in Southeast Asia's perceptions of American interests or responsibilities in the region. In this era of relative peace or noncrisis, the United States plays a major role in assuring that the former era of constant crises will not return.

Notes

1. Khatharya Um, "Thailand and the Dynamics of Economic and Security Complex in Mainland Southeast Asia," *Contemporary Southeast Asia,* vol. 13, no. 3 (December 1991), p. 260.

2. Perry L. Wood, "Interface: Regional Security Trends Toward Enhanced Defense Cooperation in Southeast Asia." Unpublished paper delivered to Midwest Conference on Asian Affairs, Oshkosh, Wisconsin, October 23, 1992, pp. 3 and 5.

3. For a discussion of the Russian buildup in the Far East, see Tai Ming Cheung, "The Eastern Front," *Far Eastern Economic Review,* November 26, 1992, pp. 26–28.

4. See Mechai Viravaidya, Stasia A. Obremskey, and Charles Myers, "The Economic Impact of AIDS on Thailand," Cambridge, MA: Department of Population and International Health, Working Paper No. 4, Harvard University School of Public Health, March 1992.

5. The preceding paragraphs are drawn from Clark D. Neher, "Political Succession in Thailand," *Asian Survey,* vol. 32, no. 7 (July 1992).

6. See Paul D. Hutchcroft, "The Political Foundations of Booty Capitalism in the Philippines." Unpublished paper delivered at the 1992 Annual Meeting of the American Political Science Association, Chicago.

7. Ibid., p. 31.

8. Roger W. Fontaine, "The Philippines: After Aquino," *Asian Affairs,* vol. 19, no. 3 (Fall 1992), p. 172.

9. Ibid., p. 184.

10. The quote is from Foreign Minister Siddhi Savetsila, in Khatharya Um, "Thailand and the Dynamics of Economic and Security Complex in Mainland Southeast Asia," 1991, p. 247.

11. Ibid., pp. 263–64.

12. Michael Malley, "Software: ASEAN Economic Cooperation and the Security of Southeast Asia." Unpublished paper presented to Midwest Conference on Asian Affairs, October 23, 1992, Oshkosh, Wisconsin, p. 2.

13. Rodney Tasker, "End of the Sentry," *Far Eastern Economic Review,* November 26, 1992, pp. 18–20.

14. Wood, "Interface: Regional Security Trends toward Enhanced Defence Cooperation in Southeast Asia," 1992, p. 25.

7

Vietnamese Security in Domestic and Regional Focus: The Political-Economic Nexus

William S. Turley

The fall of communism in Eastern Europe, the Cold War's end, and the collapse of the Soviet Union destroyed any possibility for Vietnam to base its security on alliance or on its own military strength. These and other events left it virtually bereft of friends, foreign aid, even trading partners. However, Vietnam had begun earlier to implement market-oriented reforms, seek "dialogue" with neighboring states, and lay a basis for integration into the regional economy of Southeast Asia. Urgent pursuit of these objectives in the Cold War's aftermath won Vietnam admission to the Association of Southeast Asian Nations (ASEAN) in July 1995. In the process it joined its neighbors in abandoning a security strategy attuned to global bipolar conflict for one geared to regional and "geo-economic" concerns.

Vietnam now shares the region's peace and can expect to benefit from participation in its phenomenal growth. And yet the new era does not lack sources of insecurity. Internally, the very reforms needed to promote peace and development have potential to cause social unrest and political instability. The price of growth and openness is change and vulnerability, which will tend to loosen the grip of the ruling Vietnam Communist Party (VCP). Externally, Vietnam is Southeast Asia's front line against Chinese assertiveness, especially in the South China Sea and on the border that Vietnam shares with China. Here geopolitics still matters: the power disparity confronts Vietnam with hard choices as it does no other Southeast Asian state. In the interest of its own security and independence, Hanoi must somehow accommodate China without threatening other Southeast Asian states, and it must strengthen ties with major powers like Japan and the United States without antagonizing China. Vietnam also shares a disputed border on both land and sea with a prickly and unstable Cambodia, and its rivalry with Thailand for influence in the states between them may be in abeyance rather than dead.

The Cold War's end improved the prospects of regional stability and growth, but not without complications that Hanoi will find difficult to manage. Over the rest of this decade, Vietnam faces two major challenges. One, already largely met, has been to shift the basis of national security from military might and the Soviet guarantee to diplomacy and reconciliation with neighbors. The other more enduring and unfamiliar challenge for the current generation of leaders is, as they see it, to extract maximum benefit from a merger with the world market economy without becoming overly dependent on any one power within it.

Perceptions of Global and Regional Power

Assuming that the Vietnam Communist Party will remain in power at least until the end of the decade, the relevant Vietnamese perceptions are those of the party elite. For this elite, the central geostrategic priority for decades was controlling the mountain interior in order to withstand attack from Great Powers enjoying easy access to Vietnam's long coastline, as well as Laos and Cambodia. Unable to defend the coast, the communists concluded that they could win national independence and unity only if they excluded foreign influence other than their own from Laos and Cambodia. The doctrine of "security interdependence" among the three Indochinese states flowed from this conclusion and was a basic plank of Vietnamese strategy throughout Hanoi's intervention in Cambodia during the 1980s; a residue of this strategy survives in Vietnam's relations with Laos. The underlying geostrategic assessment, however, has not provided Hanoi much help in coming to terms with post–Cold War shifts in global and regional power.

Winding Down the Cold War

The Cold War structure of power was in a sense reassuring for Vietnamese communist leaders. Although it put Vietnam almost continuously on the front lines of global conflict, it induced the Soviet Union to support Hanoi's goal of reunification with the South and later to provide it with the means to eliminate the perceived threat of a Chinese-backed government in Cambodia. Soviet economic assistance was also vital to Vietnam's economic survival. Vietnamese assessments of global and regional power shifted in response to changes in the Cold War power structure and Soviet economic support.

From the late 1960s to the mid-1980s, Hanoi subscribed to the Soviet doctrine of the "three revolutionary currents." This doctrine identified the growing power of the socialist countries headed by the Soviet Union, the national liberation and independence movements in the Third World, and the struggle of the working class and working people in capitalist countries as the three principal trends shaping the global balance of forces. The historically inevitable development of these broad movements supposedly moved world affairs in a direction favorable to socialism.[1] Secure in the faith that they had caught the wave of the future, Vietnamese leaders calculated that Moscow's support would outlast China's hostility, denigrated noncommunist neighbors in ASEAN for dependency on the United States, and expected ASEAN governments to remain mired in poverty, inequality, and disunity, unable to resist Hanoi's ascendance.[2] The policy consequences of these perceptions split the region into opposed blocs that mirrored both the Cold War and Sino-Soviet disputes.

Soviet vacillation (beginning with Leonid Brezhnev's offer of an olive branch to China), Vietnam's frustration in Cambodia, and Vietnam's economic stagnation under central planning while ASEAN boomed, induced Hanoi to modify these views. By the mid-1980s, Vietnamese calls to "internationalist duty" (i.e., for the Soviet Union to help Vietnam shore up fraternal parties in Laos and Cambodia) masked a hope that détente and Sino-Soviet normalization would not undercut Vietnam's own security and paramount influence throughout Indochina.[3] But Mikhail Gorbachev's "new thinking" and growing demand for reform at home forced the Vietnamese to abandon this hope. In May 1988 the VCP Political Bureau adopted "Resolution No. 13 on External Policy," which propounded a doctrine of "comprehensive security" based on economic strength, military capability appropriate for defense, and "expanding international cooperation."[4]

The present era began disturbingly for Hanoi with the disintegration of communist regimes in Eastern Europe and the reduction of Soviet commitments abroad, symbolized most dramatically by Moscow's decision to withdraw from Afghanistan. These events destroyed any pretense of a socialist community or sense of internationalist duty on which Hanoi might depend. The suspension of Soviet military assistance and the January 1991 shift to hard currency denomination for Soviet-Vietnamese trade, closely followed by the collapse of the Soviet Union itself, completed Vietnam's abandonment. Improved Sino-Soviet relations and fissures in ASEAN unity paved the way to a Cambodian settlement without completely ending Sino-Vietnamese tensions.[5] Thrust by events into an extremely exposed position, Hanoi adopted the simple pragmatism of seeking "more friends, fewer enemies." As General Secretary Nguyen Van Linh put it in his report to the Party's Seventh Congress in June 1991:

> The over-riding task in *foreign relations* in the immediate future is to firmly maintain peace, expand relations of friendship and co-operation, create favorable conditions for the building of socialism and defending of the homeland, contributing an active part to the common struggle of the peoples of the world for peace, national independence, democracy and social progress.
>
> We stand for equal and mutually beneficial co-operation with all countries regardless of sociopolitical regimes, on the basis of the principles of peaceful co-existence.[6]

By then Vietnam already was seizing every opportunity to redirect trade from the ex-Soviet bloc toward any willing partner, to remove remaining obstacles to improved relations with ASEAN, and to normalize relations with China.

Major Powers and the Global Balance

From the time of the Persian Gulf War until the Soviet breakup, the dominant view in Hanoi was that the international system was still distinctly hierarchical, with the USSR and China after the United States being "indispensable" to shaping the new world order. Europe and Japan in this view were unable to exert "decisive influence" on either regional or world politics.[7] Six months later, a new analysis perceived a "diverse and multipolar direction" of change in global power that would check American aspirations to construct a unipolar world. With the United States checked, China could emerge as the only "indispensable factor," and this imbalance might force Japan to reconsider its continued restraint from exercising "decisive influence" in Asia. That unwelcome possibility lay in the future, however; for the moment the international system, freed from the constraints of bipolarity, had become more fluid, presenting opportunities for "Vietnam's policy of befriending all nations" to score "initial and positive results."[8] In other words, the emerging structure of power was fraught with uncertainty, but that very quality provided Vietnam a chance to break out of isolation from the West, ASEAN, and Japan—imposed since 1978–79 for the intervention in Cambodia—that it could not afford to miss. Seizing the day required Hanoi to swallow its profound distrust of major powers and former enemies.

The Vietnamese are most ambivalent with respect to China, which presents a Janus face of successful reform socialism and military threat. Ideology once cemented relations, but the Vietnamese concluded as early as 1954 that China would always treat them as pawns or obstacles in larger games. Whether aiding or attacking Vietnam, Beijing's behavior was consistent, so far as the Vietnamese were concerned, with prerevolutionary manipulation, bullying, and dividing of peripheral states to keep larger threats (the Mongols, the French, the Soviet Union, the United States) at bay. China's diplomacy to the present has appeared to Hanoi to involve more sticks than carrots, more toying than bargaining in negotiations, more demand for tribute than dialogue between sovereign equals, presenting Hanoi with a choice between capitulation and resistance. If Vietnam and China share a sense of beleaguerment as two of just five communist party–led states remaining in the world, this has been insufficient for the Vietnamese to accept the curbs on their independence that closer relations might entail.

The bilateral relationship with the People's Republic of China is nonetheless the most important one for Vietnam. Proximity plus huge material inequality make this so whether the issue involves military or economic security. Vietnam lies in the direct path of China's growing power and assertiveness, and no other country has China's potential to manipulate Vietnam internally. This potential lies in China's links with highland minorities, ethnic Chinese residents, high-ranking members of the Vietnamese Communist Party and military who worked, studied, or trained in China, and, over the long term, the attraction of growth in

China's south coastal provinces. Nor do the domestic politics of any other country reverberate the way China's do in Vietnam. The PRC's phenomenal economic growth, military modernization, hegemonic ambitions, and political example constitute enduring threats.

To manage relations with China, Hanoi has few practical options. One, a military alliance of regional states, has no support within the region and would not equal China in power resources anyway. The tested option of relying upon a distant superpower brings risk: any power with global interests is certain to treat Vietnam as less important than China in its own larger strategy. Besides, this option is not viable so long as the world system is not polarized and no power needs Vietnam's help to contain China. The alternative of bandwagoning with China also lacks appeal as it would place Vietnam in China's sphere of influence, compromise Vietnam's independence, and antagonize other Asian states. Finding a middle way with the Middle Kingdom is Vietnam's central strategic conundrum. Hanoi's clear preference is to avoid strong commitment to any option, balancing China as best it can through a *tout azimuths* foreign policy.

One of the powers this policy seeks to draw in is Japan, reversing a long-standing antipathy. From the war with America into the 1980s, Vietnamese strategists considered Japan's role as America's "unsinkable aircraft carrier" a threat to supply lines from the Soviet Union. As the United States drew down its presence in the region, these strategists speculated that a China that converted its economic growth into military power would provoke Japan to rearm.[9] Compared with Japan's striking out on its own to confront China in a regional contest for power, its continued dependence on the United States for security seemed preferable. The Vietnamese were ambivalent about Japan's economic role as well, recognizing Japan's potential to be Vietnam's most important economic partner on the one hand, and fearing economic domination on the other. The fear was hypothetical so long as Japan's association with the American-led embargo constrained Japanese businessmen, but it helped push the Vietnamese to highly value diversity in economic partnerships.

Hanoi appreciated Japan's facilitation of the Cambodian peace process, and in 1990 it turned to Tokyo for help in seeking normalization of relations with the United States as well. Although the Japanese responded by urging Vietnam to cooperate with the United States on resolving the issue of missing American prisoners of war (POWs) and soldiers missing in action (MIAs), the Vietnamese discerned that Japan had influence in Washington and could help Vietnam in other venues.[10] Japan resumed official assistance to Vietnam in November 1992, and its economic importance to Vietnam began to grow. In 1993 Japan took 31 percent of Vietnam's exports (up from 23 percent in 1990 but down 2 percent from 1992) and accounted for 13 percent of Vietnam's imports (up from 9 percent in 1990), overtaking Singapore as Vietnam's largest trading partner.[11] Yet in the same year it was only the fifth-largest foreign investor, a rank it maintained in 1994. Japan is virtually certain to emerge eventually as Vietnam's most important economic partner, but not lopsidedly or in a political context that would arouse Vietnamese fear of domination.

Attitudes toward the United States are more complex than casual American visitors to Hanoi tend to believe. The warm welcome they encounter reflects a focus on interpersonal relations, not feelings toward the U.S. government and its role in the Second Indochina War. Hanoi's early reaction to the Gulf War was that the Soviet "compromise" with imperialism had freed the United States to intervene against smaller regional powers, which someday might include itself.[12] But after the dust settled, Vietnamese assessments recalled that the United States had suffered harsh lessons at Vietnamese hands and now was additionally subject to the constraints of multipolarity.

With the closure of American bases in the Philippines, Vietnamese perception of an American military threat gave way to the belief that American engagement was needed to maintain a balance among outside powers and instill determination in ASEAN to resist Chinese assertiveness. Vietnamese media ignored the Thai-American "Cobra Gold" military exercises near the Cambodian border in the spring of 1993. Vietnamese statements about possible American use of Cam Ranh Bay were vague or contradictory, probably because the Vietnamese themselves had not formally decided the question. However, Hanoi apparently gave serious consideration in 1993 to allowing naval vessels from a variety of countries to use Cam Ranh on a fee basis,[13] subject perhaps to consultation with ASEAN.[14] If Hanoi perceived any threat from the United States after Washington lifted its embargo in February 1994 and established diplomatic relations in July 1995, it was not military so much as the ideological contamination that it expected to result from closer contact with the large Vietnamese-American community. Hanoi also values the United

States as an economic partner, needed to balance other advanced industrial countries in certain sectors.

Russia has little to offer Vietnam, least of all security reassurance under the terms of the Treaty of Friendship and Cooperation signed in 1978. During 1991–92 Moscow suspended aid (in fact, in February 1992 Vietnam donated nearly half a million dollars' worth of food to Russia!), abandoned plans to build a Pushkin Institute for cultural exchange in Hanoi, began sending Vietnamese workers and students back home,[15] and wrangled with Hanoi over how to settle Vietnam's ten-billion-ruble debt. The VCP's cadre training institute adopted a Western-style political science curriculum, and Japanese, Chinese, and Thai manufactured products largely replaced Russian ones in Vietnamese markets. Trade with all the countries of the former Soviet Union declined from a Cold War high of around 80 percent of Vietnam's total to just 8.6 percent of its exports and 4.9 percent of its imports in 1992.[16]

Throughout the 1980s the Soviet Union acted as the helpful "barbarian to the north" of China, as one Foreign Ministry official expressed it,[17] but in small ways the relationship was disillusioning. Soviet machinery broke down, maintenance costs skyrocketed, Soviet advisors behaved boorishly, and—incredible to the Vietnamese—Soviets found Vietnam a good place to shop. After 1989, Vietnamese analysts dissected the Soviet and East European reform attempts mainly to discover how *not* to dismantle central planning. By early 1992, not much linked the two in the minds of officials on both sides except Cam Ranh Bay.[18] As the deputy head of Vietnam's State Planning Commission put it, "coolness and standstill" marked the relationship.[19]

Hanoi was keen, however, to salvage what benefit it could and preserve some shred of the security tie for possible later use. Thus in 1992 it apparently softened its demand for $350–400 million in rent for Cam Ranh to replace lost military aid.[20] But the Vietnamese must have known that Russian offers to guarantee regional stability in return for continued use of the facility, considering the parlous state of Russia's Pacific fleet, were meaningless. Diminished power, economic weakness, political instability, unsteady purpose, lack of global mission, and repudiation of Marxism-Leninism, not to mention Moscow's sale of arms to China and its release of erroneous documents on American POWs, made Russia an unreliable partner.

From Confrontation to Cooperation with ASEAN

Vietnamese revolutionary hubris must take as much blame as the Sino-Soviet dispute for the regional polarization that kept ASEAN and the Indochinese states apart after 1975. The Cambodian conflict from the outset involved a contest between China and Vietnam over Vietnam's hegemony in Indochina. Hanoi's striving for "special relations" and "security interdependence" among all three Indochinese states clashed with China's drive to be the arbiter of Southeast Asian international relations. The Sino-Soviet dispute overlay this conflict by causing Beijing to fear encirclement as a result of Moscow's alliance with Hanoi and by causing Moscow to support Vietnam's goals in Indochina. Thailand, which shared Beijing's interest in preventing the consolidation of an Indochina bloc under Hanoi's leadership, facilitated the international support of local forces opposed to Vietnam. When Moscow resigned from the global contest, both Beijing and Hanoi lost part of the reason (and in Hanoi's case the means) to pursue their maximum aims. Compromise became possible, and Southeast Asia's division into opposed blocs could end. But developments within Southeast Asia eventually did as much as (or more than) did changes in the structure of global power to transform Vietnamese perceptions and Hanoi's relations with regional states.

After the disintegration of the Soviet bloc, nothing made a deeper impression on Vietnamese leaders than the astonishing economic performance of its noncommunist neighbors (the Asian newly industrializing economies, or NIEs). The perception of a widening gap in wealth and power between Vietnam and its regional adversaries was one of several factors that motivated party leaders to accelerate market-oriented economic reforms and the opening to foreign trade and investment after 1986.[21] The sense of urgency to overcome the gap deepened as Vietnamese gained awareness of its dimensions. Prime Minister Vo Van Kiet warned the National Assembly in October 1994 that "[Even if] we can reach the target of U.S. $450 per capita in 2000, the development gap between our country and most of the other regional countries will still be widening. It's a matter of life or death. . . ."[22]

Once objects of Hanoi's scorn, the ASEAN six showed Vietnam the way to market-oriented growth. They were also attractive partners because they did not impose human rights conditions or demand democratization. Prime Minister Kiet's tireless trips to all the ASEAN countries and solicitation of economic advice from Singapore's former prime minister Lee Kuan Yew exemplified Hanoi's profoundly changed attitude.

Vietnam's sense of place within the region also has depended on its relations with China. Sino-Vietnamese frictions propelled Hanoi into an abortive peace offensive toward ASEAN capitals on the eve of its 1978 intervention in Cambodia and subsequently into courtship of Indonesia, which shared Hanoi's regard for China as the primary threat. Even state-supported scholarly research emphasized Vietnam's Southeast Asian rather than East Asian identity. With the normalization of relations but territorial disputes continuing, Vietnamese leaders acknowledged their cultural debt to China[23] but looked to ASEAN for help in coping with Chinese pressure.

Hanoi valued ASEAN members, moreover, as economic partners to help balance expected heavy reliance for markets and finance on the West and Japan, toward which it had an ingrained distrust. The new emphasis on commerce was apparent in emerging trade and investment patterns that sat oddly alongside older political ties. For example, of all the ASEAN countries, Indonesia had the longest and warmest political relations with Vietnam; yet in 1994 Indonesian investments in Vietnam had just one-seventh the value of those from tiny Singapore, which had been ASEAN's most vocal opponent of Vietnam's intervention in Cambodia.[24] Singapore's nearly U.S. $1.4 billion trade with Vietnam in 1993, moreover, dwarfed Indonesia's U.S. $224 million.[25] Financial resources and comparative advantage counted for more than sentiment and shared security perceptions in the new political economy.

With respect to security, however, Hanoi had historical reasons to be apprehensive about some ASEAN members' relations with extraregional powers. Thus it echoed Indonesian and Malaysian concerns about suggestions that "some countries" might let the United States use their territories or facilities for naval bases.[26] Vietnamese also blamed the organization's lack of effective security cooperation on the greater importance some members attached to relations with Beijing and Washington than with Hanoi. Nonetheless, membership and "comprehensive" relations with ASEAN were an "important and long-range strategic goal."[27] Problematic relations with China and wariness toward great powers generally could make Vietnam, along with Indonesia and Malaysia, the most committed of all Southeast Asian states to regional security cooperation and the concerns of a Zone of Peace,

Freedom, and Neutrality (ZOPFAN) and the Southeast Asia Nuclear Weapons Free Zone (SEANWFZ). Vietnam strongly supported closer association among all ten Southeast Asian states in an expanded ASEAN and participated in the July 1994 inaugural meeting of the ASEAN Regional Forum.

However, while achieving full membership in ASEAN a year later, Vietnam was no more ready to become involved in defense cooperation than it was to meet ASEAN's timetable to create an ASEAN Free Trade Area. Such cooperation had been limited among ASEAN members anyway, but Vietnam faced constraints of doctrine, equipment, and resources not faced by Indonesia, Malaysia, and Singapore, for example, in mounting joint exercises and cooperating to combat piracy.

Hanoi, moreover, has only begun to develop trust in its new partners. The ASEAN member Vietnamese historically have trusted least is Thailand. Thailand is the only Southeast Asian country with which Vietnam had major conflicts before the colonial era; it was a major base of American operations during the Second Indochina War; and Thai post-war behavior—supporting insurgents in Laos and the Khmer Rouge in Cambodia—reinforced Vietnamese suspicion that Bangkok would, if the opportunity presented itself, replace Hanoi's influence in Laos and Cambodia with its own.[28] Whether motivated by insecurity brought on by witnessing the revolutions in Indochina, or because it was too weak to resist pressure from the patron of the moment, Thailand seemed, to the Vietnamese, determined to exclude Hanoi's influence from the states between them by conniving with any great power that was hostile to Vietnam.

Great power détente and disengagement did much to soften that view. Equally important was Bangkok's own willingness beginning in August 1988 to compromise on Cambodia and, in former prime minister Chatichai Choonhavan's words, to "turn Indochina from a battlefield into a marketplace." Standing alone, Thailand posed no threat, and Hanoi welcomed Thai offers of assistance, trade, and investment. But suspicion lingered on both sides, impeding agreement on the terms of Thai-Vietnamese economic cooperation, most notably with respect to fishing and natural gas exploration in overlapping territorial waters, which impinged on coastal security, and reconstitution of the Mekong Committee, which had implications for each state's power to determine the use of a vital resource.

The suspicion has been apparent as well in competitive bidding between Hanoi and Bangkok for influence in Laos. Poor as it is, Hanoi persists in building hydropower installations, bridges, roads, and agricultural projects in Laos, subsidizing up to 1,500 Lao students in Vietnam each year, promoting trade,[29] fostering province-to-province aid and exchange, and entering long-term agreements with Laos on energy, forest resources, telecommunications, and more. Although ideological solidarity and the psychological rewards of playing patron to a weaker state help to explain this persistence, it seems unlikely that Hanoi would have defined Lao-Vietnamese relations as based on "comprehensive cooperation" if Thailand had not inaugurated its own aid program for Laos in 1991 for the express purpose of weakening Vietnam's influence.[30] Thai economic dynamism and cultural bonds with Laos, and, of course, Chinese aid to Laos, challenged Vietnam's hard-won predominance. Thus Thailand has evolved, in Vietnamese perceptions, from an insecure ally of hostile great powers into a competitor capable of exercising magnetic attraction on Laos (and Cambodia) in its own right. For the present, Vietnamese regard this trend benignly because of the relaxed international environment, but they have to wonder whether Thailand's pull on Laos (and Cambodia) and schemes to focus regional development on Bangkok, particularly in the context of projects that will link the kingdom with Laos and southern China, will leave Vietnam much influence across the mountains at its back.

The Military Dimension

Hanoi's perception of a much reduced military threat is evident in the contraction of its military establishment. In the four years following the inauguration of a "strategic adjustment" in mid-1987, cutbacks in manpower of about 600,000 (from a high of around 1.2 million plus reserves and militia) included 200,000 officers, "specialists," and workers in national defense industries. Regular ground forces stabilized at about half a million. In 1991 the International Institute of Strategic Studies reduced its estimate of MiG-21s in Vietnam's air force from 206 to 125, of ground attack aircraft from 176 to 60, and main battle tanks from 1,600 to 1,300.[31] While China was beginning to develop a blue water navy and a naval air force oriented toward Taiwan and Southeast Asia, Vietnam had only seven aging frigates and fifty-five small coastal combatants in its navy of 12,000 seamen.[32]

Three years later, these estimates were unchanged.[33] Defense spending, both in absolute terms and as a percentage of GDP, declined after 1985, picked up slightly in 1989, and then declined again until 1992.[34]

Following the communist collapse in Europe and the Tiananmen Square incident in China, the VCP intensified "the political and ideological tasks to ensure that the Army can stand firm politically" and gave sympathetic attention to problems of military pay and living conditions.[35] Assuring the political reliability of the army in the event of domestic turmoil took precedence over plans for modernization. Besides, the termination of Soviet military assistance left little choice.

All this was a major turnabout since the decade after 1975, when Vietnamese armed forces about equaled those of all the ASEAN states combined and helped to provoke defense buildups throughout the region, particularly in Thailand, Malaysia, and Singapore. Whatever the threat Vietnamese military capability once posed to the other ASEAN countries, it has evaporated. Still large and no doubt formidable in the defense of its home territory, the People's Army of Vietnam (PAVN) lacks the external support and economic base to do much more than stabilize its present reduced strength. To be sure, the Council of Ministers decided in 1992 to raise allocations for defense in response to tensions in the South China Sea,[36] and in July 1993 Deputy Prime Minister Phan Van Khai reported that a part of rising revenues would be "put aside to satisfy the newly emerging needs of national defense and security."[37] And the increase in the proportion of military spending in national income from 6.6 to 8.4 percent of gross domestic product in 1993 put Vietnam at a level of defense spending well above the ASEAN average.[38] But Vietnam's small GDP (less than one-half that of Thailand's), pressing development needs, and lack of military relations with countries capable of assisting the PAVN's modernization will constrain procurement of expensive technology for years to come. Barring an oil discovery of fantasy proportions, Hanoi cannot hope soon to match its neighbors' buildups.

Poverty and weakness force Hanoi to seek economic ties and cultivate political support wherever it can find them. However, perception of greater danger from China than from other major powers causes Hanoi to seek friends particularly among members of ASEAN who share this perception. From Vietnam's perspective, a continued inability of ASEAN to cooperate on security, and Chinese success in keeping the Association divided, would be serious limitations and could

cause Hanoi to accept the tacit or indirect involvement of outside powers in the maintenance of regional stability.

Sources and Kinds of Insecurity

Despite the collapse of and abandonment by its allies, Vietnam today
is more secure from military attack and insurgency than at any time
since the Vietnamese Communist Party began its armed struggle for
power in 1941. Diplomacy, trade, investment, and acceptance of interdependence in all its forms have replaced alliance and armament as the
main guarantors of Vietnam's security. Although some Vietnamese
leaders still see the world in Manichean terms, global political, ideological, cultural, and economic currents loom larger than military
threats in their perceptions of the sources and kinds of insecurity.
There is still potential for armed conflict with neighbors, particularly in
the South China Sea and in Cambodia, but the more dangerous processes are "intermestic" ones that could shape events inside Vietnam.

South China (Eastern) Sea

The South China Sea disputes stem from overlapping claims by all
littoral states plus Japan and Taiwan. The dispute involving islands,
reefs, and continental shelf claimed by China and Vietnam came to life
in 1974 when China seized an island in the Paracels (Hoang Sa) from
Saigon government forces. Verbal sparring followed, and in March
1988 Chinese naval forces seized seven islands and sank three
Vietnamese supply ships, causing the deaths of seventy-two Vietnamese seamen. The easing of Sino-Soviet tensions had no effect except
perhaps to embolden the Chinese.

For Beijing, the stakes are prestige, China's role as a regional
power, and strategic position astride a major sea lane. For Hanoi, they
are the security of Vietnam's 3,400–kilometer coastline and approaches to its major ports. Vietnam would face a Chinese presence on
all sides were China to dominate the sea and extend its influence into
Laos and Cambodia. Both countries have an interest in the area's mineral, fishing, and other natural resources, which are proportionally
much more important to Vietnam than to China, and both base their
claims on long historical usage.[39] Vietnam, like China, has sought to
involve foreign oil companies in exploration for oil in the Spratly

archipelago (Truong Sa) and feels that rights under the Law of the Sea strengthen its hand.

The dispute flared again in February 1992 when China passed a law reaffirming its sovereignty over the Spratlys. Chinese vessels apparently landed troops on one Spratly island at the same time.[40] In Hanoi's view these acts contradicted an agreement reached with China the preceding November to take no action regarding territorial disputes that would "complicate the situation."[41] The actions certainly aroused fear throughout Southeast Asia that China had reversed itself on seeking resolution of such disputes through negotiation and was now trying to fill the vacuum left by the U.S. withdrawal from the Philippines.

While both China and Vietnam proceeded to court ASEAN—Beijing to allay ASEAN fears and isolate Vietnam, Hanoi to capitalize on those fears and rally support for its position—they also continued to shore up their claims materially. In early May 1992, Vietnam's Ministry of Defense installed satellite relay stations on three islands in the Spratlys to serve troops already stationed there.[42] Days later, the PRC's National Offshore Oil Company signed an agreement with Crestone Energy Corporation of the United States to explore for oil in disputed waters, provoking Hanoi's denunciation. A workshop hosted by Indonesia in late June and the ASEAN Foreign Ministers Meeting in July provided fora for both Hanoi and Beijing to woo ASEAN but failed to cool their dispute. In early July Chinese vessels landed troops and materials on a Spratly reef, eliciting a note from Hanoi describing the action as a "grave violation of Vietnam's territorial sovereignty."[43] Two weeks later Vietnam opened a fishing port on the main Spratly island, and later the same month Beijing turned down a Vietnamese proposal for a high-level meeting to settle the issue. In October, after an inconclusive meeting of experts in Beijing, Hanoi announced the formation of a team to conduct geological, meteorological, and natural resource surveys in the Spratlys and shortly thereafter unveiled plans to construct an "economic, scientific, and technological complex" on the same reef that Beijing had contracted to Crestone.[44] Following Chinese prime minister Li Peng's visit to Hanoi in early December, Vietnamese foreign minister Nguyen Manh Cam described efforts to defend Vietnam's sovereignty and territorial integrity at sea as a "most complicated struggle."[45] Although talks on the land border proceeded well in August 1993, a Chinese oil rig operating during the same period in waters claimed by Vietnam provoked a spate of angry notes from Hanoi. Both sides organized geological and archaeological surveys and installed equipment in disputed areas. In July 1994 Vietnamese patrol boats seized three Chinese fishing vessels and took fire from two Chinese vessels, resulting in the wounding of two Vietnamese sailors.

Meanwhile, Hanoi strove to win ASEAN support by seeking agreements on joint exploration in overlapping claims outside its continental shelf and where third parties were not involved. China for its part insisted upon settlement of all disputes on a bilateral basis; rebuffed Vietnamese and ASEAN suggestions for a multilateral approach; rejected an Indonesian proposal for involvement of Japan, the United States, and Europe in discussions; and warned ASEAN not to take Vietnam's side. In all of these respects, Beijing had its way. Neither ASEAN nor any outside power was prepared to risk confrontation with China. If China wished to precipitate a clash with Vietnam to intimidate other claimants, it was clear Vietnam would stand alone. Hanoi finally concluded it had no choice but to accept Beijing's demand for a bilateral solution, and in November 1994, during President Jiang Zemin's visit to Vietnam, the two unveiled an agreement to set up an expert's group to discuss their sea disputes.

The realpolitik is clear. Until the Crestone deal, Hanoi sought to defuse tension through conciliatory diplomacy. Afterward it took a harder line while seeking coordination with ASEAN, and later still it accepted the bilateral approach when ASEAN support failed to materialize. Vietnam simply is in no position to oppose China at sea with force, and it has a more urgent need than China to settle differences over boundaries, cross-border trade, and the status of citizens and ethnic minorities in each other's territory. Considering the weakness of its hand, Hanoi's consolidation of a presence in contested areas, strong affirmation of its claims, and willingness to skirmish indicate that much more than just mineral rights is at stake.

Cambodia

In return for abandoning its Cambodian client to the uncertainties of a UN-supervised peace, Vietnam gained normalized relations with China, China's abandonment of the Khmer Rouge, and improved relations with ASEAN, Japan, and the West. The reform-driven need of *both* China and Vietnam to expand ties with the market economies and curry favor with ASEAN was a powerful motive for each to back away from the Cambodian conflict and, subsequently, to implement the peace agreement scrupulously. These facts, along with the evaporation of the global rivalries that polarized the region, augur well for noninterference by regional states in Cambodia's internal affairs.

Vietnam for its part has additional reasons for restraint. Declining Soviet support and commitment to domestic reform after the mid-1980s made the material cost of military engagement in Cambodia increasingly burdensome. For the Vietnamese military, as one officer put it, the Cambodian campaign was "a bitter experience," and a party official remarked that "Cambodia has been a painful lesson ... an error we never want to repeat again."[46] It is hard to conceive of problems spinning so far out of control that Hanoi would address them by repeating the error.

But Vietnam faces threats from Cambodian instability that it will not be able to ignore. Three possibilities could draw it back in. One is mistreatment of Vietnamese nationals residing in Cambodia.[47] Pervasive Khmer antipathy to the settlers translates into tolerance of violence against them.[48] Not wanting to appear soft on the Vietnamese during the May 1993 elections, few Khmer leaders dared to condemn the Khmer Rouge for massacring Vietnamese civilians and carrying out attacks around the Tonle Sap that caused some 20,000 people to flee downriver to Vietnam. Hanoi limited its response to verbal condemnation and demands for investigation, punishment, and recompense, determined not to take action that might provide a pretext for another power to intervene[49] or be held responsible for the collapse of the 1991 Paris agreement that ended the Cambodian conflict.[50]

The electoral outcome did not solve the problem, for not only did the Khmer Rouge remain outside the process, but competitive politics institutionalized the pandering to ethnic prejudice. Halting if not reversing Vietnamese immigration became a requisite of nationalist legitimacy. One of the first policy statements by the new government of Prince Norodom Ranariddh and Hanoi's erstwhile protégé Hun Sen—delivered by the latter—listed the "immigrant issue" as a top priority.[51] In 1994 the National Assembly passed an immigration law that Hanoi considered so prejudicial to the rights of ethnic minorities that it mobilized King Norodom Sihanouk and UN Secretary General Boutros Boutros-Ghali to request modifications. The Assembly resisted the pressure, forcing Ranariddh and Hun Sen to promise there would be no mass expulsions or cantonment of foreigners.[52] With 6,000 Vietnamese refugees from Khmer Rouge violence still in camps near the Vietnamese border, the legal status of the settlers was a festering sore, and the very real possibility of turbulence degenerating into a pogrom, as in 1970, would provide Hanoi a compelling reason to reintervene.

The second problem for Vietnam would be Cambodia's slide into another civil war or protracted ungovernability. Khmer Rouge sway over 10 to 15 percent of the countryside might seem to present the most probable cause, but decay and division on the government side are equally likely. Seven provincial leaders refused to accept the May 1993 election results,[53] and the same individuals who instigated that refusal led an attempted coup in July 1994. Cambodians themselves acknowledge that King Norodom Sihanouk's death could intensify power struggles within the fragile governing coalition, which is composed of persons and parties that were deadly enemies only a few years ago.[54] Chaos in Cambodia would impose real costs on Vietnam in the form of refugees, lost economic opportunities, banditry, spillover of fighting along the border, and raids on Vietnamese villages. All of these things happened before, providing Hanoi a reason (in addition to larger strategic considerations) to launch attacks into Cambodia in 1977 and finally remove the Khmer Rouge regime by force in late 1978. Hanoi must be concerned as well about the effect turmoil in Cambodia would have on the approximately 900,000 ethnic Khmer who comprise 10 percent of the population in five key Mekong Delta provinces.[55] In a fluid situation, both Thailand and Vietnam might feel compelled to become involved, with polarizing effect in Cambodia and on the region.

Vietnam's third Cambodian nightmare would be a Khmer Rouge return to power. Fortunately, this is unlikely. The Khmer Rouge refused to participate in the 1993 elections and so were excluded from the Provisional National Government based on a coalition of their enemies. Apparently fearing defeat, they calculated it was better to bargain for a place at the table after the elections, offering to join a "quadripartite" national army and allow access to Khmer Rouge zones of control as required by the Paris agreement to induce concessions from Phnom Penh.

In fact the Khmer Rouge was playing with a weakening hand. Over the previous decade Khmer Rouge combat forces had fallen from around 40,000 to perhaps 10,000 troops in the spring of 1993. After the May elections, with cached supplies dwindling and the Thai government curbing the gem and timber trade,[56] straggling Khmer Rouge soldiers began begging for handouts from UN peacekeepers and defecting, some of them to find better conditions in Phnom Penh's new army based on the merger of factional forces, which now qualified for international assistance. The Khmer Rouge had become a patronage machine since its ouster from Phnom Penh, and dependence on external support was its Achilles' heel.[57] Up to 2,000 Khmer Rouge troops crossed over to the government side by mid-September, according to UN sources.[58] In December 1994, 400 Khmer Rouge fighters turned in their weapons in Siem Reap province alone to beat the January 15 amnesty deadline.[59] Increasing resort to recruitment by impressment and hostage-taking, and to shooting people who refused to cooperate, seemed acts of desperation.[60] Khmer Rouge attacks may even have helped the coalition parties in Phnom Penh keep their differences in check. The ultimate fate of the Khmer Rouge could be to follow the Malayan and Thai communist parties into gradual extinction.

Still, the Khmer Rouge is a force to be reckoned with because of corruption, incompetence, repression, and malfeasance on the Phnom Penh side. The two largest parties to emerge from the elections, Prince Ranariddh's royalist Funcinpec and the ex-Hanoi client Cambodian People's Party, were enemies in war and are themselves split into patron–client cliques. The norms of tolerance, compromise, proceduralism, and rule of law so essential to stable multiparty politics are largely absent. Popular indifference to the government's fate combined with factional strife could present the Khmer Rouge with an opportunity to recover. In this way the second possibility above could develop into the third possibility. With a little luck and the sustenance of Thai business and military connections, the Khmer Rouge could well prolong the division, stagnation, and misrule that have made Cambodia vulnerable to decay and intervention in the past. Although Vietnamese leaders have said Hanoi would not intervene even if the Khmer Rouge returned to power,[61] this is the kind of commitment that statesmen tend to forget in changed situations.

Vietnam can afford to ignore the Cambodian backwater so long as its social and political conditions get no worse and other powers, particularly Thailand and China, respect the Paris agreement. But it cannot be indifferent to the forcible expulsion of Vietnamese settlers, spillover from civil war or breakdown of government, or the manipulation of Cambodian internal affairs by outsiders.

Domestic Dilemmas

A special category of insecurity arises from Vietnam's domestic economy, society, and polity. At the center of this category lie several "reform dilemmas" that are the consequence of shifting from central planning under tight political control to a market-oriented economy and a more open, though still authoritarian, political structure. The central dilemmas, of course, are how to liberalize the economy without restoring capitalism and how to separate the party and state society without inviting instability; in other words "to achieve change within the framework of socialism without eroding the bases of socialism itself."[62] Even Vietnamese who take ideology seriously have acknowledged that the models of other socialist countries are "inapplicable" and that Vietnam's own past experience provides little guidance. The one point on which they seem to agree is that it was an "illusion to wish to advance directly to socialism without going through the stage of capitalist development," and therefore Vietnam will have to pass through a period of "state-initiated capitalism."[63]

Several issues that stem from the core dilemmas loom in leaders' minds as sources of insecurity. One is corruption, fueled by the declining purchasing power of state salaries, opportunities to compensate through the expanding free market, and ineffective checks on official power. No institution is untainted, not even the People's Army.[64] Awareness of corruption's impact on popular confidence in the regime caused leaders in the early 1990s to use such terms as "scourge," "crisis," and "alarming,"[65] and to describe a situation that was "so severe it may even endanger the existence of our regime."[66] As troubling as the sheer scale of corruption was the inability of the central government to bring cases to trial, obtain convictions, and impose stiff sentences. "No bold measures have been taken against cadres in high positions," former party general secretary Nguyen Van Linh wrote in May 1993, because "nobody is bold enough to take action for fear of causing influential officials to get involved."[67] And yet, in spite of increased prosecutions and tougher punishments a year later, corruption had increased.[68] The scale of corruption may be no worse than what other Southeast Asian countries experienced at a similar level of development, but it discredits reform and the communists' pretension to purity.

An associated problem is smuggling, which corrupts officials and thwarts efforts to protect domestic production. The value of smuggled goods arriving in the first nine months of 1992 was estimated to be 3 trillion dong, or U.S. $250 million.[69] One-third of this inflow came over the northwestern border with China, two-thirds through the southern land and sea borders, and it accounted for perhaps 20 percent of all retail sales.[70] Smuggling may result from a misguided attempt to tax trade, but it also reveals the state's weak control over borders, officials, and agencies, and the national economy's increasing vulnerability to international market forces.

Reform also has exacerbated inequalities, which violate the VCP's compact with society, particularly with that portion of it that long served as the party's main base of support. Many state employees, poor peasants without sideline occupations, and inhabitants of former revolutionary zones in mountainous areas have seen their incomes stagnate or decline. The people most likely to get rich, or so it is commonly believed, have done so by "illegal activities" and "cheating the people."[71] Although rural inequalities in Vietnam are lower than in any other Asian country,[72] the trends are worrying. As Mark Selden has observed, "Particularly significant are growing income differences between North and South, between the densely populated and dynamic Mekong delta and other regions, between predominantly agrarian and agro-commercial industrial areas, and between Vietnamese and minority peoples."[73] A 1994 survey by the General Statistics Department found that average income in the countryside ($103 per year) was less than half of that of city dwellers ($242 per year), while a slight majority of all people had experienced an improvement in income since reform began.[74] If most people are content with improving incomes they may not care much about growing inequality across space, sectors, and classes, but the trend has been the subject of intense debate among government analysts and figured in a backlash against proposals for private land ownership in 1991.[75]

While urban-rural, lowland-mountain, and other spatial inequalities have widened, the one that poses the greatest challenge to central control and national unity is between North and South. More accurately, this is an inequality between two core power domains centered on the deltas of the Red and Mekong rivers. By comparison with the

North, the South has better infrastructure, more recent experience with a market economy, a larger pool of entrepreneurial talent, better links to the outside world, more productive agriculture, little experience of socialism, and so has responded more quickly to the growth opportunities of reform. The South, or rather the Ho Chi Minh City, Danang, and Ba Ria–Vung Tau municipal areas, also benefited from receiving three-fourths of all foreign investment up to 1993. Over 45 percent of all foreign investment went to Ho Chi Minh City alone, 3.2 times as much as to Hanoi.[76] This was partly because the area offered a more attractive investment climate but also because "capitalists of Chinese origin," who accounted for two-thirds of the total foreign capital invested in the country,[77] found it easier and safer to operate through family and clan networks. Industrial growth in the greater Ho Chi Minh City area, sparked by this investment, was reported in mid-1993 to have been over twice the national average for three consecutive years.[78] Although skyrocketing land prices in Ho Chi Minh City and desire for access to the central government influenced investors to channel more capital toward Hanoi in 1994, long-term trends favor more rapid accumulation of wealth, and therefore of power, in the South.

The investment and trade activities of overseas Chinese also should revitalize Vietnam's own ethnic Chinese *(Hoa)* community. In 1978, nearly all of the North's 200,000 ethnic Chinese left, mostly for China, where many of them reside to this day. The northern *Hoa* had been a privileged minority, "bastions of free enterprise in an otherwise socialist economy."[79] Although their status has remained a point of friction between Beijing and Hanoi, some have returned to resume roles as middlemen in the China-Vietnam trade. In the South, "boat people" and orderly departures seriously depleted the *Hoa,* and socialization measures in the late 1970s weakened their economic power. But the state never succeeded in bringing their commercial activity completely to heel, and they were quick to take advantage of private business opportunities under *doi moi,* or renovation, as Vietnam's process of reform is known.[80]

By the late 1980s, all of this no longer mattered because relations with China were improving and reform made the revival of *Hoa* commercial activities acceptable. The *Hoa* community's partial assimilation and reduced numbers—to 961,700 nationwide in 1989,[81] or about half of their pre-1978 percentage in the total population—also alleviated Vietnamese concerns. However, the Vietnamese have an abiding fear of manipulation by Beijing via the *Hoa,* and Hanoi's attitude toward them could change quickly in the context of a crisis in relations with China. Vietnamese concern also might grow if *Hoa* commercial transnationalism seemed to draw Vietnam too tightly into South China's economic orbit or to exacerbate North–South differences in Vietnam.

One of these differences is the comparative weakness of southern attachments to the party and state. The number of new members admitted to the Ho Chi Minh City Party Committee declined by one-third in 1991,[82] and its secretary observed in early 1992 that "the situation of degeneration in party and state organs has reached an alert level."[83] For two weeks in February half of the Political Bureau met in Ho Chi Minh City to discuss the party's "fading" leadership role in the South, which was the result of members' focusing on advancement in jobs where opportunities for material gain had improved, and neglecting party work.[84] Nationwide the VCP recruited 37,000 new members in 1992, an increase of 4 percent over 1991, and 21,000 in the first half of 1993, an increase of 30 percent over the same period in 1992,[85] but the South appears not to have contributed to the improvement. Much more holds the regions together than pulls them apart, but uneven party strength across regions and dissimilar popular attitudes toward central authority are sensitive matters to the leadership.

Finally, the combination of communist collapse abroad and reform at home had corrosive effects on party members' faith, dedication, and obedience. In 1991, only a quarter of the base-level membership was sufficiently active to merit description as carrying out the VCP's "exemplary vanguard role."[86] The party's youth wing, the Ho Chi Minh Youth Union, suffered a "downturn" in the quantity and quality of members and in the union's prestige.[87] Although total party membership stabilized, demographic turnover and the climate of tacit pragmatism could only further weaken interest in ideology. Increasing representation in the Central Committee of individuals with power bases in provinces, combined with the breakup of provinces into smaller ones, contributed to "the increasing fragmentation and decentralization of power" and "the rise of independent kingdoms" in both the party and state.[88]

One cannot predict how the leadership will respond to these stresses or say with confidence what the outcome will be. But the general nature of its predicament is clear. Failure to achieve sustained economic growth will discredit the Vietnam Communist Party in the eyes of members and population alike, whereas success will nurture a civil society and pressure to end the party's power monopoly. The contradiction does not have to resolve itself in the VCP's overthrow or evolution into liberal democracy, but it does make the party's survival hinge on compromise with the groups and forces growing around it.

The Diaspora

Reform and openness unleashed in Vietnam an "explosion of interest" in foreign ideas and technology, evoking erratic, ambiguous responses from the government.[89] One connection with the world that presents Hanoi with an especially prickly mix of challenge and opportunity is the over 2 million Vietnamese who live overseas (nearly half live in the United States) and maintain ties with half a million families in the homeland.

On the one hand, the diaspora is a source of modest foreign investment (a total of U.S. $70 million by 1994) and remittances that rose from about $500 million in annual hard currency in 1990 to perhaps $1 billion in 1994.[90] With some 50,000 overseas Vietnamese now visiting their homeland each year and experiencing the more relaxed atmosphere, Hanoi can reasonably hope to blunt some of the antipathy that has prevailed in the overseas community as well.

On the other hand, the travails of socialism worldwide encouraged dogmatic anticommunists abroad to smuggle subversive literature and infiltrate small bands of commandos into Vietnam to "carry the flame back home." Emigrants returning to visit families and friends have provided a constant stream of ideas, knowledge, and customs that conflict with regime norms. Since the large majority of overseas Vietnamese, including "reactionaries" of the former Saigon regime, are from the South, party leaders have expected the effect to be strongest there.[91] But the North has not been immune. Students and workers returning from former socialist countries confirmed socialism's failure with personal testimony, and Vietnamese émigrés aimed radio broadcasts at Vietnam from Russia until June 1993. Debate among diaspora intellectuals over the country's future has blended with debate inside it, fueling dissidence. Although officials' worst fears appear to have subsided, it is "too early to say what the political, social, and cultural implications of all these first-hand accounts of life in both West and East will be on the Vietnamese public at large."[92] Leaders have regarded the interaction between diaspora and homeland with apprehension, some of them questioning whether the "open door" to any source of "cultural venoms" is worth the long-term risk.[93]

Peaceful Evolution

Hanoi's perception of insecurity stemming from the interplay of international and domestic environments has been most striking, as it has been for Beijing, in the theory that the West generally, and the United States specifically, are attempting to complete the conquest of socialism through "peaceful evolution." In the Vietnamese view, this strategy looks beyond world communism's disintegration and aims to induce collapse in the remaining socialist states and create a new world order based on "pure capitalism." As Minister of Defense Doan Khue has put it:

> Following the failure of socialism in Eastern Europe and the Soviet Union, the adversary forces have been . . . stepping up their offensive against the remaining socialist countries, which include Vietnam. Their plot and action are aimed at accelerating the combined use of unarmed and armed measures against us to undermine in a total manner our politics, ideology, psychology, way of living, and so on, and encircling, isolating, and destroying us in the economic field, with the hope that they could achieve the so-called "peaceful evolution" and make the revolution in our country deviate from its course. They have been trying to seek, build, and develop reactionary forces of all kinds within our country; at the same time to nurture and bring back groups of armed reactionary exiles to join with the reactionaries within our country; and to combine armed activities with political activities, hoping to transform the socioeconomic crisis in our country into a political crisis and to incite rioting and overthrowing when opportunities arise. They may also look for excuses to effect an intervention, to carry out partial armed aggression, or to wage aggressive wars on various scales.[94]

In some writings, almost any form of contact with the West—imports that compete with domestic manufactures, economic aid, foreign investment, bribes by businessmen, cultural exchange, invitations to attend scholarly conferences abroad, tourism—may be an instrument of "peaceful evolution."[95]

American triumphalist rhetoric provided proponents of the thesis a rich mine of material for to cite as "proof" of its validity. So did efforts to attach conditions regarding democratization and human rights to normalization. Acceptance of these conditions, one analyst wrote, would result in "a transfer of power . . . by peaceful means. The socialist state will be finished. There has been a precedent for this in the world. We need to foresee this danger and find a method of doing away with the pragmatic trend now existing in socialist countries."[96]

It is hard to tell just how seriously Hanoi officials took all this. Members of the military and security establishments produced by far the largest proportion of commentary on "peaceful evolution," seeming to reflect institutional interests and obsessions. Civilian officials, by contrast, invoked the term much less frequently and with less imputation of Western conspiracy. Civilian discourse on "peaceful evolution" moved quickly from the notion of a diabolical American plot consciously pursued to the abstract forces of economic, technological, and cultural interdependence seen as operating to capitalism's advantage. While the intensity of conviction clearly differed across bureaucracies, the priority given to democratization and human rights in the Western agenda made "peaceful evolution" seem an apt description of a real threat, even to Vietnamese who recognized that this was a risk the nation would have to take in order to survive and prosper in the modern world. Normalization with the United States did not completely alleviate the uneasiness and in some ways sharpened it, as the American concept of "engagement" continued to subject economic relations to political criteria and supported training and educational programs designed to encourage Vietnam's transition toward democracy.

Patterns of Stability and Accountability

A popular misconception about Vietnam is that it has continued to reform economically while ceasing to reform politically. The misconception is understandable. Shocked by events abroad in 1989, Vietnam's leaders concluded that circumstances left them no choice but to proceed with marketizing the economy while, in politics, emphasizing stability. General Secretary Nguyen Van Linh stepped up attacks on "bourgeois liberalization" and "multiparty politics," the VCP tightened media controls, and security forces rounded up nearly 10,000 people in just one week of an "anticrime campaign" in December 1989.[97]

The Central Committee's Eighth Plenum in March 1990 unveiled measures to renew "the party's leadership over the masses" and expelled Tran Xuan Bach from the Political Bureau for publicly demanding synchronization of political reforms with economic reforms.

Other leaders agreed that political reforms were needed, but they feared a public debate on them would be difficult to contain. Premature and excessive political liberalization, they believed, had destabilized the Soviet Union before economic reforms could show results, while Romania and China showed what would result from denying participation to professionals and intellectuals. Learning from these and other upheavals, they determined to co-opt groups formerly excluded from the "worker–peasant alliance" and restore public confidence through a gradual modification of the links among the party, state, and people. Vietnam was thus the *only* communist country to have *continued* systematic political reform after 1989. To say that this reform happened not to be in a pluralist, multiparty direction is not to suggest that it was not meaningful.

Vietnam's political reform thus developed into a multifaceted process involving all institutions of the state, party, and mass participation.[98] Much of this was simply an effort to reverse the corruption and incompetence that had undermined the regime's legitimacy, and to adapt the state machinery to the requirements of a market economy through purge and bureaucratic streamlining. But along with efforts to make the existing structure work better, other reforms had deeper structural implications. These included measures to disaggregate party and state functions, open the VCP to a greater degree of public scrutiny and criticism, downplay class struggle, enhance the role of technocratic elements in policymaking, decentralize management of state enterprises and agencies, introduce limited competition into the election of popular representative organs, increase the legislative independence of the National Assembly, and create a "law-ruled state." Revisions to the constitution and the law on government organization in 1992 gave the National Assembly authority over appointments to the Council of Ministers, for which party membership was no longer a requisite. In the July 1992 elections for the National Assembly the ratio of 1.52 candidates per seat was down from 1.67 per seat in 1987, but still higher than the ratio of 1.24 per seat in the 1981 prereform elections. A few independents and non-VCP members ran in the municipal elections of November 1994, winning six seats in Ho Chi Minh City and four in

Danang. Effort also has been made, with mixed results, to revitalize mass organizations as institutions of corporatist representation.

None of these measures comes close to liberal democratization. The screening of candidates for the National Assembly virtually eliminated thirty-eight of forty "self-nominated" candidates,[99] and while the new constitution dropped reference to the "dictatorship of the proletariat," it continued to reserve the "leading role" for the Communist Party. A description of the People's Councils as organs of popular representation in early drafts of the new constitution was changed in the final one to make them "the basis of the state's power in the regions."[100] A new publishing law adopted in July 1993 provided for licensing of private printing and publication, albeit subject to strict content guidelines and state censorship.[101]

The task party leaders have set for themselves is to "lead" without governing or, as outgoing general secretary Linh put it to the Seventh Congress in June 1991, to "secure adequate democracy under one-party leadership." But the changes represent movement away from rigid Leninist emphasis on centralization, hierarchy, and tight inter-locking directorates between party and state. Both the nature of the changes and intense debate over them suggest there is a fairly strong constituency within official circles for further evolution. Overwhelming support for emphasizing professional competence over party membership in employment practices,[102] for example, paved the way to a government decision in 1993 to peg civil service ranks and wage levels solely to professional qualifications. The constituency for political reform *inside* the party and state in Vietnam is probably stronger than it is in China, in no small measure because the infusion of reform ideas from Eastern Europe and the Soviet Union through study abroad continued right up to 1991, while in China that infusion ceased thirty years earlier.

The direction of evolution is broadly consistent with the East Asian, or neo-Confucianist, model. The Vietnamese may call their particular version of this model "socialist democracy," but a more descriptive term is "mobilizational authoritarianism," which captures the Leninist elements of citizen participation in state affairs through institutions dominated by a single party exercising a constitutional monopoly of power. The main difference between this and non-Leninist single- or one-party dominant systems is the emphasis in Vietnam on organizing popular assent rather than depoliticizing public affairs. In this respect,

Vietnam has something in common not only with China, but with Singapore and Taiwan. In these noncommunist examples, the dominant party (a Leninist structure in the case of the Nationalists in Taiwan) employed mobilization, cooptation, and a tutelary notion of government to limit demands from particularistic groups during the crucial early stages of industrialization, maintaining political stability while achieving high rates of economic growth. And in both countries growth generated internal pressures for political change which the parties have found expedient to accommodate. A similar trajectory seems in store for Vietnam, with the party reinventing itself along the lines of, say, the People's Action Party of Singapore or Golkar of Indonesia.[103]

Asian communist systems are not destined to follow the European ones into collapse and resurrection as pluralist democracies. Fundamental differences of history, culture, and level of economic development set the Asians apart. An important source of Vietnamese communist resilience is the attainment of power through war and revolution. In the course of these struggles the VCP rooted itself in hamlets and villages and in popular patriotism without serious competition at the mass level from its elite nationalist rivals. These origins secured for the regime as a whole, distinct from the individuals who serve it, a degree of popular acceptance that not even corruption and incompetence have been able to destroy completely.

Moreover, the regime faces no serious internal opposition, and not only because it stifles dissent. By comparison with almost all other Asian countries, Vietnam is more agrarian, less industrialized, and a good deal poorer. A middle stratum of merchants, managers, entrepreneurs, and professionals capable of articulating alternative policies and organizing opposition nationwide has just begun to develop. There is no national church or movement like Poland's Solidarity to provide leadership or a focus of loyalty outside the party, state, and affiliated mass associations. A civil society of the kind that played such an important role in the political upheavals in Eastern Europe and the Soviet Union can hardly be said to exist in Vietnam. The Unified Buddhist Church, the Catholic Church, and religious sects in the South offer a measure of associational life apart from the party-state, but these are mutually exclusive, internally divided organizations. Frictions in 1993 between the state and the Unified Buddhist Church—the vanguard of protests against the Saigon regime in the 1960s—revealed the fragmentary nature of opposition and the government's skill in managing it. Only a split within the VCP itself could present a serious challenge to the party's dominance. Moreover, the party's disintegration might no longer imply the collapse of the state.

Vietnam has no practical alternative to its existing framework of change. No party or political movement in modern Vietnam besides the VCP has ever had a mass membership in the countryside as well as in the towns and cities of all regions. No state besides the Socialist Republic has governed all of Vietnam as a single nation since France divided it three ways in the nineteenth century. The only political organizations that might spring up (were truly competitive politics permitted or the existing structure to lose its integrative force) would be personality-based cliques, small bands of dissident intellectuals, religious sectarian movements, and region-based parties. Although there is unprecedented international pressure for relaxation of controls, in Asia this pressure can also legitimize strong, paternalistic states. The present regime therefore is assured survival for the rest of the decade—and probably beyond, if it delivers steady economic growth, an equitable distribution of social welfare, and suitable professional opportunities for the intelligentsia. The international community should welcome this prospect, as the alternatives of instability or collapse would close the door on trade and investment and unleash a new flood of "boat people" onto foreign shores.

Initiatives for Cooperation or Conflict

Since deciding to leave Cambodia and concentrate on reform, Hanoi has emphasized conflict avoidance, risk minimization, and cooperation with neighbors. This strategy involved the ardent pursuit of bilateral agreements on trade, investment protection, taxation, maritime transport, civil aviation, and cultural, scientific, and technological exchange with all of the ASEAN states, and in its signing (along with Laos) of the Bali Treaty of Amity and Cooperation on July 22, 1992. In July 1995 it became a full member of ASEAN. Hanoi has campaigned as well for acceptance in the General Agreement on Tariffs and Trade (GATT), the Asia-Pacific Economic Cooperation (APEC) forum, and other international bodies. All of these initiatives have been part of a larger effort to break out completely from its Cold War isolation, expand freedom of maneuver, and float on the rising tide of regional development.

Borders

As noted above, the potential for conflict with China over claims at sea goaded Vietnam to seek cooperation with ASEAN members both collectively and bilaterally. But Vietnam and China have also disagreed regarding their common land border. The disagreement stemmed from differences over the contemporary relevance of a boundary drawn by France on behalf of Vietnam in the nineteenth century, and from "land grabbing" during the decade of armed confrontation following China's 1979 punitive invasion. Both Vietnam and China have an interest in opening the border to trade and bringing the smuggling across it under control, but Vietnam charged that China had moved border markers, military outposts, and even peasants into some one hundred square kilometers of Vietnamese territory scattered in 132 different places.[104] The Vietnamese customs post at Lang Son in 1992 was located nearly half a kilometer south of where it stood in 1979.[105] The dispute is a point of considerable friction, but Vietnam felt much more pressured than China to settle because of the proportionally much great potential that trade across the border had to lift the Vietnamese economy. In 1993, while both Vietnam and China continued to militarize islands in the South China Sea, negotiations on the land border progressed sufficiently to warrant reopening several gates to trade.

Another territorial dispute centers on the border between Vietnam and Cambodia. Although Vietnam and its client, the State of Cambodia in Phnom Penh, reached a border agreement in 1982 (about the same time that Vietnam and Laos also formalized some minor changes), all Khmer factions felt constrained during the 1993 elections to promise they would reexamine it. The Khmer Rouge demanded redrawing the border as it was prior to Prince Sihanouk's ouster in 1970, while Sihanouk himself extracted a commitment from Hanoi to address the issue after the installation of a new government. Hanoi's foreign minister Nguyen Manh Cam acknowledged that border delineation was one of the "outstanding problems between the two countries" while making clear that Vietnam saw this as a matter of clarifying details rather than making major adjustments.[106] Since Vietnam benefited from the 1982 agreement, pressure to redraw the boundary has come from Phnom Penh. In January 1995, during Ranarridh's visit to Hanoi, the two sides agreed to settle the issue through the establishment of a special joint commission.

Military Security

For military security Vietnam must depend largely on its own means, and these are likely over the next decade to diminish compared with those available to neighboring states. With one-third to one-half the per capita income of China (income figures are fuzzy for both countries) and chronic budget deficits, Vietnam has lacked the economic resources to make significant purchases on the international arms market. No power with the means to do so has shown an interest in supplying Vietnam with arms and equipment gratis on any significant scale. Hanoi's most likely prospect for upgrading armaments would be to use hard currency earnings from the export of rice and crude petroleum to buy arms from former communist suppliers that presumably would sell at friendship prices. Arms and cooperation in defense industries were subjects of discussion in Slovakia during Deputy Prime Minister Tran Duc Luong's five-nation tour of Eastern Europe in August 1994. Vietnam's debt to Eastern Europe of 500 million transferable rubles and a debt twenty times that size to Russia constrain deal-making, however.

Although the 1978 Treaty of Friendship with the Soviet Union runs until 2003, Russia can make only limited use of Cam Ranh Bay. Nor would a "conservative" takeover in Russia lead soon to closer security relations between Russia and Vietnam, as such change would keep Russia inward-looking and focus its attention on the "near abroad." India has long-term potential to contribute to Vietnam's security by supplying arms and balancing China's regional presence, and in 1992 it gave Vietnam U.S. $48 million in economic aid. But of course India will not soon have the resources or domestic stability to substitute for the Soviet guarantee. Hanoi's best opportunity for expanding defense relationships may lie in bilateral ties with other ASEAN members, with whom it has exchanged defense attachés. Vietnam has also discussed training, visits, and technical cooperation with Indonesia and Malaysia. While important as confidence-building measures, these ties make little material contribution to Vietnam's defense.

Vietnam's most substantive security relationship today casts it in the role of patron rather than client. This relationship, with Laos, is based on a Treaty of Friendship and Cooperation that mimics Vietnam's treaty with the USSR and on mutual interest in policing areas inhabited by border-straddling ethnic minorities. Its scope is much reduced from the days when the PAVN stationed 50,000 troops along the Lao portion of the Ho Chi Minh Trail and directly supported operations of the Lao People's Army, but it is not without political as well as military significance. Defense cooperation is the one terrain on which Hanoi can compete with China and Thailand for influence in Laos from a position of strength, thanks to long-standing ties between the military establishments of the two countries. Although the last contingents of PAVN troops in Laos returned to Vietnam about the same time as the withdrawal from Cambodia, the PAVN maintains a mission in Laos of indeterminate size and assists the Lao People's Army in training and "party building and political education."[107]

Regional Cooperation

Weakness, poverty, and vulnerability are compelling reasons to emphasize cooperative relations with other states in the region. From Vietnam's perspective, regional organizations and conferences provide the only frameworks through which it realistically can seek help to balance China, discuss collective measures to limit major power involvement in the region, join with others in responding to the emergence of trade blocs, and participate in regional development schemes. These are powerful incentives to be a joiner and play by the established rules.

Hanoi is enthusiastic about cooperation on issues of "low politics" as well. The rapid spread of drug use and opium production, for example, has led Vietnam to seek help with drug suppression, partly in anticipation that drug trafficking will follow the expansion of trade. ASEAN has recognized the need to draw all three Indochinese countries into drug suppression efforts, and in 1993 Thailand agreed to share with Vietnam its experience with crop substitution. Hanoi also has declared solidarity with ASEAN and other Third World countries on environmental issues.

Simple lack of resources places a practical brake on Vietnamese enthusiasm, however. The main impediment to admitting Vietnam to full membership in ASEAN by 1995, for example, was doubt about its ability to pay the $1 million contribution to the regional fund and to supply staff and resources for some 300 working group meetings per year. As a member Vietnam also will have difficulty complying with ASEAN agreement to harmonize trade regulations and slash tariffs to 5 percent or less by 2003.[108] These are challenges, of course, for other poor countries left behind by the explosion of interaction among the region's wealthier ones.

Concern about limited resources and domestic impact lay behind Hanoi's initial reactions to proposals for an ASEAN Free Trade Area (AFTA), an East Asian Economic Caucus (EAEC), and Indochina-wide development. Vietnamese (and Lao) commentary on AFTA pointed out the familiar difficulty of reducing trade barriers among existing ASEAN members so long as they directed much more of their trade to the rest of the world than to one another.[109] Pressure to protect infant industries and inefficient state enterprises from foreign competition (for five months ending in February 1993 Hanoi banned the import of seventeen types of goods to stem the flood of mainly Chinese consumer items) made it necessary to delay consideration of reciprocal tariff reductions. Besides, as Hanoi was no doubt aware, ASEAN members have shown little enthusiasm for free trade with a country that foreign investors have targeted as Asia's next cheap-labor export platform. Hanoi could afford to be more positive about the EAEC because the concept was more inchoate and probably would demand less adjustment on Vietnam's part than AFTA.

As regards plans for Indochina-wide infrastructure development, in which Thai, Japanese, and international lending agencies are heavily involved, Vietnam could only respond to others' initiatives. And in these there have been seeds of discord as well as harmony. Hanoi has looked with favor on any proposal that might benefit Vietnam's economy and incidentally complement its long-standing wish to integrate the economies of the three Indochinese countries. But all of the regional states have perceived the potential of these schemes to affect alignments and power and have taken stances accordingly. The rivalry between Hanoi and Bangkok to shape the political economy of their security over the long run—to draw advantage from economic cooperation without ceding strategic position—thus has complicated initiatives for regional development.

Negotiations to reactivate the Mekong Committee dragged on until February 1993 because of Thai-Vietnamese disagreement over Cambodia's reinstatement. In the end Bangkok obtained agreement to offer membership to China and Burma, which could shift the balance within the Committee in favor of the upstream members.[110] In the same period, Bangkok shifted its attention from a proposal of the

Asian Development Bank to build roads linking the kingdom with Laos and Vietnam to the concept of a "development quadrangle" linking Thailand with Laos, Burma, and South China. Even former premier Chatichai Choonhavan, who, as noted above, had offered in 1988 to "turn Indochina from a battlefield into a marketplace," dropped that idea to mount the northern-oriented quadrangle bandwagon. The reason was plain: Thai business interests had a much greater stake in South China than in Vietnam, and Thai security officials saw the quadrangle as a way to adjust to growing Chinese influence in Burma.[111] If implemented, the scheme would create a transnational economic zone in the interior, consolidate a Thai-Chinese condominium over Laos, and marginalize Vietnam. In the end, the Asian Development Bank succeeded in bringing Burma, Cambodia, China, Laos, Thailand, and Vietnam to agreement on plans for a $1.2 billion road system based on both concepts. In the first stage, roads linking Vietnam and Thailand via Laos and Cambodia will be upgraded; in the second, roads will be built between Thailand and southern China, one through Laos and one through Burma.[112] Although roads that tie Indochina together with Thailand have priority, all roads in the final system will converge on Bangkok. For balance—that is, a comparable focus on the development of Vietnam and Indochina to match the Thailand–China axis—Hanoi must depend on support from outside the region, particularly Japan. Just such support seemed forthcoming in former Japanese prime minister Kiichi Miyazawa's January 1993 proposal for a "Forum for Comprehensive Development of Indochina," which emphasized support of transnational programs and projects involving two or more of the three Indochinese countries. A group of seventeen donor countries led by Japan supported the Mekong River Commission's plan to spend $232.3 million on ninety-four projects in 1996.

International Economic Imperatives

The Cold War's end and Soviet collapse forced Vietnam into an abrupt and profound reorientation of its economic relationships. Whereas for decades Vietnam had relied on the Soviet bloc for up to 80 percent of its two-way trade, economic turbulence and Moscow's decision to denominate trade in U.S. dollars forced Hanoi to reverse that pattern in the space of a year. This reversal and the broader

Table 7.1

Vietnam's Direction of Trade, 1993

	Exports percentage	Imports percentage
Asia Total	62	82
NIEs (Korea, Taiwan, Hong Kong, Singapore)	21	54
ASEAN	7	9
Europe	18	11
CIS	5	2
Others	15	5

Source: International Monetary Fund, *Direction of Trade Statistics,* Washington, DC: 1994.

implications of market-oriented reforms made keeping Vietnam's economic door open a matter of survival.

Considering the obstacles, the effort was spectacularly successful (Table 7.1). The figures do not include smuggling, but if they did the table would show an even smaller CIS share and a larger Asian share in Vietnam's trade in 1993.

Much of the $1.4 billion trade in 1993 with Singapore was reexports, while unrecorded smuggling would add significantly to the ASEAN and Chinese figures.[113] Therefore the distribution of trade among partners was more even than the figures would suggest. Especially intriguing was the burgeoning tie with the Republic of Korea, with which Vietnam's trade grew from $80 million in 1989 to over $400 million in 1992, by Vietnamese government estimate, making Vietnam the ROK's third-largest present or former communist trade partner after China and Russia. By comparison, Vietnam's trade with Thailand was about $140 million in 1993.[114]

Vietnam has been boosting the value of its exports by 20 percent per year, eliminating its trade deficit in 1992. Since then growth and construction have begun to suck in imports, foreshadowing a slowly widening deficit, but expected increases in exports should be sufficient to reduce the debt service ratio.[115] With trade growing at a rate higher than GDP growth, Vietnam's stake in the international and particularly the Asian regional economy must grow as well.

The "open door" to investment also enjoyed some success despite the U.S. embargo. Beginning with the amendment of the foreign in-

Table 7.2

Foreign Capital Investments over U.S. $100 million, by Country of Origin in Rank Order, to November 10, 1995

	Number of Projects	Total Capital (U.S. $ millions)
Taiwan	231	3,290
Hong Kong	181	2,130
Japan	175	1,920
Singapore	113	1,600
South Korea	130	1,440
United States	48	1,030
Malaysia	42	836
Australia	47	703
France	69	636
British Virgin Islands	40	608
Switzerland	15	585
Britain	19	477
Thailand	55	423
Sweden	7	375
Netherlands	20	367

Source: *Vietnam Economic Times,* No. 20, December 1995, p. 9.

vestment law in 1987, investments from the convertible area crept up steadily from an accumulated total of a little over $500 million in 1989 to nearly $18 billion at the end of 1995, the bulk of this coming from diverse sources in Asia. Through 1995, Taiwan topped the list with 18.5 percent of the total, thanks to Taiwanese government promotion and the large role played by ethnic Chinese as investment channels throughout the South China–Hong Kong–Taiwan area (see Table 7.2). In fact, "overseas China"—consisting of Taiwan, Hong Kong, and Singapore plus ethnic Chinese investors in the rest of Asia—accounted for 45 to perhaps 50 percent of the total.

However, the American trade embargo's end set the scene for all players to increase their stake, and permitted U.S. firms in particular to raise their share in foreign capital invested from nearly nil to almost 6 percent of the total, the sixth largest share, by late 1995.

Whether in trade or investment, the important facts were that Vietnam adjusted quickly to post–Cold War economic realities because it literally had no choice. The effects were to accomplish in one year a shift in external orientation that otherwise would have taken a decade, effectively locking the Vietnamese economy into the ASEAN–East

Asia market area. The shift also increased the urgency of obtaining an end to the embargo and access to Western and Japanese aid, finance, and investment. Especially significant was Japan's announcement in late 1992 that it was resuming aid, starting with a $370 million commodity loan at 1 percent interest, with American assent. With Japanese businessmen accounting for 40 percent of all visits by foreign businessmen to Vietnam,[116] it was only a matter of time before the scale of their investments ranked alongside the scale of Japan's trade with Vietnam. Henceforth Vietnam's own limited capacity to absorb aid and inadequacies of infrastructure, finance, and law would far outweigh international factors as restraints on its economic growth and integration into the world economy.

Vietnam and the United States

Vietnam's withdrawal from Cambodia and concessions on MIAs in 1992 removed what little justification remained for the American embargo and withholding of normal relations. The embargo kept American business on the sidelines of a new opportunity, while it provoked resentment from allies, who increasingly acted without reference to American wishes. With the establishment of full diplomatic relations between Hanoi and Seoul in December 1992, Vietnam had normal relations with all countries of Asia. ASEAN support of American policies had evaporated with Thailand's decision to stand down from confrontation over Cambodia in 1988. Whatever the domestic constraints on policy change in the United States, the embargo was an anachronism. The time had come to think of Vietnam as a normal country with which Washington should have normal relations, and to consider what relevance Vietnam might have to American interests.

Vietnam's external orientation is not only a bellwether of larger dynamics that affect American interests in the region, but it exercises some independent influence on those dynamics as well. Hanoi's role in polarizing the region by providing the Soviet Union strategic access and pursuing hegemony in Indochina is the obvious case in point. At present, Vietnamese capitulation to China would expose all of Southeast Asia to increased Chinese pressure, while Sino-Vietnamese conflict could suck in or split ASEAN. Either extreme in Vietnam's orientation would lead to requests from within the region for American involvement, fuel the regional arms race, and add to the factors encouraging Japan to rearm. The United States would not welcome any of these developments. Therefore it has an interest in seeing Vietnam obtain assurance from close ties with countries that share its concern about Chinese assertiveness but have no wish to confront Beijing openly. Although the risks to Vietnam of veering toward either extreme keep it on a moderate course, a day could come when the United States might want to collaborate with Vietnam in the tacit "containment" of China.

Washington is already engaged in two major sources of insecurity to Vietnam, ironically in ways that parallel, rather than oppose, Vietnamese interests. One is Cambodia, where instability poses more problems for Vietnam than for other regional powers. American demands that Thailand cut links to the Khmer Rouge irritated Bangkok but pleased Hanoi (although neither the Vietnamese nor the Thai care much whether democracy and civil liberties flourish in Phnom Penh). The other source of insecurity is Sino-Vietnamese sparring over claims in the South China Sea, particularly the Spratlys. The danger here is not so much the exceedingly remote possibility of a multisided armed conflict among all of the littoral states, or polarization between China and ASEAN, but a Vietnamese retreat, which would clear obstacles to China's control over the entire sea. Other claimants would then come under strong pressure to make bilateral accommodations with Beijing. Alternatively, an agreement between Beijing and Hanoi to divide the major islands and resources between them would also marginalize other powers. American access to the region might then diminish, and pressure on Japan to extend the defense of its sea lines of communication would grow. In the sea as in Cambodia, American interests should tilt Washington toward Hanoi.

Thinking of Vietnam as a normal country in which the United States might involve itself positively requires bringing images into line with the contemporary reality. An experiment in "reform socialism" in a post-socialist world, Vietnam has ceased to be a revolutionary state. It is instead moving toward the Asian model of "soft" authoritarianism and state economic interventionism. Elsewhere in Asia this model over the long term has been open to change in the direction of broader popular participation, greater tolerance of organization outside the state, and freer expression of ideas. The same forces of industrialization, urbanization, education, technological development, and global flows of information that have set South Korea, Taiwan, Thailand, the

Philippines, and even China on courses toward change have begun to exercise their influence on Vietnam. These forces are especially potent in Vietnam's case because it lacks the external support it would need to withstand them: their impact is apparent in the NIEs it would emulate. The real cause of lasting change is thus "modernization" working internally, not the conditions that Western, particularly American, leaders have sometimes been tempted to impose as requirements for fuller development of bilateral relations.

Notes

1. Communist Party of Vietnam, *Fifth National Congress: Political Report,* Hanoi: Foreign Languages Publishing House, 1982, pp. 127–130.

2. William S. Turley, "Vietnam's Strategy for Indochina and Security in Southeast Asia," in Young Whan Kihl and Lawrence E. Grinter, eds., *Security, Strategy, and Policy Responses in the Pacific Rim,* Boulder, CO: Lynne Rienner, 1989, pp. 172, 174–175.

3. Communist Party of Vietnam, *Sixth National Congress: Documents,* Hanoi: Foreign Languages Publishing House, 1987, pp. 118–130.

4. Takayuki Ogasawara , "Vietnam's Security Policy in the Post-Cambodia Period, Diplomatic Dimensions," in *Asia-Pacific and Vietnam—Japan Relations,* Hanoi: Institute for International Relations, 1994, p. 107.

5. William S. Turley, "The Khmer War: Cambodia after Paris," *Survival,* September 1990, pp. 438–439.

6. Communist Party of Vietnam, *Seventh National Congress: Documents,* Hanoi: Foreign Languages Publishing House, 1991, p. 41.

7. Phan Doan Nam, "How to Perceive Features of the Current World Situation," *Tap chi Cong san* (The Communist Monthly), September 1991, translated in Foreign Broadcast Information Service, *Daily Report: East Asia* (hereafter referred to as *FBIS-EAS*), October 10, 1991.

8. Phan Doan Nam, "Vietnam and the New World Order," *Quan doi Nhan dan* (People's army daily), March 28, 1992, Broadcast over Voice of Vietnam Radio, March 27, and translated in *FBIS-EAS,* April 22, 1992.

9. Turley, "Vietnam's Strategy for Indochina and Security in Southeast Asia," 1989, p. 174.

10. Yoshihide Soeya, "Japanese Diplomacy Toward Vietnam: The International Context," paper presented at a workshop on "The Reemergence of Vietnam," Maui, Hawaii, January 5–6, 1995, pp. 30–31.

11. International Monetary Fund, *Direction of Trade, 1994 Yearbook.*

12. Hanoi Radio, January 17, 1991, in *FBIS-EAS,* January 18, 1991.

13. *Business Times* (Singapore), July 26, 1993.

14. This is what VCP General Secretary Nguyen Van Linh appears to have had in mind in a 1990 interview broadcast over Japanese television. NHK General Television Network (Tokyo), May 2, 1990, in *FBIS-EAS,* May 3, 1990.

15. Vietnamese residing in the Soviet Union declined from 6,777 in 1988–89

to 1,945 in 1989–90 and to a smaller but apparently too unstable a number to count in 1990–91. Tong Cuc Thong Ke (General Statistical Office), *Statistical Data of the Socialist Republic of Vietnam 1986–1991,* Hanoi: Statistical Publishing House, 1992, p. 126.

16. Vietnam News Agency, January 22, 1993, in *FBIS-EAS,* January 25, 1993.

17. Turley, "Vietnam's Strategy for Indochina and Security in Southeast Asia," 1989, p. 173.

18. *The Nation* (Bangkok), January 11, 1992, in *FBIS-EAS,* January 13, 1992.

19. Vietnam News Agency, July 25, 1992, in *FBIS-EAS,* July 28, 1992.

20. Sophie Quinn-Judge, "Cam Ranh Mushrooms," *Far Eastern Economic Review,* January 23, 1992; and *Far Eastern Economic Review,* January 21, 1993, p. 9.

21. Reform in Vietnam had roots in piecemeal adjustments including product contracts in agriculture in 1979–80. The comprehensive program launched at the party's Sixth Congress in December 1986 is known in Vietnamese as *doi moi,* or "renovation."

22. *Indochina Digest,* VII, October 21, 1994, p. 42.

23. More telling than the recognition of China's help in winning the war with the United States was the boost for scholarship on the Sinitic elements of Vietnamese civilization, but with an emphasis on Vietnam's indigenization of these borrowings. Twice in 1992 Premier Vo Van Kiet made well-publicized "working visits" to Hanoi's Institute for the Study of Nom Script, a Vietnamese adaptation of Chinese ideographs, to make allusive commentaries on the relationship between national culture, development, and defense. Voice of Vietnam Radio, March 3, 1992, in *FBIS-EAS,* March 6, 1992; and Voice of Vietnam Radio, June 28, 1992, in *FBIS-EAS,* July 13, 1992.

24. *Vietnam Business Journal,* January/February 1995, p. 9.

25. International Monetary Fund, *Direction of Trade, 1994 Yearbook.*

26. Voice of Vietnam Radio, March 4, 1992, in *FBIS-EAS,* March 10, 1992.

27. Dong Thai, *"Ve Van de An ninh trong Quan he Viet Nam-ASEAN"* (On the security problem in Vietnam–ASEAN relations), in Duong Phu Hiep, ed., *Quan he Viet Nam-ASEAN* (Vietnam–ASEAN relations), Hanoi: Asia and Pacific Institute, 1992, p. 43.

28. William S. Turley, "Thai-Vietnamese Rivalry in the Indochina Conflict," in Lawrence E. Grinter and Young Whan Kihl, eds., *East Asian Conflict Zones: Prospects for Regional Stability and Deescalation,* New York: St. Martin's Press, 1987, pp. 149–176.

29. Vietnam News Agency, February 13, 1992, in *FBIS-EAS,* February 14, 1992.

30. *The Nation* (Bangkok), March 25, 1991, in *FBIS-EAS,* March 26, 1991.

31. International Institute for Strategic Studies, *The Military Balance,* London: Brassey's, 1990 and 1991.

32. Ibid., 1992.

33. Ibid., 1994.

34. Carl Thayer, *The Vietnam People's Army under Doi Moi*, Singapore: Institute of Southeast Asian Studies, 1994, p. 36.

35. *Tap chi Quoc phong Toan dan* (All people's national defense monthly), June 1991, in *FBIS-EAS,* July 25, 1991.

36. Carl Thayer, "People's War and All-People's National Defence: The Vietnam People's Army under Doi Moi," paper presented at the Workshop on Arms and Defence Planning in Southeast Asia, Institute of Southeast Asian Studies, Singapore, June 18–19, 1993, p. 42.

37. Voice of Vietnam Radio, July 14, 1993, in *FBIS-EAS,* July 16, 1993.

38. Thayer, "The Vietnam People's Army under Doi Moi," 1994, p. 36.

39. Nguyen Q. Thang, ed., *Hoang sa, Truong sa* (Paracels, Spratlys), Ho Chi Minh City: Ban Tre Publishing House, 1988; and Vu Phi Hoang, *Hai Quan Dao: Hoang sa va Truong sa, Bo phan Lanh tho Viet Nam* (The Paracel and Spratly archipelagos, pieces of Vietnamese territory), Hanoi: People's Army Publishing House, 1988.

40. Agence France-Presse, July 16, 1992, in *FBIS-EAS,* July 16, 1992.

41. Agence France-Presse, February 28, 1992, in *FBIS-EAS,* February 28, 1992.

42. Voice of Vietnam Radio, May 6, 1992, in *FBIS-EAS,* May 7, 1992. In the Spratlys' 33 islands plus 400 islets and atolls, Vietnam is said to deploy about 1,000 troops on 25 islands (it admits to 21), compared with the Philippines, which has troops on 8, China on 7, Malaysia on 3, and Taiwan on 1 (Kyodo News Service, June 29, 1992, in *FBIS-EAS,* June 30, 1992; Antara News Service, July 1, 1992, in *FBIS-EAS,* July 1, 1992).

43. Voice of Vietnam Radio, July 7, 1992, in *FBIS-EAS,* July 8, 1992.

44. Voice of Vietnam Radio, October 26, 1992, in *FBIS-EAS,* October 27, 1992.

45. *The Bangkok Post,* December 14, 1992, in *FBIS-EAS,* December 14, 1992.

46. Jaques Bekaert, "Cambodian Diary: The View from Hanoi," *The Bangkok Post,* March 14, 1992, in *FBIS-EAS,* March 19, 1992.

47. Estimates of the number of Vietnamese settlers in Cambodia vary wildly from the low of 100,000 cited by Hanoi to the absurd allegation by the Khmer Rouge that 1 to 2 million Vietnamese civilians—or 3 million around the time of the UN-sponsored elections in May 1993—provide cover for 40,000 Vietnamese troops. The actual number is impossible to determine, and Vietnamese officials make the plausible observation that efforts to limit migration combined with the deterrent effect of Khmer hostility have kept the number below the half million that resided in Cambodia before 1970. Independent estimates in 1994 were between 150,000 and 400,000 (*Indochina Digest,* VII, October 14, 1995, p. 41). Whatever the correct figure, even the low estimate would represent a threatening presence in the eyes of many Khmer.

48. Nate Thayer, "Not So Secret Agenda," *Far Eastern Economic Review,* November 12, 1992, pp. 12–13; Nayan Chanda, "Easy Scapegoat," *Far Eastern Economic Review,* October 22, 1992, p. 18; Nate Thayer and Susumu Awanohara, "Cambodia Takes a Bath," *Far Eastern Economic Review,* October 15, 1992, pp. 56–57; Richard S. Erlich, untitled article, *The Bangkok Post,* August 17, 1992, in *FBIS-EAS,* August 17, 1992; Nayan Chanda and Nate Thayer, "Rivers of Blood," *Far Eastern Economic Review,* April 8, 1993, p. 22.

49. General Doan Khue, "On the Occasion of the 47th Anniversary of the October Revolution and National Day . . . ," *Tap chi Quan phong Toan dan* (All people's national defense monthly), August 1992, in *FBIS-EAS,* September 15, 1992.

50. Minh Hien, "Persistently Build the Vietnam-Cambodia Border Into a Region of Peace and Friendship," *Tap chi Quoc phong Toan dan* (All people's national defense monthly), June 1992, in *FBIS-EAS,* July 20, 1992.

51. Samleng Pracheachon Kampuchea Radio, July 1, 1993, in *FBIS-EAS,* July 2, 1993.

52. *Indochina Digest,* VII, September 23, 1994, p. 38.

53. The murkiness of this farce did not disguise the role of family ties and personal animosities in shaping political events. The leader of the breakaway was Prince Norodom Chakkrapong, a deputy premier in the previous, Hanoi-installed Phnom Penh government and estranged half-brother of Prince Norodom Ranariddh, winner of the elections. The secession movement crumbled after Hun Sen prevailed upon his brother Hun Nheng, governor of Kompong Cham province, to accept the election results. The subsequent agreement between Ranariddh and Hun Sen to divide the new state's presidency may have been the price Ranariddh paid to obtain Hun Sen's help in ending the secession. Throughout these events Hanoi stood by its pledge to support the electoral outcome, taking no part. See Agence France-Presse reports, June 10–15, 1993, in *FBIS-EAS,* June 10–15, 1993.

54. Seki Tomoda, "Vietnam's Relations with Cambodia," paper presented at a workshop on "The Reemergence of Vietnam," Maui, Hawaii, Jaunary 5–6, 1995, p. 26.

55. Vien Dan Toc Hoc (Nationalities Institute), *So tay ve cac Dan toc o Viet Nam* (Notes on the nationalities of Vietnam), Hanoi: Social Sciences Publishing House, 1983, p. 34; Tong Cuc Thong Ke (General Statistical Office), *Statistical Data of the Socialist Republic of Vietnam 1976–1989,* Hanoi: Statistical Publishing House, 1990, p. 9.

56. Thailand imposed this embargo at the request of the Cambodian Supreme National Council and the UN Security Council in February 1993 to pressure the Khmer Rouge into participating in the peace process. At the time, the Khmer Rouge was taking in an estimated $1 million a month from this trade (Agence France-Presse, February 10, 1993, in *FBIS-EAS,* February 10, 1993). While the Thai government in Bangkok, especially the Ministry of Foreign Affairs, was determined to implement the embargo, the complicity of Thai army and local government personnel with traders, gem dealers, and loggers made it impossible to seal the border. In November 1994, U.S. secretary of state Warren Christopher obtained assurances from Thai leaders that disciplinary action would be taken against Royal Thai Army officers who assisted the Khmer Rouge in any way. *Indochina Digest,* VII, November 18, 1994, p. 46.

57. The Vietnamese were certainly aware that the distribution of material benefits to the rural poor steeped in traditional concepts of obligation to benefactors was crucial to preserving the Khmer Rouge popular base. External assistance and income from trade, distributed by patrimonial commanders, sustained Khmer Rouge forces in battle and bound families to them. As a Vietnamese who served five years in Cambodia put it, "the strength of the Khmer Rouge rests on its ability to infiltrate and win grassroots support through the money and rice it handed out" (quoted in *The Bangkok Post,* November 27, 1992, in *FBIS-EAS,* December 1, 1992). Also see Serge Thion, "The Cambodian Idea of Revolution," in David P. Chandler and Ben Kiernan, eds., *Revolution and Its Aftermath in*

Kampuchea: Eight Essays, New Haven: Yale University Southeast Asia Studies, Monograph Series No. 25, 1983, pp. 11–14, 28, 29.

58. Reuters, September 16, 1993.

59. *Indochina Digest,* VII, December 20, 1994, p. 52.

60. *Indochina Digest,* VII, November 18, 1994, p. 46.

61. Seki Tomoda, "Vietnam's Relations with Cambodia," 1995, p. 25.

62. David W.P. Elliott, "Dilemmas of Reform in Vietnam," in Turley and Selden, eds., *Reinventing Vietnamese Socialism: Doi Moi in Comparative Perspective,* Boulder, CO: Westview Press, 1993, p. 53.

63. Tran Nham, "Resolutely Follow the Socialist Path . . . ," *Nhan dan* (People's daily), January 24, 1991, in *FBIS-EAS,* February 19, 1991.

64. Nguyen Thi Dinh, untitled article, *Tap chi Quoc phong Toan dan,* January 1992, in *FBIS-EAS,* March 11, 1992.

65. Vo Van Kiet on Vietnam Television, October 1, 1992, in *FBIS-EAS,* October 5, 1992.

66. Voice of Vietnam Radio, December 19, 1991, in *FBIS-EAS,* December 24, 1991.

67. Voice of Vietnam Radio, May 10, 1993, in *FBIS-EAS,* May 12, 1993.

68. *Indochina Digest,* VII, October 28, 1994, p. 42.

69. Voice of Vietnam Radio, November 11, 1992, in *FBIS-EAS,* November 16, 1992.

70. Voice of Vietnam Radio, June 14, 1992, in *FBIS-EAS,* June 17, 1992.

71. Voice of Vietnam Radio, October 25, 1992, in *FBIS-EAS,* November 2, 1992.

72. In 1989, Vietnam's Gini coefficient for rural inequality, on a scale of zero to one in which zero signifies perfect equality, was 0.11, compared with 0.23 for China in 1982, 0.26 for Taiwan in 1975, 0.38 for the Philippines in 1975, 0.39 for South Korea in 1981, 0.42 for Indonesia in 1981, 0.44 for Thailand in 1981, and 0.49 for Malaysia in 1979, according to Ngo Vinh Long, "Reform and Rural Development: Impact on Class, Sectoral, and Regional Inequalities," in Turley and Selden, eds., *Reinventing Vietnamese Socialism,* 1993, p. 195, citing the Hanoi journal *Tap chi Xa hoi Hoc* (Sociological review).

73. Mark Selden, "Agrarian Development Strategies in China and Vietnam," in Turley and Selden, eds., *Reinventing Vietnamese Socialism,* 1993, p. 242.

74. *Indochina Digest,* VII, September 2, 1994, p. 35. While these figures accurately reflect income disparities, they underestimate purchasing power. Adjusted for purchasing power parity, Vietnam's per capita income is estimated at $1,263, as compared with Thailand's $5,890 and Indonesia's $2,970. Than T. Nguyen, "Rising to the Challenge: Vietnam's Opportunities for Economic Development," paper presented at a conference on Vietnam and Japan, Centre for Asia Pacific Initiatives, University of Victoria, British Columbia, November 17–19, 1994.

75. Ngo Vinh Long, "Reform and Rural Development: Impact on Class, Sectoral, and Regional Inequalities," in Turley and Selden, eds., *Reinventing Vietnamese Socialism,* 1993, pp. 191–194, 202.

76. Vietnam News Agency, January 17, 1993, in *FBIS-EAS,* January 21, 1993.

77. Voice of Vietnam Radio, December 10, 1992, in *FBIS-EAS,* December 11, 1992.

78. Vietnam News Agency, August 13, 1993, in *FBIS-EAS,* August 13, 1993.

79. Charles Benoit, "Vietnam's 'Boat People,' " in David W. P. Elliott, ed.,

The Third Indochina Conflict, Boulder, CO: Westview Press, 1981, p. 146.

80. Lew Stern, "The Eternal Return: Changes in Vietnam's Policies Toward the Overseas Chinese, 1982–1988," *Issues and Studies,* 24, no. 7 (July 1988), pp. 118–138.

81. *Tong Cuc Thong Ke* (General Statistical Office), *Statistical Data of the Socialist Republic of Vietnam 1976–1989,* Hanoi: Statistical Publishing House, 1990, p. 9.

82. *Saigon Giai Phong,* March 21, 1992, in *FBIS-EAS,* April 14, 1992.

83. *Saigon Giai Phong,* February 2, 1992, in *FBIS-EAS,* March 18, 1992.

84. Voice of Vietnam Radio, February 19, 1992, in *FBIS-EAS,* February 24, 1992.

85. Voice of Vietnam Radio, May 12, 1993, in *FBIS-EAS,* May 14, 1993; *Indochina Digest,* September 17, 1993.

86. Do Muoi, speech at Hai Hung provincial second round party organization congress, August 15–17, Voice of Vietnam Radio, August 19, 1991, in *FBIS-EAS,* August 26, 1991.

87. Vietnam News Agency, October 17, 1992, in *FBIS-EAS,* October 22, 1992.

88. David W. P. Elliott, "Vietnam's 1991 Party Elections," *Asian Affairs: An American Review,* 19, no. 3 (Fall 1992), pp. 162–163.

89. David G. Marr, "Education, Research, and Information Circulation in Contemporary Vietnam," in Turley and Selden, eds., *Reinventing Vietnamese Socialism,* 1993, p. 337.

90. Hanoi Radio, July 1, 1991, in *FBIS-EAS,* July 5, 1991; *Indochina Chronicle,* VII, August 19, 1994, p. 33.

91. *Saigon Giai Phong,* December 29, 1991, in *FBIS-EAS,* February 12, 1992.

92. Marr, "Education, Research, and Information Circulation in Contemporary Vietnam," 1993, p. 350.

93. This may be inferred from Vo Van Kiet's defense of the open door in a letter to a national conference on news and publication in Ho Chi Minh City, Voice of Vietnam Radio, February 24, 1992, in *FBIS-EAS,* March 2, 1992. For a detailed discussion of the party's changing policy toward the overseas Vietnamese and tendency to "vacillate between distrust and a practical understanding of the importance and advantages of cooperating. . . ," see Lew Stern, "The Return of the Prodigal Sons: The Party and the Viet Kieu," *Indochina Report* (Singapore), April–June 1992.

94. General Doan Khue, "On the Occasion of the 47th Anniversary of the October Revolution and National Day . . . ," *Tap chi Quoc phong Toan dan* (All people's national defense monthly), August, in *FBIS-EAS,* September 15, 1992.

95. Colonel Tran Van Khoa, "Heighten Vigilance Against Peaceful Evolution Schemes of the Hostile Forces," *Tap chi Cong san,* January, broadcast over Voice of Vietnam Radio, January 9, 1993, in *FBIS-EAS,* January 13, 1993.

96. Nguyen Khanh Bat, "Fighting Peaceful Evolution in Cooperation and in the Economic Struggle," Voice of Vietnam Radio, February 4, 1993, in *FBIS-EAS,* February 9, 1993.

97. Hanoi Radio, December 10, 1989, in *FBIS-EAS,* December 12, 1989.

98. See Lew Stern, "Toward a Kinder, Gentler Organization: Party Reform under Nguyen Van Linh," paper presented at the Annual Meeting of the Association for Asian Studies, Washington, DC, March 19, 1989; William S. Turley, "Party, State,

and People," in Turley and Selden, eds., *Reinventing Vietnamese Socialism,* 1993, pp. 257–275; and William S. Turley, "Political Renovation in Vietnam: Renewal and Adaptation," in Börje Ljunggren, ed., *The Challenge of Reform in Indochina,* Cambridge, MA: Harvard Institute for International Development, 1993.

99. Voice of Vietnam Radio, June 22, 1992, in *FBIS-EAS,* June 23, 1992.

100. Greg Lockhart, "Vietnam: Democracy and Democratisation," *Asian Studies Review,* 17, no. 1, July 1993, p. 140.

101. Voice of Vietnam Radio, July 24, 1993, in *FBIS-EAS,* July 29, 1993.

102. Political Bureau member Le Phuoc Tho, in a 1993 speech to party members, quoted remarks Ho Chi Minh had made in 1947: " 'Suppose we have to choose between two applicants who are the relatives of a party member and a nonparty member. The second candidate is better than the first in terms of intelligence and behavior. Which of these two candidates should we select?' (Everybody in the conference hall unanimously responded: The relative of the nonparty member)," from *Nhan dan,* May 18, 1993, in *FBIS-EAS,* July 9, 1993.

103. In 1992 the party's Nguyen Ai Quoc Institute launched a research program to "perfect and concretize a theoretical basis for the building of a firm political system in our country during the transition period toward socialism" under the patronage of Political Bureau member Nguyen Duc Binh. Vietnam Television Network, October 31, 1992, in *FBIS-EAS,* November 9, 1992; and Vietnam Television Network, November 2, 1992, in *FBIS-EAS,* November 10, 1992.

104. Agence France-Presse, October 26, 1992, in *FBIS-EAS,* October 26, 1992.

105. Agence France-Presse, April 1, 1992, in *FBIS-EAS,* April 2, 1992.

106. Voice of Vietnam Radio, July 23, 1992, in *FBIS-EAS,* July 24, 1992.

107. Vietnam Television Network, November 3, 1991, in *FBIS-EAS,* November 12, 1991.

108. *Indochina Digest,* VII, September 30, 1994, p. 37.

109. Voice of Vietnam Radio, February 9, 1992, in *FBIS-EAS,* February 19, 1992.

110. *The Bangkok Post,* March 8, 1992, in *FBIS-EAS,* March 10, 1992.

111. *The Nation,* (Bangkok) April 11, 1993, in *FBIS-EAS,* April 26, 1993.

112. *Indochina Digest,* VII, September 16, 1994, p. 37.

113. The IMF recorded Vietnam's two-way trade with China in 1993 at U.S. $415 million. But an estimate of Sino-Vietnamese land border trade alone based on interviews with Chinese officials fixed the amount in 1992 at $497.3 million, not including smuggling, which augmented that amount by perhaps one-third. Annual estimates from these sources suggest that the border trade has grown from 2 percent of Vietnam's total trade in 1989 to 7 percent in 1992. See Brantly Womack, "Sino-Vietnamese Border Trade: The Edge of Normalization," unpublished paper delivered at Cornell University, October 1993, pp. 5, 10.

114. Voice of Vietnam Radio, December 22, 1992, in *FBIS-EAS,* December 22, 1992.

115. Nguyen, "Rising to the Challenge: Vietnam's Opportunities for Economic Development," p. 30.

116. Kyodo News Service, November 6, 1992, in *FBIS-EAS,* November 6, 1992.

8

A Postscript on U.S. Policy

Sheldon W. Simon and Richard J. Ellings

One of the sources of potential instability in Southeast Asia is the decline of U.S. credibility in the region, a decline that has been faster than would seem justified. After all, it was just in 1991 that United States–led forces expelled Iraq from Kuwait in what can only be described as an extraordinary display of sheer power, global reach, technological prowess, and strategic genius. Why would peace-loving nations in other parts of the world not be reassured?

Several factors compelled America to respond so decisively in the Persian Gulf, but the one that may have struck Southeast Asians most was the kind of clear U.S. interest in the Middle East, namely oil, that does not exist on the same scale in their region. Southeast Asians also perceive, rightly or wrongly, other problems with U.S. credibility. They question America's commitment to their region because of the closing of the Philippine bases; the election of a new, Vietnam War–generation president for whom Asia appears of tertiary interest; the downsizing of the U.S. military; the closing of consulates, U.S. Information Service posts, and Agency for International Development missions in the region; the reduction of Foreign Service officers; and the dismissal of local staff. The United States is seen as a power in retreat when it closes its facilities in Medan, Indonesia, one of the most important economic centers in that country; or Cebu in the Philippines for the same reason; or Kyoto, the cultural capital of Japan. The United States is also seen as a marginal actor with regard to key issues such as the conflict over the Spratly Islands and the future of Burma.

In contrast, as the United States downsizes, the United Kingdom,

France, Australia, and even Germany all seem to be increasing their official presence in the region. And, of course, China and Japan are perceived as ever more influential on more and more issues. In fact, U.S. economic, political, and security interests in Southeast Asia are significant and growing, as official U.S. policy statements reiterate ad nauseam. But these interests are not vital in the sense that Middle East oil is.

Southeast Asians understand this, but still believe that their region can be vital to the United States, as it was deemed in 1941 and for much of the Cold War. They also understand that the United States has foreign policy goals in Southeast Asia other than security. From September through November 1995, Sheldon Simon conducted extensive interviews in seven East Asian countries.[1] Respondents were senior research staff at influential think tanks who specialize in their countries' foreign and security policies. The interviews, among other things, were designed to tap their views of the U.S. presence and future engagement in the region. Many of the questions asked dealt with three major U.S. foreign policy objectives in the post–Cold War period: *security, democracy,* and *prosperity.*

Security

Virtually all interviewees (with the partial exception of Korean and Taiwanese) believed that the short- to medium-term external security environment (five to ten years) was benign. Indeed, they felt that it was the best it had been since the end of World War II. They agreed that no regional power in the next ten years has the intention or capability of becoming a new hegemon. Therefore, external security concerns were focused on relatively minor territorial disputes regarding land and sea boundaries, problems of illegal refugees, smuggling, drugs, piracy, fishery poaching, and Exclusive Economic Zone (EEZ) patrol capabilities.

In line with these concerns—as well as longer-term considerations about the possible increase in Chinese and Japanese military might—many of these states are acquiring naval and air forces that can at least protect their 200–nautical-mile EEZs. Indeed, East Asia is a major arms market for the United States and other suppliers. While it would be an exaggeration to refer to these arms acquisitions as an arms race, the interviews suggest that they could be described as "competitive arming": each country appears to justify its acquisitions at least partly in terms of what its neighbors are doing. On the up side, these modern capabilities could become the basis for joint cooperative patrols of EEZs and sea lanes, thus contributing to regional security over time. In all probability, the ASEAN Regional Forum and such neighbors as Malaysia, Singapore, and Indonesia will be discussing these prospects. On the down side, the newly acquired capabilities have already been used to pursue and attack neighbors' fishing craft allegedly poaching in others' waters. In this context, the U.S. naval and air presence in the region is either enthusiastically welcomed or at least tolerated by all the respondents to the questionnaire.

For those most positively inclined (Japan, Taiwan, Singapore) the U.S. presence was seen as a kind of general deterrent, preempting any potential hegemon, causing all regional members to think twice before contemplating the disruption of regional tranquillity through military action. The less enthusiastic, (Indonesia, Malaysia, China), while not openly opposed to the U.S. presence, were skeptical of its actual utility in situations of regional tension—for example, the Spratly Islands, disputes among neighbors, or even a PRC threat to Taiwan. Regional specialists questioned whether the United States would have either the political interest, the political will, or even the military capability to dominate regional military situations given the downsizing of its presence over the past five years. (The exception to this skepticism was regarding the Korean Peninsula, where it was uniformly believed the U.S. commitment and capability were firm.) Many regional specialists questioned the relevance of the U.S. military presence for Asian security conflicts in the post–Cold War era. Many predicted that America's domestic priorities and budget problems would lead to additional downsizing of its Pacific forces over the next several years. Hence, the need to prepare their own defenses.

Additionally, the survey revealed broad regional interest in new multilateral security discussions, best represented by the ASEAN Regional Forum, or ARF. Much to most participants' surprise, the ARF has already gone beyond its debate format to obtain some interesting diplomatic outcomes in its July 1995 Brunei meeting. The ARF is also a venue for Japan to begin to play a security role in the region.

China has made what appears to be significant security concessions within the ARF setting. At the July 1995 meeting at which the ASEAN states raised the Spratlys issue, China's deputy foreign minister—facing a united ASEAN which now included Vietnam—agreed to multilateral discussions on the Spratlys for the first time. China also stated that the 1982 Law of the Sea could be the basis for these discussions. This is important because it seems to contradict a 1992 National People's Congress law that declared the South China Sea to be national waters. If the Law of the Sea is accepted, then China must negotiate its 200–mile EEZ claims with other littoral states—in effect acknowledging the legitimacy of those claims.

Of course, China's "concessions" could just be rhetorical, a way of buying time, defusing tension, and weakening the ASEAN united front. But the concessions also seem to be a recognition that the PRC's hard-line position in the South China Sea, combined with its saber rattling against Taiwan, could isolate Beijing throughout the region. The concessions, then, are a way of avoiding isolation at a time when relations with Taiwan are particularly prickly and U.S.–China relations are also sensitive.

Democracy and Human Rights

There is a mixed reaction among Southeast Asians to the U.S. emphasis on democracy and human rights in the region. Those states already practicing democracy (particularly those who are recent converts) are generally favorably disposed to American diplomatic efforts to pressure authoritarian states. These democratic states (Thailand, Philippines, South Korea, Taiwan) seem to accept America's Wilsonian approach to the expansion of democracy, agreeing with the propositions that democratic states will not fight one another and that democratic states are favorably disposed to a global market. Interestingly, even the Indonesian respondents were somewhat favorable to the idea of the United States vocally defending democracy. They believe that U.S. diplomatic pressure was partly responsible for the creation over the past two years of a human rights mechanism in Indonesia and the fact that the army is now actively prosecuting soldiers (e.g., in East Timor) who are guilty of egregious human rights violations. By contrast, the authoritarian states of China, Singapore, and Malaysia strongly oppose America's democracy/human rights agenda. The mildest criticism is that it is an unwarranted interference in the domestic politics of other countries and a kind of American hubris. The more severe critics, especially in China, argue that the U.S. emphasis on human rights and democracy is part of a hidden agenda designed to justify trade sanctions against lower-priced local products produced with low-cost labor and to undermine and ultimately overthrow the government.

Prosperity

Throughout Southeast Asia, regardless of regime type, there is a strong commitment to economic development and the role of the market and global economy in that development. All respondents want the United States to continue to play a major role as regional trade partner and investor. All fear the prospect of U.S. protectionism because the U.S. market has been so important to their economic success. There is a general recognition of the need for the United States to improve its balance-of-payments situation; but there is considerable resentment of the economic nationalism displayed by the current administration. The United States is increasingly seen as a trade bully, threatening unilateral sanctions unless its interpretation of open markets is accepted by America's trade partners. Moreover, bilateral U.S. trade negotiations are seen as a violation of the multilateral commitments the United States was instrumental in putting into place with the creation of the World Trade Organization (WTO). These concerns about U.S. trade strategy are also exhibited in the Asia-Pacific Economic Cooperation (APEC) forum, where U.S. efforts to formalize and set a specific timetable and sector specific commitments are seen by a number of Asians as a kind of hijacking of what they believed would be a voluntaristic, flexible trade group. At the same time, intraregional Asia-Pacific trade and investment are burgeoning, and the relative U.S. presence in both these categories is declining even though the absolute levels of U.S. trade and investment are increasing.

Disengagement?

Unfortunately, America's commitment to the region is seriously doubted. While perhaps no administration can make the same case for the importance of Southeast Asia as a vital interest that it can for the Persian Gulf, each administration, as well as the U.S. Congress, must more carefully align America's policies and commitments with its power and interests. Attention needs to be paid to Southeast Asian views and issues, and to America's civilian as well as military presence there. American business must be encouraged to invest and otherwise participate in the region's economic dynamism. Absent such reassurance of a strong American interest and presence, the United States risks marginality in one of the world's most vital political and economic regions as the twenty-first century dawns.

Note

1. These interviews were conducted as part of an ongoing project of The National Bureau of Asian Research entitled "Security, Democracy, and Economic Liberalism: Implications for Peace and Post–Cold War Policy in the Asia–Pacific." The project is supported by the United States Institute of Peace and the United States Information Agency. The opinions, findings, and recommendations expressed in this chapter are those of the editors and do not necessarily reflect the views of the NBR, United States Institute of Peace, nor of the United States Information Agency.

About the Contributors

Karl W. Eikenberry, a colonel in the U.S. Army, is currently the senior country director for China and Mongolia in the Office of the Secretary of Defense, International Security Affairs. Colonel Eikenberry has commanded and served in infantry units in the United States, Europe, and Asia. Several of his articles on Asia-Pacific security issues and army tactics have appeared in the pages of *Military History*, *Parameters*, *Military Review*, and *Infantry*.

Richard J. Ellings is executive director and cofounder of The National Bureau of Asian Research. Previously he was a faculty member and assistant director of the Henry M. Jackson School of International Studies at the University of Washington. Dr. Ellings, who specializes in the political economy of international relations and national security, has also served as a legislative assistant in the U.S. Senate. He is the author of many publications, including *Embargoes and World Power: Lessons from American Foreign Policy* (1985), and is coauthor of *Private Property and National Security* (1991).

Donald K. Emmerson is professor of political science at the University of Wisconsin–Madison and associate fellow at Stanford University's Asia/Pacific Research Center. He has published and consulted extensively on Southeast Asian security and political economy. He is coauthor, with Sheldon Simon, of *Regional Issues in Southeast Asian Security* (1993), and the editor of *Indonesia Beyond Soeharto* (expected 1996).

Clark D. Neher is professor and chair of the political science department and associate of the Center for Southeast Asian Studies at Northern Illinois University. A specialist in Southeast Asian comparative politics, his most recent books include *Southeast Asia in the New International Era* (1994) and *Democracy and Development in Southeast Asia* (1995). Professor Neher has also held visiting posts in Thailand and has served as a consultant for the U.S. Agency for International Development in Thailand and the Philippines.

Kenneth B. Pyle is professor of history and Asian studies at the University of Washington, where from 1978 to 1988 he was also director of the Henry M. Jackson School of International Studies. Dr. Pyle is also president of The National Bureau of Asian Research. One of the nation's leading specialists on modern Japanese history, he was founding editor of the *Journal of Japanese Studies*. He has published many books and articles on modern Japan, including *The Making of Modern Japan* (1978), *The Trade Crisis: How Will Japan Respond?* (1987), and *The Japanese Question: Power and Purpose in a New Era* (1992).

Sheldon W. Simon is professor of political science at Arizona State University. A specialist in comparative Asian foreign and security policies, he is the author of numerous works including *The Future of Asian-Pacific Security Collaboration* (1988), and *The ASEAN States and Regional Security* (1982) and was the editor of *East Asian Security in the Post–Cold War Era* (1993). Professor Simon also is a member of the Advisory Board of The Asia Society, and was recently a vice president of the International Studies Association.

William S. Turley is professor of political science at Southern Illinois University at Carbondale. One of the nation's leading analysts on Vietnam, he has published widely on issues of contemporary Vietnamese politics, reform, and foreign affairs. He is the author of *The Second Indochina War* (1986) and coeditor of *Reinventing Vietnamese Socialism: Doi Moi in Comparative Perspective* (1993). Professor Turley has held visiting posts at universities in both Thailand and Vietnam.

Index

A

Adulyadej, King Bhumipol, 154
Afghanistan, 109, 178
AIDS, 156, 173
Anand Panyarachun, 157, 168
Aquino, Corazon, 162
Asian Development Bank (ADB), 108, 209
Asian multilateralism, 14–15
Asia-Pacific Economic Cooperation (APEC), 4, 14, 145–46, 204, 225
Eminent Persons Group (EPG), 18, 19
Association of Southeast Asian Nations (ASEAN), 4, 16–17, 21–22, 66, 75–78, 81–84, 149–50, 172–73
ASEAN Free Trade Area (AFTA), 14, 19, 20, 167–68
ASEAN Regional Forum (ARF), 26–30, 81, 113, 145
ASEAN Treaty of Amity and Cooperation, 22, 30
defense spending within, 57–63
relations with China, 23–24, 36–37, 75–76, 81, 113
Australia, 18, 20, 28, 29, 71, 222

B

Balanced disparity, 54–57, 62, 80, 83
Bali, Treaty of, 204

Bangkok Declaration (1967), 66
Banharn Silpa-archa, 52, 159
Bolkiah, Hassanal, 52, 60
Brunei, 50, 52, 59, 60, 61
Burma. *See* Myanmar

C

Cambodia, 29, 190–94
  as "front line state," 43–44
  Vietnamese immigration to, 191–92
  Vietnamese occupation of, 42, 72
Cambodian peacekeeping operations, 134
Cam Ranh Bay, 181, 182, 206
Canada, 30, 146
Catholic Church, 203
Central Military Commission (China), 104
Chatichai Choonhavan, 166, 167, 168, 185, 209
China. *See* People's Republic of China
Chuan Leekpai, 158, 159, 160, 168
Clark Air Base, 77, 168–69, 170
Clinton Administration, 15–16, 22–23, 78
Coalition Government of Democratic Kampuchea (CGDK), 72
"Cobra Gold," 172, 181
Cold War, 21, 56, 99, 127, 138, 176–77
Collective security, 126, 135
Commonwealth of Independent States (CIS), 150